Michael Kuhn

The Social Science of the Citizen Society
Volume 1: Critique of the Globalization and
Decolonization of the Social Sciences

BEYOND THE SOCIAL SCIENCES

Edited by Michael Kuhn, Hebe Vessuri, Shujiro Yazawa

ISSN 2364-8775

1   *Michael Kuhn, Shujiro Yazawa (eds.)*
    Theories about and Strategies against Hegemonic Social Sciences
    ISBN 978-3-8382-0586-1

2   *Michael Kuhn*
    How the Social Sciences Think about the World's Social
    Outline of a Critique
    ISBN 978-3-8382-0892-3

3   *Michael Kuhn, Hebe Vessuri (eds.)*
    The Global Social Sciences
    —Under and Beyond European Universalism
    ISBN 978-3-8382-0893-0

4   *Michael Kuhn, Hebe Vessuri (eds.)*
    Contributions to Alternative Concepts of Knowledge
    ISBN 978-3-8382-0894-7

5   *Kazumi Okamoto*
    Academic Culture: An Analytical Framework
    for Understanding Academic Work
    A Case Study about the Social Science Academe in Japan
    ISBN 978-3-8382-0937-1

6   *Ngambouk Vitalis Pemunta (ed.)*
    Concurrences in Postcolonial Research
    Perspectives, Methodologies, and Engagements
    ISBN 978-3-8382-1154-1

7   *Michael Kuhn*
    Die Sozialwissenschaft der Bürgergesellschaft
    Band 1: Kritik der Globalisierung und De-Kolonialisierung
    der Sozialwissenschaften
    ISBN 978-3-8382-1465-8

8   *Michael Kuhn*
    The Social Science of the Citizen Society
    Volume 1: Critique of the Globalization and Decolonization of the Social
    Sciences
    ISBN 978-3-8382-1575-4

Michael Kuhn

THE SOCIAL SCIENCE OF THE CITIZEN SOCIETY

Volume 1: Critique of the Globalization and Decolonization of the Social Sciences

Bibliografische Information der Deutschen Nationalbibliothek
Die Deutsche Nationalbibliothek verzeichnet diese Publikation in der Deutschen Nationalbibliografie; detaillierte bibliografische Daten sind im Internet über http://dnb.d-nb.de abrufbar.

Bibliographic information published by the Deutsche Nationalbibliothek
Die Deutsche Nationalbibliothek lists this publication in the Deutsche Nationalbibliografie; detailed bibliographic data are available in the Internet at http://dnb.d-nb.de.

ISBN-13: 978-3-8382-1575-4
© *ibidem*-Verlag, Stuttgart 2021
Alle Rechte vorbehalten

Das Werk einschließlich aller seiner Teile ist urheberrechtlich geschützt. Jede Verwertung außerhalb der engen Grenzen des Urheberrechtsgesetzes ist ohne Zustimmung des Verlages unzulässig und strafbar. Dies gilt insbesondere für Vervielfältigungen, Übersetzungen, Mikroverfilmungen und elektronische Speicherformen sowie die Einspeicherung und Verarbeitung in elektronischen Systemen.

All rights reserved. No part of this publication may be reproduced, stored in or introduced into a retrieval system, or transmitted, in any form, or by any means (electronical, mechanical, photocopying, recording or otherwise) without the prior written permission of the publisher. Any person who does any unauthorized act in relation to this publication may be liable to criminal prosecution and civil claims for damages.

Printed in the EU

BEYOND THE
SOCIAL SCIENCES

The social sciences, what do they let us know about the world's social, a place of war, of poverty, *and* of wealth? Certainly, one cannot make them responsible for what is going on in the world. Is there any spot on the globe that is not somehow involved in a war? Is there any place in the world, where the growth of wealth does not exist next to the growth of poverty? Certainly, war, wealth, and poverty are the major essentials of "modernity" and they have been in the forefront of social concern for more than 200 years. The social sciences have been researching the social world with a multitude of professional thinkers also for over two centuries. Has the knowledge they gained helped to make anything better, or at least helped to reduce wars and poverty? Obviously not. Or is even the opposite is the case? Again, one cannot accuse the social sciences for this, knowledge is knowledge, but what is their impact upon the world? Not much, one must conclude, considering the fact that we still live in a world of war, wealth, and poverty. Hence, we have to raise the question what social thought under the regime of the social sciences is all about then.

The book series "Beyond the Social Sciences" publishes social thought and invites readers and writers to reflect on the social sciences and their approach to social thought, the theories they contribute to understand the social world, and how to go beyond the social sciences' way of thinking about the world.

It particularly invites contributions that critically reflect upon:

- the disciplinary structure of social sciences
- key theories founding global social science theorizing
- epistemological and methodological issues of global social sciences
- institutional aspects of global social sciences
- international collaboration practices
- the global social science structure
- international discourse practices
- international science policies
- alternative approaches to social thought

Series editors are:

Michael Kuhn, World Social Sciences and Humanities Network (World SSHNet), Achim

Hebe Vessuri, Universidad Nacional Autónoma de México (UNAM), Mexico City

Shujiro Yazawa, Seijo University, Tokyo

Preface

200 years of critical social science theories, two hundred years of poverty, two hundred years of war, 200 years of colonialism and imperialism, constantly criticized by the professional thinkers of the social sciences—how does this two-hundred-year coexistence of critique and criticized go together?

These two books on the "social science of the citizen society" accuse the latter, which social science theorists do not believe to be possible, of producing not only occasionally, presupposed, that is false theories about the world—wrong, because they criticize the world as a failure of the ideals imputed to it, thereby critically affirming them and thus pursuing the coexistence of critique and the criticized.

The first book on *the "Critique of Globalization and De-colonization of the Social Sciences"* shows that the arguments with which they justify both what globalization and the de-colonization of their sciences are supposed to be are nothing but preoccupied, false justifications legitimizing the concerns of individual nation-state views of the world. The second book on *"The Nature of the Social Science of the Citizen Society—Sketches of a Theory"* shows that in the way in which the disciplinary social sciences create their theories by looking at the practical concerns of citizen society, how it thereby produces preoccupied, i.e., false theories about the citizen society, in particular about their state—with the result of this never-ending coexistence of the critical and the criticized.

Such a project that sets out to criticize social science thinking for not only producing occasional false theories, but for being the nature of this kind of thinking about societies, for producing false theories, false theories that, thanks to their false thought, spread critically affirmative legends about the goals and purposes that govern this world, this project is doomed to failure from the outset—at least from the point of view of this social science thinking.

Thanks to its concept of knowledge, social science thinking is in fact immune to a critique that criticizes wrong thoughts. Social sciences are convinced that thinking about the social—and since the interpretation by the social sciences of T. Kuhn's book about the natural sciences also the natural sciences' thinking about nature—cannot produce correct knowledge, but only relative correct knowledge, relative to the meta-theories, definitions and methods this thinking applies. Social science theories can indeed be criticized, but this criticism cannot be a criticism of a false theory, but a criticism that argues against all the ex-ante definitions, ethical, scientific-theoretical and methodological assumptions, ex-ante decisions about the object of a theory and about the way in which thinking intends to tackle it, ex-ante decisions that social science thinking must make and whose reasoning it must disclose. The critique that a theory creates wrong thoughts is not an option in social science thinking, because theories can only ever be relatively wrong or right theories measured against all their assumptions and definitions.

Nonetheless, since even all the resulting tautological cognitive operations of a critique of theories that are wrong in this relational sense, like any scientific argumentation, require a plausibility, because they are operations of scientific thinking, these tautological operations of relational critique also cannot do without reasoning. No scientific thoughts can do without their reasoning, which explain why a theory thinks what it says.

And this, the inescapability of theories from the reasoning of scientific thoughts is the weak point in the social science immune system against criticism of false theories, because not least of all, this critique immune concept of criticism, immune against the criticism of false theories, must itself also reason why there can be no right and wrong theories and why this theory about the impossibility of criticizing false thoughts, which makes social science thinking immune against criticism, is itself a right theory.

This, the inevitability of reasoning theories, of scientific thought, also of reasoning why it is right that theories can only ever be relatively right, is the reason why it is still worth trying to criticize social science theories for creating wrong theories, although wrong theories—following the social science theories about social science thinking—do not exist in social science thinking.

Contents

Preface 7

Introduction: The "Globalization" and "De-colonization" of the Social Sciences 11

Globalization 11
De-colonization 17

1. The "Globalization" of the Social Sciences—the Introduction of Nationalist Thinking into Social Science Thinking 23

    1.1 Social sciences before their "globalization": Idealizations of citizen societies and their state 26
    1.2 Globalized theories—nationalistic self-portraits of states 48
    1.3 Comments on life in the world of national citizen societies and its social sciences legends 72

2. The Final Worldwide Enforcement of the Social Science of the Citizen Society through its "De-colonization" 89

    2.1 The adoption of the knowledge concept of social sciences in the former colonized world through the critique of "Eurocentrism" 92
    2.2 The place of thinking as the "contextual" source of knowledge 106
    2.3 From the critique of capitalism to its anti-critique —from Marx to Heidegger 123

3. **Indigenous Knowledge—Contributions to the Ideological Armament of States** 139

   3.1 State self-portraits of indigenous knowledge 139

   3.2 Indigenized Knowledge in global discourse 152

   3.3 How the de-colonized social sciences view the world of science—and its ideological harvests 167

4. **The Final Scientific Highlights of the Masterminds of Globalized Post-colonial Thinking** 177

   4.1 Imperialisms as a methodological instrument of social science theory-building 179

   4.2 Imperial theories—for morally clean wars 186

5. **Old and New Mistakes and Their Sources: Theoretical Legacies of the Globalization and Decolonization Debates under the Preparatory Work of HistoMat** 197

Introduction: The "Globalization" and "De-colonization" of the Social Sciences[1]

Around 50 years after end of World War II, the social sciences next to creating their theories began another round to reflect on themselves. The discourses that the social sciences then conducted around the end of the 20th century across all disciplines and equally worldwide under the title of a "globalization" of the social sciences, countered by a discourse on their "de-colonization" that was as worldwide as it was across disciplines, could not be more paradoxical, if one considers alone the fact that it takes 50 years after the end of the war to discover that the world had become a world of nation states after the colonized part of the world had adapted the very society model of capitalism of the old colonialists and then the alternative society model, called real socialism, had declared to be finished in a very unspectacular way and had also put their societies back to the regime of capitalism.

With these discourses about "globalization" and "de-colonization", discourses on what their essential tasks and challenges are in a world of capitalist societies, especially when these discourses are discussed in the social sciences around the world and across all social science disciplines, these sciences, thanks to all the paradoxes of these discourses and their theories, provide insights into what makes social science thinking around the world today concerned.

Globalization

Social sciences call this world of states and market economies "globalization" and at the latest at the beginning of the new century, this discovery of a "globalization" leads to a comprehensive self-critique and social science thinking makes, if one follows the worldwide debates of the social sciences, a discovery and accuses itself of having so far been a "zombie science" in its previous history, because it has

---

[1] In this book, the concept of a plurality of "social sciences" refers to the disciplinary social sciences and thus to the specific form of social science theories of citizen societies. Their nature and their current progresses in theory building is the subject of the book "The Social Science of Citizen Society 2, The Nature of the Social Sciences—Sketches of a Critique".

closed itself to thinking about the "globalized" social and as a consequence of this self-critique propagates, as social sciences would call it, a "paradigm shift" of its thinking, so to speak a complete revolution of its theory creation. Globalization' is the keyword that signals the overthrow also in the social science theory production and this 'globalization' is—according to the view of the social sciences—not only the hitherto wrongly ignored, all-shaping characteristic of the social, but also the reason for the necessity to fundamentally transform social science thinking itself and to 'globalize' the social sciences themselves in order to finally produce theories about the world instead of their previous "Zombi-science."[2]

This self-critical judgment of the social sciences and the "paradigmatic" transformation it heralds raises a few questions about this program of transformation, even before one takes a closer look at this project of a globalized science, because it contains at least two errors of thought and a meaningful confession—bought with a discreet lie—a confession that allows a few insights into the nature of thinking in the social sciences.

To start with the latter: The fact that the social sciences are currently highly busy arguing about the necessity of a "globalization" of thinking is as strange as it is informative, because it confesses that thinking about everything social beyond state-constructed societies does not constitute for social scientific thinking an object of social scientific thinking, i.e., for social scientific thinking all state-constructed societies and the social are identical. For this self-critical confession cannot be without the mistake that today's discovery of a "globalization" claims that the social was not globally, i.e., worldwide, constructed before the observed "globalization". Just as if there had not been a "global" social in the period preceding "globalization"—colonialism—the discovery of a "globalized" social only makes sense from the point of view of a thinking, if this thinking equates all state-constructed societies with the nature

---

2   A "zombie science" is the social science thinking according to Beck, because it practices a "methodical nationalism". This accusation of a "methodical nationalism" does not criticize nationalist thinking, but wants to say that thinking must be "cosmopolitan", i.e., directed at the world beyond individual national societies, and this cosmopolitanism is perfectly compatible with nationalist thinking, yes, as we will see later, it is the more clever nationalism praised by Beck. (See also chapter 5 in this book) http://www.ulrichbeck.net-build.net/index.php?page=cosmopolitan.

of society, a discovery because it is beyond state-constructed societies, with which the social sciences obviously deal quasi naturally, for this thinking obviously only with the de-colonization, i.e. only with the worldwide establishment of state-constituted societies, a worldwide social exists, with which to have to deal theoretically social scientific thinking as a new task of the social sciences only discovers when the world is a world of state societies.

Obviously, therefore, the model of state societies had to be implemented worldwide in order for social science thinking to discover the existence of a social world at all. A social world that is not a world of nation-state societies, one must conclude from the current discovery of societies alongside one's own national society, is not a "global" world for the social sciences. As strange as it may sound, it is only the postcolonial transformation of the world into a world of nation-states that allows social science thinking to discover that there is a world beyond its own national society, so for social science thinking, everything social begins with state societies.

And this, the abstruse insight that sociality should only exist after the world has become a world of nation states, contains on top of it a small, equally paradoxical lie of the social sciences about itself: the social sciences knew and know very well a social world beyond nation-state societies before the de-colonization, i.e., before the transformation of the colonies into the very state societies of the colonizers. Social science thinking had even created a special social science discipline, anthropology, a discipline that was responsible for thinking about the "uncivilized social", that is, for thinking about everything social that is not nation-state societies, and which, now that the world consists of state societies, has found a new disciplinary task with the establishment of cultural studies. And it is as paradoxical as it is telling that, with the exception of anthropology, which was reserved for thinking about the non-state social and which today, after the worldwide "civilization" of the world as state-constructed societies, puzzles over what its object might be, for the social science thinking of all other social science disciplines a social world was non-existent until it was transformed into a world consisting of nation-state constructed societies, only to then demand the "globalization" of their thinking.

This concept of a "globalization" characterizes this picture of a strange discovery of worldwide existing societies by the social sciences after the creation of a world of nation-state societies, just as if there had not been a world until now, i.e. the discovery of a world consisting of state societies, just as if this, the world as a world of states, was the final completion of the social nature of the world, and offers to social scientific thinking only with this world of states its object of thinking, frees the world so to say from its untheorizable non-social spots. "Globalization", this worldwide spatial spread of something that neither knows a subject that operates this global spread nor wants to name an object, a something that is spread globally, and a concept that does not reveal which subjects are responsible for the mysterious global spread of this subject—an objectless something, nor for what reasons and for what purposes it spreads, is therefore the appropriate synonym of social science thinking for the discovery of a world, under the condition that it is a world of nation states, because for this thinking the world has finally become, quasi by itself, for this thinking, what it has always had to be as its very nature: Everything social in the world has thus matured quasi naturally towards its nature as citizen societies, has somehow come to itself. That is why the idea of a "globalization" of the social needs neither a subject that pursues this globalization, nor an object that this subject wants to bring about. It is to be imagined with this monstrous concept of a "globalization" that the social as a state constructed social develops quasi naturally into what it has always wanted to be as its very nature.

One must therefore conclude from the fact that the social sciences today proclaim the necessity of globalization that it took 200 years of social science thinking in the imperial world before, with the decolonization and transformation of colonized societies into state-constructed societies, a social world beyond the imperial world of states was discovered.

And this discovery also reveals what social science thinking is coming to terms with the nature of the formation of state societies in the imperial world of states. As if the emergence of imperial states was not the result of their colonial oppression and exploitation of the world, an exploitation of the colonized world which created the economic foundations for the economic wealth and political power of the imperial world in the first place, as if the creation of a world of states and their imperialism subjecting the social world to their domination purposes was not the way to build and live the world of nation-states, the social sciences realize, more precisely, the social sciences in the imperial world, the existence of a social world beyond their own national societies, and this only then and because and only after the science policies of their imperial states have discovered science as a new lever for global competition for economic growth and for global political power and therefore also drive the social sciences to extend their activities to the social world beyond their national societies. The fact that it was indeed the national science policies in the imperial states that, together with science as a whole, had to motivate the social sciences to do more international work tells all about the thinking about the social world in the social sciences of the imperial states of the world. It obviously needed and still needs such political instructions so that after 200 years of the social sciences, social science thinking can discover an era of "globalization", almost as if the world until then had consisted of national social biotopes sealed off from one another and having nothing to do with one another.³

For the social sciences, especially in the imperial states, their discovery of the existence of a social world beyond their national societies, after their politics have pushed them there, is therefore still a trip to an in this sense categorically exotic elsewhere. Despite all the debates about the necessity of globalizing or internationalizing social science thinking, the essential part of social science theory production continues to produce knowledge that not only continues to cultivate the unworldly notion of theories about nationally isolated societies as the basis of its theorizing, but that also continues to produce social science knowledge that arises from perspectives that interpret everything social through the particular, mostly historical, forms of the construction of nationhood of the imperial world of states and, as will be shown later, bring in these nationally constructed theories from the imperial societies as their contribu-

---

3   It is not by chance that the social sciences in the imperial state that supervises all imperial states, the USA, make an exception here. Long before the discussions on the necessity of a globalization of the social sciences started, the social sciences in the USA knew about the world beyond their national society with the rise of their country to the global world power and developed the idea of "area studies" that do not make a big fuss about their imperial missions. The unworldly idea of a social world established as a world of states, of wanting to imagine itself as a social world of social units untouched by each other, is the privilege of the social sciences in the imperial states, which under the global supremacy of the USA practice their imperial policy above all as global economic policy, and which must therefore receive a wake-up call from their national science policy, to "internationalize" their science, after their economic policy had noticed that science had become a new lever in the global struggle of capital for markets.

tion to their globalization. Theories which, in their search for explanations for social phenomena of national societies, encounter the necessity of having to study the world of states, or which even recognize the phenomena practically defined by state sovereignty as practices of national politics and in order to do so therefore direct their social-scientific thinking towards the world of states as a whole, elsewhere also called imperialism, remain an exception and enjoy a reputation of scientific exoticism, despite, or rather because of, all the debates about a "globalization" of the social sciences. And that this, the nationalization of social science thinking, that this is what constitutes its "globalization", will be shown later along the products of its "globalized" theory-building.

Less inspired by their intellectual curiosity about what is happening in the world, not to mention the discovery of theoretical necessities to be able to understand social phenomena only by thinking about them as an imperially made world, social sciences that are challenged and urged by their national political elites, of course not to analyze the social world as a whole beyond the national islands, but to participate in presenting the national knowledge resources as an attractive resource for investment seeking global capital, this rather mundane task, to prepare science as a source for international business investment, to present this as a new challenge of a discrete "globalization" as a virtually purposeless, purely scientific, self-critically presented imperative of a globalization of the social sciences, cleansed of all political and economic calculations, reveals nevertheless that the theoretical preoccupation with a nation-state constructed world beyond the individual nation-state societies is obviously a hitherto unknown phenomenon and field of activity for the social sciences, especially for the social sciences in the imperial world of states beyond the USA.

Consequently, and this is the next paradox of "globalized thinking", the internationalized or globalized social science knowledge that deals with the newly discovered world of states consists, as before, of always nationally constructed knowledge: The most common way of reflecting on the newly discovered global social, which comes to mind in social science thinking, consists of comparing nationally constructed units of knowledge about social phenomena that are always a priori strictly nationally defined. From this it must be concluded that the social sciences, confronted with the task of dealing with the world beyond their theoretical constructs of a world of social phenomena sealed off by the state, simply cannot think of anything else to reflect on the world other than to multiply what they have always done, that is to theorize about a multiplicity of societies always presented nationally, that this thinking about the world of state societies is thus only able to imagine these comparisons as the mere parallel existence of nationally constructed theories. Just as if it were not the interrelationship of states that makes societies within states what they essentially are, when the social sciences look at the world of states comparatively, nothing else seems to come to their mind but to additively juxtapose theories about individual state phenomena, just as if these state societies of the world of states had nothing to do with each other.

De-colonization

Next to the discourse on the "globalization" of social science, there is another worldwide discourse, again 50 years later than the transformation of the colonized parts of the world into nation states and market economies, the discourse on the "de-colonization" of the social sciences, which is opposed by social scientists from the so-called developing countries to the discourse on "globalization" and in which these scientists insist that social science thinking, which creates its theories about the social world from the perspective of the imperial world, is an image of the world that only social sciences can develop in the imperial world.

In fact, for social sciences in countries where there is not a single social phenomenon that does not derive its characteristics from the dependence of these countries on the imperial world, it must be a strange idea of that "zombie" science which assumes that the social in a country could be thought of as an entity untouched by the world of states and which is only able to register the social world beyond its nationally defined societies after these in turn have become state societies.

From the point of view of thinking about the societies in these countries, which are formally also nation-state societies, but which are nation-state societies in which the political as well as economic substance of their societies is under the command of imperial states and which are entirely constructed to serve the imperial states, one might think it must be, at any rate, that it is a strangely illusionary idea to want to imagine their societies as societies exclusively shaped by an individual state and untouched by other states, just as the social science globalized thinking in the imperial world wants to make it its own in its juxtaposition of comparative theories that make no comparison.

Nevertheless, instead of causing any irritation about the explanatory power of social science theories that create such illusory images of the social world, and then instead of therefore examining their theories, the advocates of a de-colonization of social science thinking not only fail to refute the theories of the sciences from the imperial world, but they in turn claim to develop theories that, in their own way, juxtapose equally nationally inspired views of their societies with the theories about the national societies of the imperial countries.

It must be the case that social science thinking, even in these countries, simply does not seem to know how social science knowledge, which is not determined by the view of state definitions of what nation-state societies are, could otherwise be such thinking about the world of state societies. It seems that the nature of social science thinking involves equating thinking about nation-state societies with thinking through the view of the social constructs, primarily through the view of the state itself, of such nation-state societies, and that the only form of this kind of thinking about this world of state societies is thinking as imagining a world of nation-state societies no differently than the mere addition of theories about such social biotopes.

The postcolonial debates, with their contributions and concerns, make these discourses even more paradoxical. If one takes a look at the critical contributions to the debate from the "de-colonized" social sciences, which come from the former colonized countries, then one has to conclude that their word-radical objections, such as those about "scientific power", about scientific "inequalities", a "scientific imperialism" and similar objections, are even more paradoxical, that all these critical contributions, for their part, do not always also operate with nationally constructed scientific subjects, be it the idea of a scientific world consisting of a "North" versus a "South", or of a "local versus global", or of a Eurocentrism or Occidentalism, all these subjects and objects of their theory-building constructed by the post-colonial debates turn out to be constructions of the same social science-trained thinking of those globalization debates which, as in those debates, consist of an agglomeration of national societies, instead of articulating any doubts about them, that the social science theories about the world of state societies operate with their a priori assumption that they can understand them as biotope societies separated from the world of nation states, in order to reject such theories as obvious false images of imperial world views.

Without even looking at the arguments of the debates about what the de-colonization of the social sciences should be, the categories central to the accusations against "globalized" thinking already show that the opposite is the case: Committed to opposing the newly discovered scientific challenge of that "globalization" of social science thinking with their discourse of de-colonization, these critical objections with their de-colonization debate interpret their objections as a plea for more "local" theories, for a more nationally contoured thinking as congenial contributions from the former colonized countries, and with this strange criticism they claim to be able to participate in the creation and debates about a new global thinking with contributions that are recognized as equal to their own nationally constructed theories about their always nationally constituted societies.

The alternative debate on the "globalization" of the social sciences, which contrasts this with its "de-colonization debate", does not know how to present this demarcation of the social sciences in the formerly colonized world with its accusation of "Eurocentrism" against the theories from the imperial world in any other way than to liberate its thinking from theories that are first explicitly attributed the explanatory power for European societies, and which then, however, for the explanation of the national societies of the former colonial world demands theories tailored to their national societies, i.e. the principle of viewing the world as individual national societies, which in "globalized" thinking are viewed through nation-state perspectives, does not reject them as a pipe dream or even as errors of the social sciences of the imperial world, but explicitly develops them further, thus confirming this nation-specific view with its critique, which does not want to criticize any of these nationally inspired theories.

But that's not all: In order to produce their post-colonial social science theories, they themselves, like "globalized" social science thinking, hypostasize not only nationally contoured questions of inquiry in thinking about their societies, decolonized social science thinking, thinking in the former colonized world that would have every reason to do so after its transformation into states, to look at the world of states and their imperialism, because their societies are all too obviously only what they are through the imperial states, the advocates of a de-colonization of social science thinking go one step further towards a nationally predetermined thinking by propagating this thinking as a thinking about nationally contoured objects and research questions, which is supposed to be able to construct its theories only through theoretically exclusive "local" perspectives, "local" views that are only accessible to those who share this exclusive, national view, thanks to their affiliation with these national societies—with the result that this kind of locally exclusive theory production, called indigenous sciences by post-colonial thinking, on nationally preconfigured social phenomena interpreted by nationally biased thinking, with such explicitly nationally inspired theories makes its contribution to that globalized scientific world as a post-colonialized theoretical contribution to theory formation—and thus finally turns this post-colonial thinking into a questionable theoretical matter.

When even renowned masterminds of this de-colonization project from the former colonial states, such as Aimé Césaire in his "Discourse on Colonialism,"[4] morally scourge the imperial states for their misdeeds, in order to work their way through this moral condemnation to the most stubborn advocates of the humanistic ideals of the state idea, as if the moral self-portraits of states, which social science thinkers and poets like Césaire like to attach to them, were ever the yardstick for any state policies, then these products of post-colonial thought are certainly among the bleak highlights in the history of social science thought and raise the question of what this decolonized thinking is all about, which is dedicated to the state ideas of those states which, under the title of these state ideals, with their old colonialism and their new imperialism, are responsible for the misery in these states and which, with their wars, ensure the maintenance of their sovereignty over this decolonized part of the world of states.

All these peculiarities of "globalized" and "postcolonial" theorizing in the social sciences are reason enough not only to take a closer look at these debates and to ask what characterizes the theories produced under the maxims of these two postwar debates, but

---

4   Aimé Césaire, Discourse on Colonialism, Monthly Review Press, New York 1972.

also to raise the question of what is actually the nature of social science thinking, which not only produces such debates, but also discovers the necessity of directing its thinking towards the world only when the world has become a world of states; and that is a thinking that then obviously seems unable to think about the world of state societies in any other way than that in which the world of these state societies, contrary to all everyday experience, is conceived as national biotopes untouched by each other, in order to reflect on these societies thus preconstructed in this "globalized" as well as in "postcolonial" thinking with nationalist perspectives.

The results of these reflections are presented in two volumes under the title "The Social Science of the Citizen Society".

In the first book on "Critique of the Globalization and De-colonization of the social sciences", these central post-war discourses of social science thinking and their legacies for science are discussed in the following five chapters:

1. The "globalization" of the social sciences—the introduction of nationalist thinking into social science thinking
2. The worldwide implementation of the social science of the citizen society through its "de-colonization"
3. Comments on life in a world of citizen societies and its social science idealizations
4. Knowledge that endows national identity—contributions to the ideological armament of states
5. The final highlights of the masterminds of the globalized post-colonial thinking
6. Old and new errors and their sources: Theoretical legacies of the globalization and de-colonization debates under the preparatory work of Historical Materialism

Book 2, entitled "The Nature of the Social Science of Citizen Society—Sketches for a Theory" analyzes the characteristics of the nature of social science thinking in four chapters:

1. Architecture and conceptual foundations of disciplinary thinking
2. Forms of telelogical thinking—progress of social scientific theorizing about itself
3. The discourse on and progress of social science knowledge
4. Beyond social science thinking

1. The "Globalization" of the Social Sciences—the Introduction of Nationalist Thinking into Social Science Thinking

For social science thinking it is a theoretical challenge when it is required to theorize beyond its national societies, especially for the social sciences in the countries where they have emerged. After

- a period of more than 150 years of colonization of the world, with the exploitation of the colonized world as the economic basis for the political and economic power base of the domination of the European capitalist states over the world,
- another half century after the establishment of the US model of imperialism, in which the former colonies have now been transformed into nation states participating in the global battle of nation states about political and economic power,
- the post-war model of imperialism with a world that now consists of a world of states, which, with few exceptions, are all constructed according to the pattern of the rationale of the American concept of nation states,
- a world divided into imperial states and states, which are under the command of the imperial states, many of which, like the former colonies, are sovereign states in a more formal sense only,
- all of which are under the supervision of the American world power,
- all committed to serve the growth of global capital and all drawing their political power resources from this global growth of capital and directing these power resources inwardly and outwardly to nothing other than this service for the growth of capital.

It nevertheless takes another half century for the social sciences in the imperial world to discover that there is a social world beyond their nation-state societies, a social world which they now, self-critically, believe they cannot continue to ignore.

The social sciences in the imperial states of Europe, in particular, thus discovered the necessity of what they call the internationalization or globalization of the social sciences—an internationalization that they henceforth put into practice as a comparison of theories of individual nation-state societies.

The reason why this "globalization" of social science theory formation is not justified as a conclusion from some shortcomings in theory formation, but rather comes across as a scientific imperative, is that this necessity of a "globalization" of social science theory formation, presented as self-criticism, is also only a euphemism for the fact that it was not the social sciences that had discovered the existence of a social world beyond their individual national societies in thinking about their objects. It was the science policies in the imperial countries, namely in Europe, later followed by those in the rest of the imperial world, as well as in some economically more important "emerging countries", which prompted the sciences under their supervision to direct their theory production also towards the social world beyond their national territories and to create social science knowledge also about other nation states and their societies, especially those in which these science policies had a political or economic interest.

In fact, the selection of societies and states to which this scientific interest in "globalized" knowledge is then directed can easily be recognized as a selection of states which they have not encountered through a scientific interest, but in which states of the imperial world of states have a special political or economic interest, such as, for example, the unfortunate fact, from the point of view of the European Union, that certain states are under the exclusive control of a competing imperial state, the United States, which other imperially ambitious powers, such as the said European Union, have started to question, and this certainly not because of any scientific interest, but for political and economic reasons. In this, questioning the exclusive grip of the US on certain states, the social sciences should also play their part. The Europeans' newly discovered scientific interest, for example, in Latin America, with which they are trying to challenge the US monopoly on this continent and this not at all primarily in matters of science, as is not concealed in their funding programs, or the interest of Japanese social sciences in South-East Asia, also being steered in the right direction by means of appropriately oriented funding programs, both cases may serve here only as two examples of why the self-critique of the social sciences is only the politically controlled interest that it elevates to a scientific mission, the already strange discovery of the existence of a social world beyond the world of imperialist states.

And even this is not yet the whole truth about the reasons why social sciences have proclaimed a new era of internationalized social science thinking. After all, it was not even the science policies in the imperial countries that forced their sciences to embark on the global voyage of discovery of the social world beyond their national territories. In fact, it was the global business world, which has always regarded the limited territories of nation states as an obstacle to its business activities and has always worked to remove the restrictions on its business to the markets of its nation states, that found its congenial partner in the nation state authorities and in the interest of these imperial states to extend their political power over other states, with the result that today's world has been turned into a world for business. So that, since this global capital, which treats the globe as its means of growth, as well as its inhabitants, with the development of new technologies in which the natural and engineering sciences play a key role in its competitiveness, this global business world has come to value science as a means of doing business, and therefore, nolens volens, also the services of the social sciences came into their sight.

And it was only following the discovery of the global business world's interest in science as an important lever for their business interests that science policies began to use their sovereignty over science to reorient science as a means for imperial states competing among themselves for their attractiveness to these global business interests. In this sense, science policies notice the new interest of the "markets" in science serving them, awaken them from the accusation of being in an "ivory tower", which has been reinterpreted only for this purpose and which rubs the goals of previous science policies and their concept of science as an accusation against science's unworldliness, and turn the whole science and its form of institutionalization into institutions for market competition for knowledge useful to the business world in a global knowledge market. It is only since then, and only because the international business world wants to see its interest in science established as a lever for its global business interests, that the reforms of the science scene initiated by science policymakers have redirected it towards these interests of the global capital in science and reformed it in line with these interests.

In order to ensure this new orientation of science, the national science policies in the imperial states, under the expert advice of the business world, have transformed their science scenes into a politically controlled national economic resource, according to the dictates of the business world and its thinking, and have forced their sciences to do so by making accordingly constructed 'offers' to redesign science as a national knowledge market as a contribution of the states to their establishment as an attractive location for the global business world, a national knowledge market that sociological thinking emphatically.[5]

As is usual in social science thinking to transform the social problems of citizens created by politics into aids for the problems of citizens, it ennobles its new economic missions in the global scientific world assigned to it by politics, as a further development of social science thinking towards "globalized" thinking, which has finally made its way self-critically to a scientific study of the world.

1.1 Social sciences before their "globalization": Idealizations of citizen societies and their state

Social science thinking before its "globalization" consists in the idealization of citizen societies and their nation state. What characterizes non-"globalized thinking" as state-idealistic thinking, i.e., thinking that attaches a raison d'être to citizen societies and their

---

[5] This transformation of science into a service to the global business community has been carried out in Europe and from there throughout many parts of the world, with the reforms known as the "Bologna Process". Each term used to describe these reforms reflects their guiding idea of transforming science into a marketable commodity, making it a tool in international competition and a lever for economic growth. As usual, the social sciences have once again discovered a "change" and, and by the theorizing about this change, have sought to find out how the invention of sweet terms could adjust their theorizing to this new political purpose. The leading theory created for this purpose, which from then on provided the entire social sciences with the euphemisms to ennoble this change as an opportunity as usual, immediately reveals in its name as "knowledge based economy" the noble opportunities that the subordination of not only science to the standards of the global business world should be also an opportunity for social scientific thinking, of course always critically, and which then actually expanded and converted its entire conceptual world to the ideas of this spleen of a knowledge based society.

state in general as the basis of its theories, beyond nationalistic scientific thinking, i.e., thinking that adopts the self-representations of individual nation-state societies, prior to this epistemic transition to "globalized" thinking, will be illustrated by a few examples.

Thinking from the perspective of the citizens—theories as a recipe for a domesticated materialism

In addition to psychology, educationalists specialize in the social science view of citizen societies through the view of the subjects of these societies.

As social-scientific thinkers who are completely committed to Weber's "concrete reality"[6] and with the assurance of not dealing with an invented reality but with the—telling—pleonasm of a real reality, thus making the existing social concerns their own as concerns of their theorizing about it, social-scientific theorizing commits itself to this reality, by making the practical concerns of the social subjects the guideline of thinking and thus to reject as mythologically speculative theoretical concerns the concerns of a non-real reality that has nothing to do with the kind of science about the really real that is so propagated as the cognitive guide of thinking.

Theories as a reproduction of the reality that is real in them, that it takes care of its concerns and forbids itself to ask why who actually has them, formulates a kind of social science thinking in which not only the state-constructed world constitutes the object of social science thinking, but this is a thinking, which, with its programmatic of self-obligation to the given reality, i.e. its methodical affirmatism, also wants to commit itself to making the real reality, i.e. this given social reality, its analytical viewpoint, i.e. commits itself to making the view of this reality its own view through the views of this reality given in this reality for the scientific views on this reality. It is no wonder that a thinking that takes on such a self-assur-

---

6   Describing the phenomenology of things, identifying the nation state fabrication of humans as their nature, as theorizing about the social is what Weber's phrases, when he says: *"The type of social science in which we are interested, is an empirical science of concrete reality (Wirklichkeitswissenschaft). Our aim is the understanding of the characteristic uniqueness of the reality in which we move. We wish to understand on the one hand the relationship and the cultural significance of individual events in their contemporary manifestations, and on the other the causes of being historically so and not otherwise."* (Weber, Max (1949), The Methodology of Social Science, translated by Edward A. Shils & Henry A. Finch, Glencoe Illinois, Free Press 1949, p 72)

ance of its methodological affirmatism not only ends up in the idealism of its theorizing, which it so resolutely denies with its pleonasm to deal only with real reality—and thus expresses this reality as the concern that drives this thinking, but also introduces a concept of reality that it calls empiricism, which originates from a rather mystical concept of reality, such as that of its actual actors.

Children, students, pensioners, employees, taxpayers, unemployed, entrepreneurs, politicians, families, scientists, all these subjects are not only state-created and regulated subjects, but, by their very nature, creatures of state defining power. Even if the individual interpretation of these creatures within the framework of what they are defined as is left to the freedom of interpretation of these creatures, their freedom is simply nothing more than to interpret them and a theory formation that is committed to the perspectives of the social world by these subjects that arise from this freedom of interpretation is a theory formation that thus makes before any thinking these concerns its own viewpoint of its thinking.

And there is no need for who knows how ingenious thought, to infer from the obligation to make the realization of all life projects dependent on the disposal of money, that this obligation is not aimed at helping these life projects to become a reality. The fact that without money you get nothing does not justify the conclusion that the practical everyday mind likes to draw, which economists also like to confirm as a scientifically sound insight, that the purpose of money is to provide citizens with the necessary things for their life projects. If this were the case, one could distribute the useful things in life to people and nothing would be more superfluous than money. The same experience in dealing with money is sufficient to know that the whole running after money only ensures that money is increased where there is already more than enough—from the point of view of such life projects—and therefore the sense and purpose of such money-calibrated societies, is not the supply of money for the purpose of realizing any life projects, but the increase of this strange use-free wealth, which is measured in the increase of itself freed from any use, and not only not by what one could do with it, but uses these concerns to get to the things of life through money to increase the wealth of money itself.

It is more difficult than to deduce this from mere experience to insist, day after day, contrary to all experience, that running and working for money must be good for achieving what one intends to do in life, if only by proving this profit and loss account by limiting one's life projects to what money is just enough for, i.e., by applying one's knowledge in exactly the same way as the obligation to acquire money as the only permissible form of living one's life demands. Everyone can decide for themselves whether and how they want to cheat themselves what the market economy and their political watchdogs are actually there for and what they are not for, when they are confronted with the fact that other views than mere grumbling are allowed, but forbidden as a practical alternative.

For social scientific thinking, such quite practical constraints to construct the world in the sense of what is prescribed do not apply, and scientific thinking which nevertheless wants to base its theory formation on the same views of those state creatures, which have been constructed out of the emphasis on practical blackmail by the established constraints, without being subjected to these constraints, is a thinking, which, without any compulsion before thinking about anything, imposes upon itself the obligation to orient its thinking towards what the social definitions of the state subjects determine as questions formulated in the sense of their purposes, that is, to renounce in advance with this commitment to the views born of the pursuit of these purposes views that cannot be committed to any pre-selected view of things.

A sequence of thoughts about "concrete reality" that is highly ordinary for this kind of thinking may illustrate how this thinking, through its adaptation to valid existing social purposes and concerns, produces theories that reproduce the considerations of the subjects of state provenance included in these social purposes, and thus not only repeat all their false considerations as scientific knowledge about them, but with this reproduction as scientific theories of their logic of forced self-deception and subservience, attest to the consecration of well-founded insights.

> "If skill requirements increase, low skilled workers will be under increasing pressure, in the industrial sector and in some service sector. Demographic evolutions could reinforce this tendency."[7]

Thanks to his sympathy for the failed materialism of the typical citizen, the social science theorist reveals in his discussion of how this citizen uses his knowledge for his concerns, how social science

---

7   Mehault, P. (2007), Knowledge Economy, Learning Society and Lifelong Learning-A Review of the French Literature, in: Kuhn, M., New Society Models for a new Millennium, New York, Peter Lang, p. 80.

thinking constructs its knowledge of the world of citizens as knowledge from the perspective of these citizens: By adapting to this view of the world, everything that a citizen does takes the form of coping with the state definitions of what they demand of the citizen, transformed into existing living conditions, and the theories of the science thus introduced about this ontological creature of suffering take the form of critical care for its concerns as precisely these creatures of suffering. Following this logic of caring, sharing of the concerns that these creatures have only because they have subordinated themselves to state concerns as living conditions that are no longer at issue, and about which their science, in its shared concern to get along with them, in no way wants to enlighten who, why and how these circumstances of life are established, the knowledge of these creatures becomes "competences", a mental ability very peculiar to these state creatures, which is characterized by the fact that the owner of such "competences" only obeys the owner only in that the mental products born from this ability must promise to those whom the owner of such "competences" wants and must obey. In this, too, is found the equally strange nature of social-scientific knowledge, which, in its caring service to such civic shrewdness, never ever wants to criticize it for its stupid as well as harmful thoughts, but makes its standpoint of critical accommodation its own as the maxim of its theory formation. Thus, and only in this way, the growing abilities of this civic creature do not become better means of giving his concerns a better chance, but rather a growing pressure for this subject to make itself servant to the additional demands of foreign concerns, whose subjects and aims are thought in these theories into the unknown as natural constraints from somewhere, constraints generating circumstances, about which this caring science better does not enlighten its "low skilled workers", but in the interest of avoiding worse in its theories advises them to better obey.

Because scientifically educated sympathizer of the "low skilled workers" knows a phenomenon, "demographic evolutions", in which he, thanks to his state-trained eye, does not regard "age" and "aging", i.e. harmless old age and aging, as quite natural aspects of life, but spells out old age and aging to his clients as the threat that it is from the point of view of state social security funds, a view that is obviously very clear to the social science thinker, in which the whole of life is thought of as a foreign challenge and any future at all as a threat, because here, too, nothing more makes sense to the thinker concerned with social science than the state's views of old age as costly, useless junk, from which he derives such threatening "tendencies" that life brings with it for this kind of thinking, for which his "low skilled workers" will have to take responsibility as a matter of course—or they should just simply not to become so old, so that they could avoid such "tendencies". Because social science thinking is the theoretical support of the practical management of citizens and produces its theories from this perspective, its idea of thinking of the population as its own threat is also not a headache for this thinking, on the basis of which such theorists who would ask themselves the question what is decidedly tendentious about their way of producing their theories, in which the nature of human life, age, is its unavoidable threat.

In short: Social science thinking, which derives its ideas from the adaptation to the viewpoint of the citizen, is able to deal with the demands of the civic life of a materialism permitted by the state—as long as it proves its usefulness for the materialism of the state and its economy—and to act as a subject for it, who strives to domesticate its materialism in such a way that it sees in the service for all requested purposes, which deny its aims in life and come to it in this thinking as if these requested purposes were the nature of all social life, the way to achieve his private aims in life, this is the view that gives birth to the theories of social scientific thinking.

It is this view of state creatures of the state-constructed social reality through the state-defined social purposes, their subjects, life programs and biographies that social science thinking does not want to analyze as state constructs, but rather presents them in their partisanship for the concerns of these subjects underhand, as if they were quasi natural conditions of life with which their subjects, who, for their part, are nothing but state creatures, have to cope as if they were natural living conditions, even though, of course, every social scientist knows very well that the state-constituted society is anything but a natural event. With this transformation of all state-constructed social subjects and their state-manufactured and cared for living conditions, in which this way of thinking unnoticed all the differences between the state's view of social life and that of its social subjects, into the idea of natural living conditions and their constraints, this thinking underhand turns the state itself into the pure reaction to "problems", in whose representation as constraints is erased, that it is the state that imposes these problems on them, with the beautiful result that the state itself, just as the citizens admonish it as a lever for their concerns, is constantly discussed as a service provider in solving such problems.

Nevertheless, social science thinking does not accommodate its theory formation to the practical views of state-defined subjects, because social science thinkers want to justify the state social order with apologetic intentions. Social science thinkers, at least those thinkers who do not yet "globalize" their theory formation, are certainly not nationalists who share and propagate the concerns of a particular state. Politically, they may be; the very basic apologetics of their theory formation, to interpret the state-made social world through the gaze of state-made subjects, is, in a certain sense, the result of a methodological apologetics of their particular way of theory formation, not the result of their political view, but arises, as it were, underhand as a result of their self-imposed way of thinking, which is justified by their scientific-theoretical gurus with their epistemological skepticism. With the commitment to reality as a measure of the objectivity of their theories, the social purposes valid in this reality become an incorporated epistemological interest in their theory formation.

Undoubtedly, social science theorists know that the subjects of a state-created social order, that citizens are a historical construct; under the hand of their methodological apologetics of subjecting their thinking to the made form of reality, all social constructs and the subjects of the social system, to which the social sciences owe their own emergence, as if they were human nature. As if it were the most natural thing in the world, social science thinkers waste no theoretical attention whatsoever on the most obvious inconsistencies of the everyday minds of those who seek to find their paths in life in the paths prescribed for them, they do not ask why, or what fore, because, for reality thinkers, this would be speculative thinking, and they reproduce not only unmoved by the view of the state creatures who try to adapt themselves to this world prescribed for them, despite all the absurdities of this view and despite all the practical failure of its practical implementation, these interpretations of their social life in their theories of social science, gained from their practical needs, but also offer them these theories as a caring service for all the "problems", which they do not want to get to the bottom of under any circumstances in order to eliminate them, in the interest of their epistemological connection to reality, so that these problems thanks to their thus guaranteed return also provide these sciences with the material for the return of their theories of problem solving. Theories of muddling through, theoretically constructed as each one on the one hand of the other hand and presented with academically twisted insights, are the insights that these theories with their thinking committed to methodical apologetics offer to their clients, clients they never criticize for the mistakes of their thought constructs, which these clients usually not only do not understand but do not even know, because these professional scientific thinkers produce this kind of sophisticated theories, with reference to their concern for the concerns of their research objects only for themselves anyway.[8]

The inevitable superficiality of this thinking cannot realize that all members of these societies, with a few exceptions, have in common characteristics of their way of life, which, despite all their superficial differences, determine them to an identical as well as fundamental form of life. Whether people are civil servants, white-collar workers, middle or higher class, blue-collar workers, pensioners, housewives, students or the unemployed, all these figures of state social definitions have in common for their way of life that they are variations of a tolerated materialism, that is to say, that they are all—with the few exceptions of those who are defined in this nomenclature far less narrowly, usually more technically as investors, because they are masters of the organization of the life of the society as a whole,—for all the differences in their political definitions, all share the substantial characteristic which consists in having to establish the materialism granted to them as a service for the growth of a wealth of those exceptional people, for whom this politically granted materialism of all those ordinary people is their essential means and their greatest obstacle. The toleration of their materialism, their freedom without the means of its realization, is paid for by all these members of society, who are all the same servants of wealth, with a life consisting of the same lifelong labor for this wealth of the "investors" which they produce and do not gain their lifetime. Such essential distinctions as commonalities escape the reality-based thinking that, with its commitment to reality, gets

---

8   Please see volume 2.

caught up in the observational observations of society and its superficial differences.

This kind of thinking committed to—its imagined empiricism—with its peculiar superficiality of its form of theory formation, which consists in a hyper-specialized knowledge of all possible facts, numbers and data, and this "empirical world", which, like every theory, are at first thought buildings, but which in this kind of thinking are thought buildings about a world, which only this kind of social-scientific thinking creates with its thinking through some kind of approaches from the arsenals of disciplinary theory formation, a world, which exists only in the minds of this thinking and in its thinking committed to the purposes of the existing world considers it to be the real reality, and which then confuses knowledge in this "empirical world" about the world with knowledge, this kind of thinking, in its superficiality, escapes all differences between what people and what citizens are, differences between the life plans and goals that people set for themselves and the life paths on which the life paths regulated by law domesticate these life plans in such a way that they prove themselves to be a service to their state and their economy.

In its way of thinking, this science not only fails to notice that there are some differences between people's life plans and their legal domestications; in its equation of its phenomenological thinking, it does not cause this thinking any headaches either, to present the limitations of such life plans, which are quite noted in it, and their adjustment to the life practices required by the state via law, forced by state power, as factually required necessities of every social life and its naturalized conflicts, and thus to ennoble the state domestications of the permitted materialism of state creatures for the benefit of the materialism of their rule as an aid to the materialism of their subjects. In this way, they ultimately discover the nation-state constructed society as the natural home of man and the view that the state takes of its society as the most natural view of social science thinking of all that is social.

Even if everyone can know that no human being ever demands the effort of work, social science thinking as the state itself, through the eyes of the authorities, present work as an offer, as a service of the authorities to their subjects, an offer to which, as this thinking finds, the state is not obliged, but always helps to ensure that this offer exists; the difference between the desire for money and the desire for means of living is not a real distinction for this thinking through the view of social life regulated by law, because the reality of this society, which is organized by the state, by law allows all its citizens to obtain food only by means of money and allows them to obtain this money only, if they sell their labor to such people who are looking for labor, that is, this service relationship of money owners and owners of work very much in accordance with the constitution as the only way to realize their life plans with money, that is, with those state-administered wealth share certificates.

Thus, for this thinking, this state stipulation that all members of this society can only get hold of the wealth produced by them if they acquire these state share certificates of wealth by selling their labor to their labor buyers, and if they accept, by this sale of their labor, that the work products of their work are owned by the buyer of their labor, for this thinking this is not a case—to put it in legal prose—of a well-coordinated hostage-taking of the society in deed unity with blackmail by the state authorities and by those few exceptional citizens, those buyers of work who, even without working themselves, have all the wealth shares as well as the products of work at their disposal, but for this thinking which is committed to reality and which is not open to any criticism, all this is the philanthropic provision of offers by the state and the economy for the realization of the individual life plans of people, without which these have-nots, who produce everything and to whom nothing of what they produce belongs, would come to nothing and thus, thanks to this provision of jobs, are be able to spend their life as a working life after all.

This realistic view of this society, for which the state is something like the embodiment of a communal organization of the supply of the food necessary for the life plans of its members, a quasi kind of communism, becomes, just like the accommodation of its thinking to the state constructions of the members of society and to their world full of all too human "problems", including their lifetime—a "social challenge", which here too reflects rather one-to-one the view of the state of the aging of its subjects. Longer life—a problem? For whom?

After the discovery in Europe and the USA—i.e., in the latitudes of the states dominating the world of states, in other parts of the world, lifetimes move in the opposite direction—that people live longer, it did not take more than a few weeks for the social science professional thinkers to get in line to rediscover one of their "problems" in a longer life as well. While the thinkers, completely in the sense of their sympathies for the concerns of the citizens of the citizen society, first dealt with questions about what one could do in this additional lifetime, after a few weeks of such distant thoughts, the methodical affirmatism of social science theorizing and its art of listening to reality and its purposes as the purposes of humanity had brought this thinking into line and recognized the lifetime of society as that of useful servants of wealth, who has his measure in his monetary growth and not in what these citizens need for their life plans and therefore rethinks the lifetime as a time for service to this wealth, consequently limits this to their period which is profitable in the sense of this monetary growth and with the extension of the remaining lifetime of the servants of wealth discovers the problem that they nevertheless have to get hold of money, which this has earned and which has been forcibly put aside for these useless times, now longer than before, i.e. of more money. That this pot of money grows with the growing age of the people is a problem for the administrators of these useless funds, useless because, from the point of view of its increase, it is a waste of wealth, so that since the extension of the life span, it is debated as the problem of an "aging population", a debate that reveals already in its concept, which view of the lifetime of whom discovers what problem in this, when it is no longer a question of a longer lifetime of people and what one could do with time, but of a population living longer, that is, the state's view of the phenomenon has entered into the theorizing about a longer lasting life. It had probably taken a few months until the social science professional thinkers had brought themselves to the line of the state's view of the lifetime of its citizens, and discovered, in the usual manner, the same invented "challenges for the community" that they then, as always and everywhere, also presented to people, who have no work and, therefore, when they live longer, have more time but no money for all sorts of things, translated into the problem of costs to the community, i.e. the state, and this problem of how can the state afford people living longer who are useless now presented towards people as their real concern about living longer.

Thus, the theories that eavesdrop on the purposes of reality succeed in taking on all phenomena defined as "problems", which they alone constantly create as "problems", i.e. as a way of thinking adapted to the practical handling of these phenomena, according to the purposes given in these problems, because they naturalize their purposes, assume them to be unquestionable, thus, share them under the hand of their care and declare their solution to be the task of politics, and then, with the political care of the monopoly power of society, to call for solutions to all these problems, all of them problems which for this way of thinking can never have been caused by this state endowed despite of all its power, but which this state must be able to solve, so that these political powers have to listen to their professional scientists incessantly and critically, so that they can finally take care of their tasks, invented by their social scientists, which only they attach to state politics. This is annoying for the political powers on the one hand, but it helps to maintain the belief that the solution to all these problems of the citizens must be the task of politics.

Lessons about "Auschwitz"—citizen societies and the refinement of the missions of their state

With its theories and contributions, the Frankfurt School, especially its exponent Adorno, can certainly be described as most influential for the social science thinking of post-war debates not only in Germany but worldwide. From these reflections on the war by Adorno, one can study how non-globalized social science thinking, even when it discusses national political activities, does not adopt the concerns of the German state or its self-representation, thanks to the idealizations of its missions—and yet, with its criticism of this state, theoretically sketches the foundations for the post-war self-portrait of this state.

Adorno's reflections on what he circumscribes as "Auschwitz" are to be discussed here as an example of how this critical social science thinking at times, when those debates about a globalization of social science thinking were unknown, does not discuss the state program of a certain state, but, using the example of state activities of a particular country, here of Germany, discusses constitutive elements of state societies and their state in general, in this example, in that for these discussions of state missions components of war activities, i.e. activities between states are first constructed as affairs of an individual state, this thinking thus fades out the world of states and their imperialism, and in that this thinking, secondly, with its critique of state war practices, then, through the critical delimitation of war practices and the idealization of what the actual tasks of states against war are, makes itself common to the principle of state politics and, through this, to the German state—in its critically contested, idealized form—and in this way shows itself exemplary, how the—not global—social science thinking does not court any individual state, but rather the concept of state-constructed societies, like that of citizen societies and their political power, and how this thinking then endows this political power with the mission to actually stop the use of warlike violence, which only these political powers are capable of.

> "The demand that Auschwitz may not happen again is the very first of education. It precedes all others to such an extent that I don't believe I need or should justify it."[9]

Auschwitz: The crushing of enemies within for the war against another state power outside that has been made an enemy, the violent subjugation of the rule of another state over land and people to its own power by destroying its means of violence and purifying its own society of citizens of its own state power within that has been made an enemy, this is how war goes—and that, war, is first and foremost a matter of what, of education?

War a matter of education? And what if one does not heed the not very squeamish admonition of this figurehead of critical sociological thinking, his view that "Auschwitz" is "first and foremost" a task of education and that this is so fundamental and, therefore, so self-evident that it does not need any justification, what if one does not obey this admonition after all and tries to trace which thoughts must have been made in order to be able to understand Adorno's view, which indeed was and still is the most common critical view about "Auschwitz" after the war, not only among intellectuals in Germany, and what if one then also tries, in spite of his admonition, to find out how it is that this view means to present it as so self-evident that one must not ask for any why and for what, in order to immunize it against any criticism, and still takes the liberty of asking for any reasons for this view?

---

9   Adorno, T.W., (1971) *Erziehung zur Mündigkeit*. Frankfurt a.M., Suhrkamp, 1. Auflage, p. 88.

In order to anticipate the result of the transgression of this Adorno's prohibition of thinking that "Auschwitz" is supposed to be a question of education, a theory that derives its entire conclusiveness of this theory about "Auschwitz" only from this prohibition of thinking: It is the state infatuation, not in Germany, but in state societies in general, which cannot be shaken by the war and "Auschwitz", especially the state infatuation of sociological thought, which, with its diagnosis and with its prohibition of thinking, precisely sketches the view of the war and Auschwitz and precisely the pattern of the post-war raison d'être of German politics, and with which this politics sets off for the next attempt, this time on the economic path after the military path failed, at least for the time being, to become a European economic superpower again, and tackles this again immediately after the war. And today, now that this economic path has been successfully taken, the question is being discussed everywhere as to whether it is still possible to stay out of the world's wars, in which one has long been involved everywhere, in other words, whether one wants to get even more involved in the military path again.

And how does a critical theorist end up with the pattern of Germany's post-war raison d'être, including its new national self-image, far from being a nationalist thinker?

It goes like this: With the synonymization of Germany's politics under the Nazi regime to "Auschwitz", Germany's war, i.e. the attempt to establish itself as a European and thus as a leading world power by destroying the political dominions in competing European states and conquering the power over them, this war is, first of all, with the help of scandalizing the destruction of all actual or supposed enemies within warring Germany, just as if there would be war without these scandalous excesses of violence, not only moved out of the focus of reflection, but, at the same time, also deprived any reflection on the connection of war, its specific forms of violence, which only states are capable of, and also on all the internal "cleansing" of the people who are considered enemies of society, of the ground for any reflection. With this scandalization, the war and everything that belongs to it is no longer an object of reflection, so removed from critical reflection, and thus also the internal "cleansing" of the population, carried out with state perfection, of parts of the population that are not considered suitable for war because they are politically and racially unreliable, all this is now no longer an object of any kind of reflection, and thus, as quite beyond the rationality of warlike actions of states, as the actual and only object of thinking about war. Isolated from war what is part of any wars because it is scandalized away, this is the arche typus of the post war (not exclusively) German way of thinking about the war. War, the kind of violence of states against states, is thus no longer the object of reflections on what is discussed by critical thinkers under the synonym "Auschwitz", the world of states and their warlike dealings, including their internal excesses of violence against parts of their population from the observations of states in war, so successfully dissected from thinking as an object of social science thinking.

With this arrangement of the object of thinking synonymized as the scandalous "Auschwitz" and then, with the separation of state interests in war by means of the condemnation of its warlike means and its victims, then, with the next step, war made a matter of misguided morality and thus a matter of education, not only are the warlike activities inwardly are separated for outwardly, but also the state, the subject of the warlike actions, is finally socio-scientifically defined: All differences of state and subjects are dissolved, all, state and citizen without distinction between the politically ruling and the subjugated subjects, are equally held responsible for "Auschwitz", and with the assignment of the internal war affairs, scandalized to the abomination, made to a mistaken educational matter, and with this in the next step they are made a question of criticizing the morality of the German citizen, so that the very state, the subject of war and the subject of "Auschwitz", can appear as the corrective authority of the misguided morality of citizens, thanks to this kind of thinking, and with this the state is assigned its educational mission and through this mission attributed the new raison d'état of the state which is thus purified and reformed.

No wonder that the political representatives, in this cleaning made from warriors into supreme moralists, rejoice over the morally corrupt citizens who are thus made the real responsible for "Auschwitz", and quickly blurt out that their hand may fall off when they reach for a weapon again.

Any questions about the state aims of things not so unusual for states, such as wars acts like the internal "purges" which, to recall briefly, no citizen, but only state and their political leaders can instigate and carry out, wars in which these states are the ones who burn their citizens, and if any citizens do not want they shoot them in line with all states war laws, wars against other states which are therefore accompanied by wars against these citizens, such as their internal "purges", which are after all not a particularly unusual event in the history of states, all such questions after all the destructions of the just finished world war, all such questions about wars, which one could also raise as a scientist, what these states aim at with their wars, what duties they enforce on the citizens in them, the very war morality states create for this, with what kind forces all this is enforced on the citizens, not to mention what the German state wanted with its war against the world powers, all these questions are buried with the help of the power of persuasion of the moral force of the misery of a defeat, buried under the mountains of dead citizens and buried under the burden of destruction, buried with the accusation of a misguided moral education of the citizens of this state, all buried together with all the war debris.

The citizen and his morals are pilloried, and the state rises from the ruins of his war confronted with a massive accusation that, the war shows for thinkers like Adorno that it has completely failed in its educational mission—and thus, as an outline of the foundations of its future reasons of state, is assigned by this critical thinker the task of learning from "Auschwitz" by fulfilling its moral mission now educating its citizens to become morally decent citizens—just as if they, the citizens were the real war criminals. What better idea could the remaining remnants of the political class have than finally taking the ever very humane aims of states into their own hands and to take on the mission of finally educating the morally depraved subjects to educate them now to be good national citizens.

Now, one also understands how good it is that the critical sociologist adds that this noble mission of a purified morality and the politics purified by it must not be doubted by anyone. With this logic, which derives from the misery of a lost war together with its hardened prohibition to interpret all its atrocities differently than as the result of a failed moral education of the citizens, and which derives from this for the political class, the makers of the war and rulers over the remaining citizens, the mission to teach the citizens now mores for their disgrace, why one now feels attempted raising the question what this sociological thinker, in his unshakable infatuation with the state in his critical conception of the state as the failed guardian of humanistic ideals, what this thinker would have thought about the state and the morality of the citizens, if this state with its citizens had not lost but won this war and had celebrated this with its victorious citizens. The answer may be thought up by everyone.

In the same way, or as the critical spirit of Adorno conceived it, post-war political propaganda in the construction of the new joint imperial project of Germany and France, called Europe, puts the remaining citizens in charge of rebuilding not only their civic morale, but also the next project of imperial ambitions: The war was branded as a heinous "crime"—because Hitler had not won it, and the "Wehrmacht" was "abused" by Hitler for this purpose, so that the reconstruction of a new Wehrmacht began without interruption. For a short time, one could also think that this branding of war as a "crime" was a position against war (as I said, arm off when someone takes up a weapon again, Adenauer), but with the establishment of the new military force, this was quickly dismissed and corrected as unrealistic pacifism and instead, with the commitment to the moral inscrutability of its state history, which, similar to and thanks to the idea of Adorno's prohibition of reflection, could not be explained by anything, with the assurance, to say it with Adorno, "that Auschwitz will not happen again", with the reconstruction of the same state and the same market economy, new plans for the next, now peaceful conquest of Europe and the world were started with the morally clean means of a successful market economy, actively militarily supported by the USA, which through this war then instead of the Germans became a world power, now also militarily repaired by them for its war goals against the same enemy. No state in the world would, of course, reject this offer and with "Never again Auschwitz" as the proof of a new purified raison d'être, and, what a surprise, the fingers that were supposed to fall off when reaching for a weapon again, thanks to the successful application and redemption of Adorno's demand for a purified moral education, not only remained on the line thanks to this ostentatious confession of a moral guilt, but were, as we can see today, the perfect garnishment of the strategy to make the German state for the time being, at least, a hegemon in Europe, with the best prospects to challenge the global supremacy of the world power USA under German leadership of Europe and to reopen an old calculation for the Russians. With this, we arrive in the ideological department of state politics in today's world, thanks to the application of the socio-scientifically critical thought patterns of thinkers like Adorno.

For in this or a similar way, critical social science reflections before their "globalization" about the war of states construct their ideas about their actual higher humane, moral missions and thus strengthen the belief that all these states, despite all this, are actually always concerned about the well-being and morals of their citizens and that it is them, these states, who always have their concerns with the morals of their citizens. The real goal of states, set with the social-scientific criticism of the German state as the failure of its educational mission to educate morally integrity-conscious citizens, endows the world of states with their critical idealism and missions in a way similar to what happened for post-war Germany, and thus provides the states of the world with their critical images of their noble missions and those of their special missions in the world of nation-states, self-portraits, which sometimes, thanks to the course of world history, such as in the case of Germany, need to be readjusted. For this, for the rescue of the idea of the state as the guardian of all values, whose persuasiveness it has called into question with its war, social science thinking a la Adorno knows how to offer its theoretical services for correction to all doubters about what drives nation states. For Adorno, for this pre-globalized thinker, it was the German politics that he critiqued for misusing the nation state and failing to do what the nation states are originally for, for the moral education of the citizens and this state mission is for thinkers like Adorno so natural that he takes for granted that it is so redundant to be justified.

The Vietnam War—a challenge for the cohesion of a citizen society

Another social scientist, one of the world's most distinguished thinkers and, a synonym for critical thinking like Adorno, is Bourdieu, another pioneer of social science theorizing before this "globalization" of theorizing.

The fact that the title of his famous book, "Homo Academicus," [10] insinuates that Bourdieu—a social scientist who, like Adorno, is certainly not suspected of being a nation-state biased thinker—announces under this title a theory about a species of man, the academics that can be found all over the world, does not in the least irritate this prominent and much-cited thinker, when his book,

---

10   Bourdieu, P., (1988) Homo Academicus, Cambridge, Polity Press.

under this general title about a human species found worldwide, presents a study that deals with investigations at two faculties of a university in France, and a study which, quite apart from any "globalized" thinking, does not say a word about who and what distinguishes this Homo Academicus as a species that can actually be found worldwide. This study, unaffected by the actual worldwide existence of his subject, a human species of every citizen society, theorizes on the question, not what distinguishes this human species, the academic, but, after he flirtatiously debates in a long introduction about whether an academic like him can theorize about the academic in order to arrive at the result, he with his broadly rolled out self-critical methodical insights can do it, in order to, after he has awarded himself the theoretical suitability, debate under this ambitious title of his book the question why academics in these two faculties, of which one, obviously following the plausibility of an assumed common sense and—anticipating the answer to his whole questioning—stands for "conservative" and the other for "progressive" academics, what characterizes these "conservative" and "progressive" faculties and why these academics joined or did not join the protest movements in France in the 1970s.

Even if it is not easy to ignore the tautological answer to the question, which is already too openly predicated on the pretentious distinction between conservative and progressive academics, it is, nevertheless, remarkable how little the social science thinking of a theoretician who is, by no means, a nationalist, how little it somehow irritates this non-"globalized" thinking to think under the title of the species of academic about the differences between academics in matters progressive versus conservative that make him concerned as a sociologist, that is, the question of whether this homo academicus is, as one would sociologically say, a retarding or progressive social subject. Social science thinking before that "globalized" version does not reflect on any individual nation-state characteristics of phenomena, here that of the academic, but on nation-state constructed objects as such, beyond any comparison of nation states and their creatures such as the Homo Academicus, even if no one knows better than Bourdieu that the academic is a creature of state science that experiences quite diverse interpretations among the states of the world, differences unlike him globalized theorizing is so keen on.

Such questions of international comparative theories about the academic are not familiar to pre-globalized social science thinking, which is interested in the creatures of states in general, here the academic, and sociological thinking is interested in the academic— in what sociologists are interested in everything and everyone, which is why they are sociologists.

What does the sociological thinker, who is one of the most cited thinkers worldwide, theorize about under this title when he reflects on the academic under the question of their progressiveness versus conservatism? What moves this critical theorist under this question, under which he analyzes the Homo Academicus?

Dealing with the question of why the two departments at the Sorbonne have different political positions on what makes the student movement concerned, a thinker like Bourdieu knows, of course, that this protest by initially essentially intellectuals was directed against the US war against Vietnam, an object of protest that he is very familiar with and personally shares, but which is not addressed anywhere in his studies of conservative and progressive departments at the Sorbonne under the topic of a "homo academicus". The Vietnam War, or rather the protest against it, is for this academic who theorizes about Homo Academicus only the political occasion promising him scientific attention, to debate the questions that interest him as a sociologist about any topic.

Vietnam War and protest against it, that is the world of politics, world politics is a subject of political science and for that reason alone it is not the subject of sociological studies. Sociological thinkers are concerned about a completely different, much more profound question, they always reflect on whatever they their object of thinking is: Bourdieu, social scientist, sociologist, left-wing thinker, what makes him concerned and what he does as a sociologist to answer the question why academics joined the protest against the war in Vietnam or not, a war, by the way, in which France, as the old colonial power, was still heavily involved—Bourdieu, who is above all whatever he thinks about a sociologist, and as sociologist, he does what sociologist always do: he digs in tons of all kinds of data, all of which have in common that they have nothing, absolutely nothing, to do with the Vietnam War or the war in general, but which are made up of all the ordinary kinds of data, the study of which provides sociologists with enlightening information about everything, really everything they study, data that sociologists find incredibly exciting, whatever they study, and which they also interpret when they are looking for an explanation, better after a confirmation of the explanation they have—which distinguishes conservativeness from its tautological opposite progressiveness—and do this through association-impregnated interpretations of data that should allow them to understand why people somewhere in the world are protesting against whatever, i.e. progressive, for him equals good, no matter what and where and why, just as the same data allow them to deeply understand why people only drink the same Coca Cola and others don't, or why some beat up their children, i.e. are conservative, i.e. are bad.

Social scientists, here sociologists, know already, thanks to their disciplinary access to the objects of their theorizing, exactly how and where they find their answers to their questions, because they already have them, thanks to their disciplinary access, here why the world knows conservative and progressive academics and dig in their data on academics, just as if these subjects were a mere sociological synonym for any citizen in matters of progressiveness versus conservativeness. As for anything they dig in data like these: the family status, i.e. married, divorced, their sex, their age, what newspapers they read (conservative or progressive, enlightening), what kind of cars they drive, Deuschewo or Peuschewo, the districts where they live, Clichy or Bois de Boulogne, the size of their apartments in square meters, the number of children, the age when they got married, etc. and so on. ; in other words, all the card indexes constructed from a profoundly nation-state perspective and the state data derived from them on information defined by citizenship and collected accordingly, which serve the sociologically trained mind of a sociologist as profound "indicators" for theorizing about what sociologists always and in everything makes concerned, namely, the question of the extent to which citizens succeed in making friends with what sociologists have defined as their deepest need, their nationally defined duties, sociologically translated as the need for conformity with or deviations from their "social roles" or similar varieties of social classifications of the wholeness of societies, in order to pursue their sociological concern and to constantly observe whether the citizen simply follows their intended classification to and their community (conservative), i.e. everything remains as it is, or strives towards new kinds of interpretation of citizens life (progressively), so that the cohesion of society might be challenged on the basis of the given "norms", and so that politics is challenged in its function, attributed to it by sociologists, of holding all and everything together, social cohesion they call the sociological top concern. Just as sociology ticks: Sociality as the noblest supreme task of state politics and sociological science as providing alarm signals for the demand for political intervention if this sociality is to be endangered. This is how sociologists look at the world, this is how they look at anything and this is how they look at academics.

For Bourdieu, in search of an answer to the question of who follows the protests and who does not, this question can thus be answered as easily as all sociologically constructed tautological questions. The fact that the objects of his research are academics can be entirely ignored; they only stand, anyway, for the only question that makes sociological thinking, no matter which genre of citizen arouses their interest concerned.

And one had almost suspected it: people who pay attention to their social status, who live in posh apartments in the Bois de Bologne, who drive fat cars, etc., etc., in other words, who have indicators pinned to them as proof of their conservatism, betray to the sociological mind that these conservatives can unambiguously only be conservatives and who—crystal clear—because conservatives, are conservative, and therefore do not join what is not conservative, i.e., the protest. And, who would have thought it, the other way round are those progressives: people who don't get married when they should, drive a 2CV, live in cheap apartments in Montmartre, read critical newspapers, are people, as you can "conclude" from the indicators, who change or swap roles and these are without doubt the ones who go to protest for exactly that reason, and are therefore clearly—progressive.

Because sociological thinking translates every question about whatever and whoever into its one and only question, how the cohesion of society is, it has no problem asking the question of who is protesting against the Vietnam War and who is not, this question of a war, of a military conflict between states, to the sociologically translated completely detached question of who is the preserver and innovator, in order to understand sociological thinking as immensely critical with its concern for the preservation of the cohesion of a citizen society, so that there are citizens who join the protesters, because they, since they are progressive, represent the society's future. And, because this sociological thinking can always use the same "indicators" for this kind of theoretical insight, which always addresses the same sociological question about everything and everyone, the competitive society is always criticized for this, with all its potential to endanger social cohesion, any society, sociological thinking knows originates from the nature of any society, any society is a society with all the invented worries about the eternally threatened cohesion of society. In line with of all the criticism, sociological thinking is also realistic enough to regard the state-made competitive society, with all its various private subjects and social conflicts, despite showing their most obvious nature as nation-state made subjects all being private property owners, as the archetype of all social life and to, therefore, keep a critical eye on it from sociological thinking to see whether anything does not cause this society to totter and require the intervention of its political violence.

Thus Bourdieu writes a book about what he, as a social science thinker, considers worth explaining about demonstrations against a war: first and foremost, himself, Bourdieu, the superior homo academicus, who ponders about homo academicus, its "social structure" or similar things that are immensely worth knowing for social science thinkers, who are all concerned about the existence of citizen societies, above all, their ever questioned cohesion and even more so about that of their representative of sociality, their state. This thinking, it must be noted, is all not nationalistic, despite all the concerns for the cohesion of the citizen society, or better not yet nationalistic, engaged by concerns about the cohesion of citizen societies and their states and committed to the sustainability of these citizen societies and their states, the more.

1.2 Globalized theories—nationalistic self-portraits of states

At some point at the end of the 20th century, the social sciences discover a new phenomenon and baptize it "globalization" and find that this phenomenon called "globalization" requires the eponymous "globalization" of their science.

That a new insight into the world, if it is then, as in the case of "globalization", considered epochal, requires a new form of thinking about the world, belongs to the peculiarities of social science thinking, a way of thinking which knows characteristics of its cognitive activities, to be taken from the objects of its thinking, with which it then approaches them.[11] In this case of globalization and the accordingly globalized thinking this means one must see everything as a matter of globalization. That is, one has to "think globally" about "globalization" and this is not considered as an obvious methodical affirmatism that inevitably produces tautologies—if the world is global, thinking has to be global thinking and to interpret the world as a global world—but as a form of thinking that sees itself as a loudspeaker of reality and therefore adjusts this thinking before thinking according to the needs of the object of theorizing, or better, to what these thinkers see as the needs of the object of thinking, as if social science thinkers were the existing world's reality spokesmen. What this phenomenon called globalization is supposed to be is already itself strange enough. As usual in the social sciences, any famous scientist has put this term into the world as a new thesis about the world, and then the scientific scene has started to wonder which reality this thesis must surely mean. From there on, theory creation is heavily engaged in finding anything in the world that allows to imagine what globalization might be about. Then, once any phenomena are found illustrating what this category is supposed to say, a new theory is created, a theory which from that time on conquers the world of theory formation. If a thinking from then on creates theories about anything without relating this to this new theory coined globalization, from then on guiding thinking, theories are considered as being outdated, just as if thinking was adjusting thought about the world to thought fashions. (See also volume II)

This is the way theory formation in social science thinking works, you either look for an already existing theory and march out into the world with your trained mind and interpret it skillfully through the glasses you have put on. What comes out of this is not obviously presupposed knowledge, but, as every student of the social sciences learns, this is how science works, only works. Or, one invents a kind of visionary theory, a hypothesis, or even just a new term, like globalization, and then one puts everything in this world in such a way that one suddenly identifies everything and anything as a worldwide spread, something that supports this thesis, because

---

[11] Since the objects of social science thinking are al objectification of any human will, requesting from social thought that it must adjust its way of thinking to the "concrete reality" is therefore nothing less but the obligation for affirmative thinking. See more about this in "The Social Sciences of the Citizen Society, Volume 2, The Nature of Social Sciences—Notes about a Theory."

it reinterprets the world through this thesis, and then, theoretically, delights in the fact that one has now understood what has happened in the world in a completely new way, justified by a renewed reality. Thus, in social science theorizing the main nature of the reality is found to be change.

After the term "globalization" was then put into the world, this already strange thought, that a subjectless something, spread all by itself worldwide, that is, in its own words, globally spread, thanks to its reflexive pronoun does not reveal who and what is done there towards which purposes, so that globalization is a self-generating, subjectless something and it must be its main nature to be spread worldwide, a being characterized by nothing else but being everywhere; and out of this thought of a being everywhere, thanks to its contentlessness inviting theorizing to the freely fantasize about of all kind of imaginations what globalization must certainly be, a new generation of theories was then generated, which wanted to understand everything everywhere from then on as a phenomenon of this concept of a self-creating, subjectless something that had been thus put into the world, and which, with this strange theoretical creation of a world from the minds of thinkers, from now on "framed" theoretically every theory about whatever ("framing" is the name of this scientific-theoretical operation to create thought through presuppositions, here it is "globalization") and thanks to this new view understood everything completely anew as a phenomenon of that "globalization". Since then, everything has been a clear case of this "globalization".

For this thinking it also no doubt, if from then on any topic was interpreted across all social science disciplines as a phenomenon of that "globalization", then finally also theorizing itself had to be— globalized. Nobody asks what this should actually be, arguing, that since simply everything was globalized, so that thinking itself also must be "globalized". Nobody wants to question this kind of conclusion from the nature of an object of thinking to the way of thinking, not to mention raising any question, if any property of any object of thinking, could at all be a property of thinking—just as if one would say, since the sky is blue, hence, thinking must also be blue. That the activity of knowledge creation about a thing depends on the property of thing, almost as if thinking about unemployment was a different thinking than thinking about poverty, for the advocates of a "globalization" of all social phenomena it seems obvious that thinking about these phenomena must in turn be globalized thinking. That this rule of social science thinking is nothing less but its affirmatisms made a methodological must for this thinking, this is also nothing that could irritate social science thinkers, when a new fashion of thinking is created, because the challenge is now how to adjust one's theories to this new fashion and to rephrase any theory now as a contribution to globalization, created through a globalized way of thinking.[12]

What then actually globalized thinking should be if it is counteracted with its opponent of local thinking, as if global thinking were taking place beyond any place, also this nonsense of attaching attributes to thinking, which as before it obtains from the object of thinking, attributes of thinking, such as geographical entities, attributes which cannot even be an attribute of thinking, all these theoretical oddities one has to accept without any further questions, if one wants to introduce the place of thinking as an epistemological instance by attaching to thinking the location of its object, i.e. the location of the cognitive activity as an attribute of cognitions, and thus create this, thinking through place, as a another special way of thinking.

And even if one were to ask whether, for example, an Indologist or a Sinologist from France, two humanities, or also a psychologist, assigned to the social sciences, who researches psychological phenomena anywhere in the world, whether these social scientists, who have been creating their theories about this and that here and there since the emergence of disciplinary social science theorizing, whether these scientists are already globalized or rather pre-globalized theorists, all this cannot irritate the idea of a geographical classification of cognitive activities, because thinking, thinking as the eternal ex post adaptation of theories to reality is so self-evident to this thinking that this thinking does not notice the theoretical nonsense of a rather free-hand epistemological categorization of locations as determinants as a way of theorizing. Globalization is the order of the day, so thinking must be globalized as well and nobody is confused about this epistemological absurdity, an absurdity not better than creating orange knowledge.

---

12 How such new fashions guiding the creation of theories are created, this is discussed in "The Social Science of the Citizen Society, Volume 2, The Nature of Social Sciences—Sketches of a Theory."

The epistemological nonsense does not interest the propagandists of a "globalization" of thinking. Whatever this may be, this "globalized" or also "internationalized" social scientific thinking wants to be understood thanks to this geographical attribute, making the location of thinking a cognitive mode of thinking, as a thinking that no longer directs its thoughts towards an individual nation state, more precisely, a thinking that directs this thinking from the national society of the nationality of the social scientist, beyond this nationality of the scientist—towards the world of states. The fact that this has always been the case, as I said earlier pointing on particular social science disciplines such as Anthropologie and all those humanities does not matter, because globalized thinking is not just simply widening the geographical sights of theorizing.

Thinking is globalized, not if—let's say—a French scientist theorizes about something beyond France. Thinking is not globalized then and by the fact that scientists think about phenomena of other nationalities beyond the state of their nationality. Globalized thinking is a particular way of cognition operating with the assumption that thoughts are, indeed must be, affected by the nationality of the thinker. Globalized thinking, i.e., theorizing affected by the location of thinking, identified with the nationality of any thinker, does not reject such assumptions as politically interested, presupposed thinking, but, on the contrary, attributes to this thinking, which is affected by the nationality of the thinker, the new quality of the very necessary progress of thinking in that "globalized" social reality, the very progress towards this "globalized" social scientific thinking, thinking has to make.

And what is the result of this operation coined globalizing the social sciences? To anticipate the outcome of this operation of a "globalization" of social science thinking: In this step of social-scientific thinking from non-globalized social-scientific thinking to globalized thinking, this thinking that discovers the world as its new object and that practices this view of the world as the comparison of individual nation-state societies actually makes a remarkable quasi-methodical transition of its theory-building, which is connected with the alleged discovery of its new object, the world of states beyond, this transition is the transition from critical state-idealistic thinking, a thinking that idealizes the citizen society and its state as such without any nationalism', i.e. a thinking without the affirmation of any individual nation state, this globalized thinking shifts to a thinking towards nationalistic scientific thinking, a thinking in which the self-representation of individual nation states and their national citizen societies becomes the methodological principle of this "globalized" thinking. This "globalized" thinking is a further development of social scientific theory formation, towards a social science that pursues social science as the creation of politically presupposed thinking and by doing so, eliminates nothing less than the difference between social science knowledge and political opinions, a difference that is constitutive for social science, i.e. it puts with these politically and no longer scientifically constructed presuppositions of its thinking an end to any forms of scientific judgement, i.e. judgements based on objectivity. And this is exactly what social sciences looks like today, in the world called "globalization", and the according globalization of the social sciences as their congenial decolonization: social science thinking, which is dedicated to the practical concerns of the individual citizen societies, of their citizens, their individual state and their economy.

The transition to internationalized/globalized theory-building, thus, as will be shown, consists, under the nebulous concept of a "globalization" of social science thinking, in the release of nationalist thinking as scientific thinking. It is this transition to nationalist thinking as scientific thinking, a thinking that adopts thinking to the concerns of individual citizen societies and their states, which the social sciences present under the title of their "globalization", a shift to ennoble nationalistic thinking to scientific thinking, a shift the critical thinker Beck, as everything critically soaped up, calls a shift to "cosmopolitanism", a shift with which social science theory formation turns nationalist thinking into a modernized methodology of social science theory formation—by the way, as will be shown later, including Beck's "cosmopolitanism", he presents as the smartest version of nationalist thinking.

And this progress of social science thinking, presented so strangely as worldwide, i.e., "globalized" thinking, is, as will be shown, is a remarkable shift, since it also finds its consistent conclusion in no more and no less than in the scientific justification of all possible nationalisms, of imperialism, up to the justification of war.

How this "globalized" social science thinking constructs its theories about the citizen societies of a world of states, how it argues in these "globalized" theories, and what the actual further development towards globalized social science thinking consists of in detail, will be shown in the following examples.

Nationalistic self-portraits of states

Globalized social science thinking, which discovers that there is a social world beyond national biotopes, directs its views to the social world beyond these national biotopes and constructs its theories about the world as a comparative addition of theories, theories about the incomparability of individualized national social biotopes, as this globalized thinking finds out in theses comparative studies. In these comparisons, not only all state constructs of social phenomena, the citizen societies, but also their political body, the nation-state, the historically specific manifestations of citizen societies and nation states are indistinguishably intertwined with their statehood as if they were the exclusive nature of these national societies. In this equation, in which all the differences between what all citizen society and all nation states share and how a particular nation state interprets the citizen society and their political body, the nation state, this insertion of globalized thinking, this thinking that is entirely conceptless about the nature shared by all individual citizen societies and states, this globalized thinking mystifies with this equitation of what all states share with their particular historical nature, with this equitation all made their exclusive nature, this new globalized thinking, which called for a new way of theorizing about the world, has since and thanks to this equitation been scientifically cherished as the individual societies and nation states culture and thanks to this view as their culture has established itself under this politicized and mystifying concept of culture as a globally new acknowledged form of social science thinking and has, coined as cultural studies, advanced to become a new approach in the social sciences across all disciplines.[13]

---

13   It is this double false equation of state forms of sociality and their nationally specific manifestations with the nature of every form of sociality that, with the de-colonization of the world as the transformation of all societies of the world into state-constituted societies and the re-transformation of the former alternative society project of the Soviet Union now all into those citizen societies and their political bodies called the nation state, that constitutes the concept of cul-

The "Globalization" of the Social Sciences   55

In globalized social science thinking, the nationally conceived societies do not only a priori constitute the object of this thinking, the individual nationally conceived societies and their individual forms of citizen societies and political bodies also constitute the theoretical view through which this globalized thinking analyzes them as an object of globalized thinking. What would be regarded in non-globalized thinking as a violation of the basic rules of social science thinking and rejected as nationally prejudiced thinking, the social sciences call this "biased" thinking, theorizing through nationally preconfigured views, is not only an everyday, universally recognized practice in globalized thinking, but is also regarded as the progressive way of a social science thinking adjusted to the nature of the globalized world, which since then, through these nationalistically shaped views, creates its globalized theories.

The generation and presentation of theories under titles that present any research question or theory under headings such as "... from a Chinese perspective" are thus not rejected in this globalized social science thinking as obviously nationally presupposed knowledge, but rather seen as an enrichment for the formation of therein globalized theories about the social world, theories that hypostasize not only individual nation-state societies as the object of their thinking, but a way of thinking that creates its theories without any reservations about its openly expressed nation-state colored view of whatever object, and which does not consider its national view as a proof of its contribution to a nationally inspired theory formation because these globalized theories contrast their nationally constructed views with other theories of the same nationalist constructed theories about other state societies.

As a result of this collection of preferably comparative country studies, which do not study a country but rather portray a national view of these countries on and about themselves, the knowledge of social science theory formation in its globalized version consists of an addition of nationalistically created theories that are only suitable for a mere confrontation because they do not even allow for

---

ture as a new epistemological theorem, naturalizing these societies, and is responsible for the mutation of anthropology into cultural theories as a theoretical means for their creation of distinctive national identities. See "The Social Science of Citizen Society, Book 2, The Nature of the Social Science of the Citizen Society—Sketches for a Theory".

comparison. Because this kind of theories, which all regard their national view of a mostly not even jointly known, identical object as their contribution to globalized thinking, consistently lack any tertium comparationis thanks to their national perspectives and therefore elude any comparison. The scientific achievement of globalized theory-building consists in the never-ending repetition of a return to its starting point, the discovery of that abstract, i.e., conceptless difference that cannot name any differences of the same thing, with which this kind of theory-building began.

What else. Because globalized social science thinking is thinking about the respective nation-state society and has no knowledge whatsoever of what distinguishes citizen societies and their political body, the nation-state, regardless of their specific phenomenology, as a particular historical form of societies and political bodies and what all these citizen societies, their states and their economy, what all these capitalist societies have in-common, its comparative theories cannot identify their differences and remain in the monstrous circle of the mere assertion of a contentless otherness, on which they insist all the more the less they can identify their national characteristics as variations of the same capitalist society.

And globalized theories cannot do this, because the theories of this globalized theory formation with their national view through their individual national society consist of the representation of those national self-portraits, i.e., of their differences, their demarcations from others, through which they distinguish themselves as national theories in that they distinguish themselves mere negatively, as demarcations from each other. Consequently, globalized theorizing about and through nation-state perspectives makes the mere, non-comprehended recognition of any peculiarities that are claimed to be national characteristics, mostly historically grown ones, as exclusively belonging to that society, a prerequisite for understanding such nation-state created insights—as well as their entire insubstantial result.

The following is an example of the inevitable impasse and nationalism of theory-building through nation-state perspectives, which, in order to share its insights, presupposes the sharing of the perspectives from which it generates them, but—naturally—cannot and does not want to do so because, as globalized knowledge, it insists on its conceptless national particularity, conceptless because, lacking due to their interests in creating demarcating images, any knowledge what these societies share, this knowledge cannot even indicate what its particularism is:

> "These difficulties are not only due to the difference between English and French. They probably also reflect the French conception of knowledge, which puts an emphasis on explicit and scientific knowledge, and the French conception of learning, which traditionally puts the emphasis on formal education and training."[14]

Since social science thinking in its international comparative studies reflects on the demarcating differences of nation-state constructs without their common concepts, these studies not only cannot distinguish between what these constructs have in common and their historical differences, but conversely consider the shared social nature of a nation-state constituted societies, about which they generate their theories, as the ontological nature that has grown into these societies.

Consequently, all social phenomena, including those that actually only originate from human nature, such as knowledge, acquire the character of an individually nation-state shaped construct and become indistinguishable from their really state-made nature for comparative social science thinking, just as if characteristics of human nature were indistinguishable from their state-made nature— and vice versa. Nationalism, the identification of individual citizen societies and their political body, the nation state, merge with the nature of all societies, and thus all this, the variations of the same historical type of capitalist societies, natural features of societies, such as in the case of this quotation, knowledge, the indistinguishable mixture of all these components shaping citizens societies and nation states across the world becomes the thought pattern through which globalized thinking creates its demarcating theories.

National comparative social science thinking thus also knows the monstrous knowledge of a "French concept of knowledge". Undoubtedly, nation-states shape the living conditions of people as they shape these people themselves, and they do so to a degree that led Marx to speak of a "character mask", a criticism of the members of citizen societies who, because they freely shape their lives, want to believe that, if they regard their actions regulated by law and their

---

14 Mehault, P (2007), Knowledge Economy, Learning Society and Lifelong Learning—A Review of the French Literature, in: Kuhn, M., *New Society Models for a New Millennium,* New York, Peter Lang, p. 67.

views as merely conditional to them, that, while they are pursuing nothing but their individual life plans, though in their lawful pursuit of these life plans execute the goals of citizen societies their nation state laid down in these laws, directing their live plans towards executing the objectives of states.

It is one thing that globalized thinking as nationally comparative thinking is not able to distinguish what is the common, shared nature of nation-state constituted societies and what are their historically particular interpretations of such capitalist societies. The fact that this kind of thinking therefore also lets all the social phenomena they discover in these state-constructed societies coincide with their constitution as nation states, i.e. anything and everything in China as manifestations of a Chinese model of state, in France everything as owed to a French nature, always strictly tautologically viewed as the national identity of an individual state and that this thinking considers even phenomena owed to human nature, such as here the theoretical political racism of a French knowledge, as a part of the national identity of an individual state, this is the consequence of this thinking through nation-state perspectives seeking for demarcating images of citizen societies and their nation states in a world all consisting of the same society model, serving with these demarcating images the politic al demarcation interest of their nation states for their foreign affair policy agendas in front of other nation states—and presents these political interests for the hostilities between nation states as nothing but mirroring the distinctive nature of their citizens and their societies.

As the above example of a global comparative theory in the field of education shows, social science globalized thinking is obviously unable to see what the national educational system discussed here shares substantially with that of other countries, and which then, caught up in thinking through national perspectives in international comparative thinking, is no longer able to separate the particular interpretations of the substantially identical educational system in France shared with the educational system of other citizen societies from an invented French nature not only of education, but also of human nature—of knowledge.

The consequence of this kind of thinking through national perspectives in international comparisons then presents what are only nationally specific manifestations of the same educational system as the essential nature of this educational system, with the result of a reciprocal, nationalistically clouded view of the educational system of all the thinkers who compare internationally in this kind of globalized thinking, a view which, ironically enough, in this kind of globalized theorizing through national views of the otherworldly national social biotopes of other states leads to a mutual indifference about what it purports to compare.

It is undoubtedly true that humanity has developed different ideas of what it considers as knowledge and what it considers as scientific knowledge. But globalized comparative thought wants to know a French concept of knowledge, a specific form of thought creation, a kind of French working mind that wants to implant a national version of knowledge and its cognitions like human nature, this political racism can only be invented by theorists for whom, thanks to their uncomprehending realism, the state nature of their social constructs coincides with their nature, and by this inevitably becomes nationalist knowledge, because their international comparative theories are inspired by the search for difference of naturalized statehood.

It is not surprising that such nationalistic thinking about this kind of concept-less comparison of nationally constituted societies is accompanied by the complaint, which cannot be eliminated, that it is never really understood by other thinkers of the same genre, if in this thinking the international comparative view of the nationally constituted societies is accessible through such a nationally inspired view only to those who share this national view and who also equate any state and its state characteristics with the nature of a nationally constituted society, as if they were its second nature.

And anything other than theorizing about state-constructed societies, citizen societies, their state and their market economy and this as theorizing about them through their specific national perspectives and the juxtaposition of the insights gained from them in their conceptless constructed uniqueness, any other thinking is obviously denied to this globalized social science thinking when it discovers the social world beyond individual national societies and directs its thinking towards its international comparative studies about this otherworld of states and, thanks to this way of globalized thinking through the perspectives of individual nation states, those theories created by such as a "French perspective", considers the citizen societies so much as their nature that it not only discovers nothing more than singularities, behind which any common ground disappears as equally state-made societies, and although the whole comparison is based on this assumed common ground, though creates, through this kind of view on the societies beyond, a knowledge that is characterized by a new global version of mutual, scientifically enlightened ignorance and of nationalist racisms, very similar to the combination of racism and ignorance that has already distinguished social science thinking while theorizing about the colonized world.

The refinement of states as a protection against the world of states called "globalization"

Globalized thinking practices nationalistic thinking, and the source of its knowledge created as nationalisms globalized social science reveals in its theories that reflect on this "globalization" itself, that reflect on the world of citizen societies and of their political powers.

For the social-scientific thinkers committed to citizen societies, the source of all evil lies in the multitude of what they individually glorify as the individual protection of mankind: the evil is that there is—and that is what the whole problem after all is all about— more than just one state in this world of all the same states and with the global enforcement of citizen societies with their nation states the entire world of states becomes a threat to each individual state. Social science calls this, the relationship between states, not imperialism, but more mystically "globalization", and, reflects, entirely in the logic of the nationalist way of thinking of globalized social sciences, on this relationship between states from the perspective of the individual state.

> "Globalisation is redefining the role of the nation state as an effective manager of the national economy. ... Can markets be the key mechanism governing modern society? ... And, what future, if there is any for the nation state?"[15]

States with their monopoly on the use of power can never, ever, be considered by social science thinkers as the power that is indeed not threatened by any internal power over their territory and over their inhabitants, which only thereby have the freedom to govern with their sovereign power into the freedom of other states outwardly. By then mystifying the worldwide enforcement of this principle, of

---

15 Boyer. R., Drache, D., (eds), (1996), States against markets, The limits of globalisation, Routledge London, p. 1.

states ruled by monopolists of power over their societies, that world of states and their societies, into their ghost called "globalization", they reveal how their globalized view of the world gives birth to their nationalism, and vice versa, why their thinking, which, no longer like the pre-globalized thinking, celebrates the social model of citizen societies as the embodiment of society par excellence, and why, as this "globalized" thinking, makes the individual state society the concern of its reflections.

Somehow one feels that in this thinker about "globalization" one hears the subjected creature of states talking, whose never giving up attempts to come to terms with his conceded materialism had been recommended by our educationalist one after another time as his arts to adapt himself to what he was forced to do, and who, for the inevitable failures of his life projects, always seeks the guilty parties for his failed materialism in some foreign states and never tires of calling upon his state authority to protect him against these worlds of states out there.

The very tone that orchestrates scientific thoughts about "globalization" as the gloomy questions about an uncertain future presents this theory as a scenario in which humanity should not be enlightened about a future without their political power, but shivered, nothing worse than a life without this "effective manager" could be imagined. The "globalized" thinking with its view of this world of states seems to speak through the views of the everyday ordinary nationalist and his logic with its nationalist state illusions, when it mystifies this world of states into this dooming subject that therefore constructed as an inscrutable, subjectless worldwide something, and by making the world of states this "mystical" subject called "globalization" makes all individual states disappear as subjects of the world of states and then, vis a vis this imagined world of states without states, pulls out of his hat in his concern for the individual state of this state-driven model of society this invented global supra-power, freed from all political subjects and purposes, to share his worries that this invented supra-power mystified towards a far away but ever present practical constraint, that this supra power could demand the obedience of his own state, which this thinker, in order to complete the gloomy scenario as a threatening chaos, celebrated towards an "effective manager", which this supra-power somewhere existing beyond all nation states now threatens to disempower, his and any individual nation state.

As these real world powers thought away from all the real political makers of the world, the states, first of all the imperial states, replaced by the invented mystified world super power beyond all the real political powers called "globalization", this thinking interprets the world of states and the societies established and commanded by the states and their economy, because acting worldwide and without any subject under the title of this globalization as a ghostly powerful global practical constraint, with the dooming end of the states as managers, and with the end of states that of mankind before its eyes. At the sight of a world of states, this world of states with all its of nothing and no one but other states of the same type, i.e. all equipped with a monopoly of power, to interpret this as an irresistible constraint on states, in order to therefore beg for the sovereignty of individual states, i.e. the political power that knows no limits of its power inside any nation state, the globalized thinking social scientist constructs this theoretical artifice as if his thinking were determined by nothing else but pure nationalism, the concern for the ability of his own state to assert itself against all other states hidden behind this cloudy notion of "globalization". "Globalization", that all states always use as the reference to all other states beyond one's own, without naming a single state, i.e., the imperialism of all states among all states, thus made into a practical constraint, which all must obey and which is the villain quoted by all states, which is responsible for all evils that never the own state causes. It is this core logic of nationalism which, in its scientific version, with its statement that "globalization" in this abstract scientific version essentially interprets the world of states beyond one's own state as coercion for one's own state and thus repeats the ordinary pub version of the same nationalistic thought and gives it a deeper scientific consecration. This, the world of states as a limitation of the power of one's own state in all its variations is what social science thinking ventilates with the term "globalization" and thus is the nationalism shared by science and the pub talk, which all states share with this globally shared idea. "Globalization" is as nothing else but the worldwide shared nationalism of the view of all individual states on the world of states.

But it is not only one's own state that, thanks to this idea of "globalization", becomes a threatened victim of the world ruled by nobody but these states. The world of worldwide profiteers set up and maintained by these states is also being re-converted with the idea of "globalization" into a danger for its state makers, thus giving nationalist thinking a second offer for its stupid conclusions about its failed materialism. The reign of states extended over the whole globe and the purpose of all these reigning nation states established by them, the increase of wealth, which increases in the sheer multiplication of national money—here for a better understanding of what this money is for the conceded materialism in substance, called wealth share titles[16]—of those who, together with their likeminded political comrades-in-arms, enforce this multiplication as the supreme goal of all social and economic life all over the world, a wealth from the proceeds of which the states take their parts, which they need to secure this political overarching goal, by means of their monopoly on the use of force, this globally enforced domination of

---

16 Even if it is nothing new: money is nothing more and nothing less than the reified social concept of capitalism, which embodies its purpose in that it shapes everything, the use of nature and everything social, and according to which it measures everything against this purpose. And nothing characterizes criticism of this concept of society better than what it means to measure everything in this society twice: Needs and the usefulness of things are a recognized, a valid point of view in this society, but the usefulness of things must always be subject to a comparison which disregards any usefulness and in which all useful things are compared as identical quantities of units of this money, disregarding this usefulness, i.e. a comparison in which nothing can be compared, because money, with its abstractions of all usefulness, makes this comparison impossible on the one hand, but nevertheless decides with this comparison of money units about the needs for useful things, because it sets the standard for what is considered usefulness socially and what is not. In the hands of those who need wealth shares to get at the useful things, what costs less overrides any usefulness in the hands of those who nevertheless need it to realize their life goals. This comparison of the non-comparable does not allow for a weighing up of usefulness, because one side of this weighing up rejects this point of view of what is useful in principle with its abstractions and at the same time is made the dominant point of view in this society by force. And a society which forbids such weighing of utilities but forces this weighing of the incomparable because it measures everything by money needs a special sort of mind, an art of comparing the in-comparable, utilities with money: This sort of thinking is the "Vernunft", that Vernunft which Mr. Kant invented for this achievement of thinking, understanding itself as the wisdom to compare useful things with money in spite of the refusal of money to compare this, this Vernunft is the ability to do the impossible and yet to decide day by day, and to reconcile this unjustifiable decision about the undecidable in the wisdom of "Vernunft". For people who have to make a living from it, money is a piece of paper which, with its numbers, fixes, beyond all usefulness, the share which they thereby receive of the wealth of these societies, with which, thanks to this Vernunft, they weigh the incalculable as the wisdom to renounce what they want under the reign of money, the wealth share certificates. For people for whom money is the means of its multiplication, this kind of Vernunft is not needed, because everything in society is oriented towards what for these money-owners is the purpose of money, the multiplication of abstract wealth, money being a title for the multiplication of wealth.

this globalized main and overarching goal of all social life, i.e. this globalized market economy enforced by the states to their societies, social science thinkers discuss all this not only as "an erosion of national sovereignty,"[17] but also as the threatening end of the principle of the nation state and thus—in this sense entirely globalized thinking—as the dooming end of their individual states.

That it is the sovereignty of the same political creature, the sovereignty of another state in a world of nation-states, which sets limits to the sovereignty of individual states, and that all the states in the world of states help the multipliers of wealth beyond their national markets to conquer the national markets of other states as sources of their business, and that they cannot govern into their national markets with the same unlimited freedom, as in their own national markets, but have to deal with the sovereignties of others, fanatics of national sovereignty, fanatics because they admire the power of states at the national level as "effective manager of the national economy", which from this point of view cannot be relativized by anything else, and therefore interpret the limitation of sovereignty through the existence of other sovereignties as erosion of state sovereignty.

And that these states then also prepare the whole world of states together with their inhabitants for the capitalists of the world as a romping place for their profiteering, so that these capitalist are offered to choose on whose territory and in which national wealth titles they conduct their business, and so that they burden the states with the competition of the nation states about attracting these profiteers, for whom they prepare their national societies, then sovereignty fanatics conclude from the free choice of the global profiteers that the future of the nation state is already called into question. In other words: Because all states want to lure the global profiteers to do business in their currency by filling the world with credits for the global profiteers in their national currency through their national banks, they consider this competition of national currencies for the profiteers of the world to invest their wealth in their national currency and to prepare countries and people with their sovereignty for this and nothing else, as the decline of their dreams of what they attribute to state sovereignty as its goals: a totalitarianism

---

17   Boyer, R., Drache, D. (eds), (1996), States against markets, The limits of globalisation, Routledge London, p. 23.

of abstract sovereignty, as if sovereignty itself was the purpose of ruling, that has no other contents but ruling.

One must therefore already be inspired by the idea that true sovereignty, which is in the same sovereignty of other sovereigns in a world not ruled by a single state and therefore relativized by that of other sovereigns, is therefore a political power that is strictly speaking the absolute world ruler and that has no other purpose with its ruling but ruling if one interprets this ruling itself as the threatened end of the whole project of the citizen societies' states, by interpreting capitalists to be able to choose between individual states as a business field for the capitalists' business in a world of states as the dooming end of these societies and of their states. And in order to make this apocalyptic idea of a market economy without its effective manager really convincing, these theorists imagine the world market managed by states, simply without their managers, see themselves as shocked as they want to be and have thus proven that without the manager, what exists only through him, is not possible to exist.

That takes some sorting out: To interpret the worldwide spread of the society system, citizen societies ruled by states for the purposes of serving a market economy, successfully enforced worldwide with the whole arsenal of state power, above all wars, as the beginning of the end of this society model, in order to create with this threatening end of this society model the nationalism of globalized social-scientific thinking and thus to give the damaged materialism of the citizens, damaged by the business world and the nation state for the sake of the business, to give to these citizens who like to blame this globalization for this damage, the blessing of scientific insights to this modernized nationalism called globalization of a world of states.

After all, these statements about what "globalization" is for social science thinking allow us to understand what this "globalized" thinking consists of: In times of the worldwide assertion of citizen societies, their nation state and their market economy, in the further development from the ontologization of citizen societies and their state in non-globalized thinking towards nationalist thinking as the methodological nationalism of social-science globalized theory formation, presented by the social sciences themselves under the title of their "globalization" to present this nationalist thinking as the epistemological imperative of the time.

Science as a global seismograph of nationalism—about the stale luck to have caught the right state

When then globally thinking idealists of state sovereignty look at the world of national citizen societies and theorize about income differences between these national societies, which they recently like to describe as inequalities, they do not do so because these income differences are worth asking why and for what they exist; they may not even examine these income differences if they want to measure such income differences in their characterization as inequality against the ideal that they should actually be equal; income differences are for the critical thinkers on unequal incomes not even a deviation from the ideal of equality that needs to be examined, but a matter that in itself does not raise any scientific questions that require any explanations.

> "In a recent book (2012), Joseph Stiglitz, a former Nobel Prize winner in Economics argues that rising income inequality is one of the main factors underlying the economic and financial crisis in the United States ... The social and economic challenges associated with rising income inequalities have gained prominence in the public debate, after the publication in 2009, of a widely cited book by Richard Wilkinson and Kate Pickett entitled "The Spirit Level, Why More Equal Societies Almost Always Do Better". Using cross-national data, the authors show that income inequality correlates with lower levels of social capital as well as with a host of other social challenges from poor health, crime, to underage pregnancies. The current report takes part in this debate by examining the bivariate correlations at subnational level (NUTS 1 level) between income inequality and indicators of education, health, criminality, political participation, social capital and happiness at the EU level."[18]

By stringing together income differences with other phenomena all characterized as "precarious" (the new scientific phrase which in pubtalk is called "shit"), one can see that thinkers of inequality are concerned with all these phenomena only because they are concerned with income differences just as they are with their observations of health, crime, or pregnancy that do not fall within a given age, whether all these phenomena, which they, because of their concerns, regardless of all differences—such as crime or unequal income—subsume under the same "precarious" behavior and string them together as if they were all somehow the same, because they are interested in

---

18 Rynko, Maja, *On the Measurement of Welfare, Happiness and Inequality*, European University Institute, http://cadmus.eui.eu/handle/1814/20694.

all these "precarious" phenomena as the same precarity. And this precarity is whether this might not undermine the sovereignty of states, as envisaged by nobody less than by the Nobel Prize winner Stiglitz in the case of the United States. To deal with the "happiness" of citizens in EU states in connection with this study by Nobel Prize winner Stiglitz is thus fed by the interest in whether here too poverty, as dissatisfaction of the poor, could possibly lead to a problem, not for the poor, of course, but to "precarious behavior" and thus to a problem for the sovereignty of European state powers.

Citizens who tell such thinkers that they are happy tell such scientific detectives, and through them their political rulers, that the sovereign states need not worry about their subservience when they succeed in so skillfully impoverishing their citizens and when these citizens continue to regard themselves as happy subservants; subservants whose good behavior the state authorities, like their scientific scholarly experts on the delicate consequences of "precarious" life for the "cohesion of societies" from the social sciences, always take good care of and detect "precarious behavior" in good time, these are the customers of these scientific investigators, who are pleased to be able to use their wise knowledge to critically request from their states for a well-dosed impoverishment, which spares the state any further serious problems. That only these scientists see the impoverishment of citizens affecting their happiness, due to their dreamy views about state politics and that the state itself does not have these problems at all, knows in any case what to do with its precarious citizens and appreciates that he is presented by these scientific caretakers of the happiness of people as if his mission was to care about the happiness of people he impoverishes, this is a different story; social-scientific snoopers in the sensitivities of all the precarious people live as theorists, at any rate, from the belief that what they find out there is important for states. As you can see, if nobody else is interested in all that stuff, at least a Nobel Prize can be won with such detective studies.

To reproach such thinkers for the fact that the creation of poverty is not only not a problem of state sovereignty at all, but the means of their political enforcement in their struggle with other states for attractive locations for the worldwide agile capitalists, with such typical sovereignty idealists, who smell threatening dissatisfaction in every poverty everywhere, open doors with such reproaches, because for these thinkers the sovereignty of states and even more so the success of their own state in relation to other states is ultimately—poverty or no poverty—the greatest happiness of the sub-servants who are dependent on their state for better or worse. Income differences, who cares, this does not matter at all, as long as the poor are happy nationalists and their ruling state is signaled by their science not to have to worry about "precarious behavior" of the "precarious" living conditions of their citizens established by him. This, caring about how states appear in the eyes of his sub-servants, is already being done by their social science thinkers, first and foremost in their globalized version with their view on the world as world of nation states, as their service to their states.

Poverty can never ever be a means of state sovereignty in the imperial confrontation with other sovereigns, but must be a problem for their sovereignty, to which social scientists point out states concerned when these sovereigns producing this poverty very sovereignly, not because they share the concerns of the poor, but because they are concerned about the state sovereignty, above all the sovereignty of the winner of the imperial competition between states, and by doing this, they once again omit the real concerns of the imperial states, with their worries about the sustainable existence of sovereignty vis-à-vis their citizens, which they, and only they—the politicians have never raised such concerns, precisely because of the poverty which the states impose as a means of their imperial concerns—consider as a threatened loss of state sovereignty, both internally and externally.

In this concern about the impending loss of state sovereignty through poverty, "globalized" social science thinkers must find out how happy the citizens living under the rule of their states and how they consider themselves to be subjects of the state they are ruled.

If one disregards what the feeling of happiness should be, not to mention how feelings of happiness should be the subject of scientific judgement, for "globalized" social science thinking, as for all other phenomena, it is clear that comparative theorizing about happiness must be analyzed not only in relation to and in comparison between nation states, but that therefore also nation states have to constitute the unit of comparison for distinguishing more or less feelings of happiness, one wants to find out in one of these typical international comparative studies what differences in feelings of happiness there are in European nation states.

"This item response theory methodology is first applied to assess the differences in happiness across selected European states."[19]

There is no question that theorizing about happiness in different EU countries is in itself an odd request that is too obviously EU propaganda, all the more so when one distinguishes the differences in happiness according to the membership of states in a community of states and when one considers that their political programs are all happy to advertise their citizens to the happy international business community as very purposefully produced, attractive human resources, as the call their people.

Nevertheless, in the context of the discussion on "globalized" social science thinking, the reference to the abstruse subject matter and politically inspired mission of such typical international comparative studies is not relevant at all. What makes this example a highly typical example of such international comparative studies is the idea underlying the research question, namely that the theorizing about people's happiness is a question that does not only sort these people according to nothing other than their national affiliation, but as a matter of course in a study on "happiness across selected European states", this national affiliation itself is assumed to be the substance of their happiness and is recorded with correspondingly constructed data, which, together with information on the country in which people feel more or less happy, disseminates the knowledge as to which "European state" is home for nationally and nothing else but as this defined people with how much happiness. Or, if the same is formulated from the perspective of the citizens, which citizens are lucky enough to have acquired the most fortunate citizenship, if one leaves aside the well-known fact that people are not allowed to choose their citizenship, but are assigned it by birth.

If there is anything else at all that, like nationality, defines itself only negatively through the demarcation from others, the other nationalities, then the abstraction art of globalized comparative social science thinking requires a comparison of separately constructed nationalities of the same political affiliation to an identical political entity on the one hand, "The European states", for a comparative thinking that is only interested in the differences within

---

19 Rynko, Maja, *On the Measurement of Welfare, Happiness and Inequality*, European University Institute, http://cadmus.eui.eu/handle/1814/20694.

this commonality, in order to imagine this commonality first of all in thinking about it in a way, just as if their common belonging to this identity did not even exist. This is a true, but highly ordinary masterpiece of the logic of "globalized" thinking, which seeks to reposition thinking about the world of state-constructed societies in its methodological nationalism as national biotopes untouched by each other—and this all the more so in societies which are characterized by their membership of a group of states in the shaping of their social, political and economic commonalities—, just as if the "globalized" thinking wanted to prove, with the justification of its research question in this study, that globalized social scientific thinking consists in nothing other than the creation of nationalistic thoughts, which therefore considers the happiness of people as nothing but a question of their nationality. Pure globalized thinking, so to speak.

To think of the European citizen as unaffected by his or her being affected by this belonging through this European citizenship, as nothing but nationally dissected people, in order to then differentiate them according to their nationality according to degrees of difference in their belonging to the identical supranational entity, characterizes the art of theorizing of a "globalized thinking", that as this "globalized" thinking best proves to be the epitome of a nationalist approach when it theorizes about the world of states in this way.

Reflections on all social things in the "globalized" social sciences, thanks to its nationalist approach, are obviously so much the same with thinking about nationally constructed societies that comparative studies of societies even within a closely connected association of nation states in which the social life of its citizens is very largely equally regulated by the well-administered interaction of this state community, whose economic life is bound together by the uniqueness of a common, supranational currency and which has a supranational government controlling these interactions, that it seems impossible for this "globalized" social science thinking to imagine the world of the citizens societies and their states other than a demarcated coexistence of then nation-state subjects even within this associated live of citizens in the association of nation states. It is impossible for this globalized social science thinking to compare citizens of the European Union, to imagine this comparison other than without their shared EU citizenship and to construct EU citizens as if they were completely nationally defined subjects abstracted from their EU citizenship: this—apart from all the abstrusities of theoretical studies that a global imperialist community of states, which does not make a big secret of its world imperial concerns, and aims at making its citizens a means for this imperial agenda, to then investigate this as nothing else but a place for happiness, and also apart from what is being investigated there under the title "happiness" as well as how this is done comparatively—this nationalistic thinking is what brings the art of "globalized" thinking of the social sciences to the particular nature of the logic of this thinking, their scientific nationalism, the commitment of their thinking to the nation-state concerns of nation-state societies in the conflicts of the global world of states and their globally operating business world, conflicts of these states including wars all over this world of nation states, which in the idea of a "globalization" is made to disappear in a world of this worldwide constraints all these states must obey, this is the epistemological principle guiding this "globalized" theory formation.

To avoid misunderstandings: the practice of nationalist theorizing as an epistemological imperative of "globalization" does not consist in the muffled celebration of the individual nation state. Globalized thinking is scientific thinking and nationalist thinking in science consists of making the concerns of the individual state, its society and its state subjects its own—usually without any reference to the international world of states—and creating knowledge which, thanks to this scientific nationalism, is committed to the individual concerns of states, to those of their societies and to those of their state-defined citizens. "Globalized" social sciences practice their scientific nationalism through a way of thinking that sees itself as a consulting service for state concerns. This "globalized" social sciences thinking in a world of states and of market economy as a service to the concerns of national subjects in the world of states works in the majority of cases as the scientific consultancy to national political, economic or social concerns, or as international comparative studies on them. It is this science, which is committed to advising state subjects and their concerns, which in this way practices its scientific nationalism as the "globalization" of its theory-building, without formulating its knowledge, like other forms of nationalism, as a hostile demarcation from other state societies. On the contrary, knowledge about other societies is thus defined as a component of nation-state thinking, "globalized" science as its response to and in the way state subjects cope with that world of states. Such as studies do when they study the happiness of people and consider this as purely a matter of their nationality.

1.3 Comments on life in the world of national citizen societies and its social sciences legends

The citizens of the world of states are national citizens. This begins right from the moment new-born people enter the world of states, strictly speaking even before that, because with its laws "for the protection of unborn life" it is the state which decides and denies parents to decide that the unborn life is already its own business and that the state decides according to its own criteria, whether the unborn becomes born life or not, and in which stage of the growth of unborn life by means of his sovereignty over the parents denies them the decision whether they want a child or not, and thus not only decides when life begins, but also what becomes life and what does not—and who has this defining sovereignty over what becomes life, as always in the case of state intervention in its citizens life, with the hardened cynicism of the decision monopolist on the use of power, who is very sure that nothing can be done against his view of things, presents this sovereignty over the life and limb of citizens as a concern for the citizen, in this case, as a concern for the "protection of unborn life", here for those citizen, which do not even exist, and as a protection against citizens who do exist, to whom he does not even want to leave the question of whether his citizens want to have children or not to their considerations, because for him every national citizen is an increase in his people, that is, it is his job to decide, a decision which he enforces on the parents with his sovereignty with the usual force of his laws.

Sure, every newborn child is born into some given world: Nevertheless, what may seem completely harmless and seems to have to do with everything but the world of states is not only not harmless, but enters as a child into the states' struggle for power in the world of states with the decision about life of a citizen of an individual state. As a child, everyone is, without being able to know what that might mean, as a *person* with all kinds of legal definitions, placed under the supervision of all kinds of legal regulations alongside his parents like these, and thus two things in particular are made clear right from the beginning of this life:

Firstly, the child, with everything and everyone that he or she does and wants to do, is defined as someone on the way to becoming a member of a state-regulated, a citizen society, whose power of definition misses absolutely nothing, right down to what is finely tuned, and thus equally regulated, as a private sphere, and even with this definition of what belongs to it and what does not, in both cases ensures that this private sphere is also a state sphere; and secondly, on every birth certificate, the embossed symbol of the respective state authority unmistakably indicates that this person is assigned this citizenship, i.e. is marked as a citizen for the rest of his or her life, who under the wings (the details of the person of child, mother and father are in the German birth certificate under the wings of the eagle covering the entire birth certificate, i.e. the state coat of arms) of this state and no other state may shape and perform his life, i.e. is object of this and no other state authority.

Already the assignment of a nationality marks in the newborn child the exclusivity of belonging to a state authority and with it the exclusion of all other state authorities from access to it and decides with this exclusion of the world of states that it regards this person once and for all as an object of his sovereign concerns in relation to the sovereign concerns of the other states in this world of states. Nothing proves the exclusivity and access of this claim to sovereignty over man as a national citizen better than the fact that a man born stateless is not a child of fortune but a true nobody in the world of nation states; either he is a national citizen or he is a nothing. So totalitarian do states take possession of their citizens at the very beginning of their lives that not being a citizen means, conversely, that these people without citizenship are regarded and treated as non-existent. From then on, from the marking as part of a national people,—a part of a Volk, as one would call this elsewhere praised subject—in these traditions of German reason of state as a Volk unmistakably defines its citizens as parts of a state subject; every citizen, regardless of whether he himself sees it that way, is a national citizen, i.e. always defined negatively to others of the same species as a national citizen, in German terminology of a Volk, these are all people of the very same category, the same on the other side all the same foreigners, defined in a purely negative way as all non-Germans, no matter to which other state they belong, and thus these negative nationals are subsumed under the matters which his national sovereignty deals with other sovereigns. The citizens of the world of states are national citizens, and as national citizens they are citizens of the world of states, and thus part of the affairs between states in the world of states. And again, it makes no difference whether or not they share these matters that states fight out among themselves. Even if they criticize their own state for any acts against other states, the question of how citizens see inter-state affairs is completely indifferent to any state, and practically all citizens are treated by their states in their state affairs completely unaffected by how they, the citizens, see it, as their state sees it.

Which nationality these citizens are irrevocably assigned, not thanks to any choice of any nationality, but with the nationality of their parents quasi as a forced natural inheritance, whether they inherit the citizenship of a country of the imperial world or that of a nation state of the so-called developing world, determines much more about their lives than about merely different living conditions. With the assignment of citizenship, the elementary life paths are in their essential content predetermined as a component of the respective reasons of state with their global agenda and the options for individual life paths designed by state programs, and are conceived and determined on all sides as levers of states in their struggle for global power. Whoever conquers which options for individual life paths as his or her highly personal biography plays only the role of shaping the options offered with the highest personal commitment as the lifelong believe that the chosen life course is the highly individual product of a highly personal life idea.

The truth looks a little different: Thanks to the frank language of PISA studies, it is no longer necessary to prove that the state education system organizes the global comparison of the education of "human capital", i.e., that it forces the youth of this world via a compulsory education into a grading race for the very predetermined ways to get money. The fact that in the worst case one does not even think up the nonsense of such spleens of life executing an individual life plan does not only become clear to those who receive the lifelong access to the life of their citizens as a means of state power and its priorities, as the non-discussable order, which came with the allocation of citizenship, for his state as a warrior, to whom this life career is imputed as a passion given with his blood, and to whom therefore nothing has a deeper quasi natural need to be, than for the warlike struggles of his state with other states for political power and economic power to give his life.

Young people, and these are most of them, to whom the failure in the competition for the better life options in their emphatically as education called career as learners has driven out the illusions, they would be the agents of shaping their life paths, rather early, are left no other choice than to submit to the not so dreamlike life careers, so that they can exist at all. But not even the experience of living one's life without such forks in the educational system, as nothing else but to follow the forced service of the state program and to lose one's life in the wars of the states of this world, is by no means who knows what kind of exception in the way of practicing one's life defined as a citizen: A glance at the world is enough to recognize it as a world in which one must first find areas which are not war zones or which have not—thanks to "globalization"—been made war zones by foreign states. Whoever wants to find people in this world of states whose lives are not shaped by wars in one way or another, has to search for quite a long time.

Even those who are spared the perception of their citizenship as a service for the warlike global state rivalries, those who fight their way through the forks of the educational system and conquer their life perspectives there, remain servants of the global state agenda and their way of life a dependent variable of it: In citizen societies, in which the pursuit of any goal in life always depends on the disposition of money, on the disposition of means of payment—slips of paper with shares of wealth numbered in figures, which no one else but again the state with its exclusive economic instruments uses in its relationship to the same slips of paper of other states according to its economic policy priorities and whose value it controls through its central banks—all conquests of money, for which most people have to spend their lives by working, especially when one has only so much of it to get at the things of daily life, to a game of sizes, in which at all corners and ends first of all the state, in accordance with its international economic-political interests, has its fingers in the pie and, in accordance with its international economic-political goals, also turns the value of money and in this way decides what one actually gets for the money one has conquered in terms of useful things.

But it is not only on the side of what one gets for one's money that the states with their political and economic interventions are approaching and turning on what one can buy for one's conquered money. Since after the end of World War II the American model of the nation state has been in force worldwide, states can no longer simply print the money they need for their political agendas, but must borrow it on the international money market like the entire business world, and in return they must adjust their national money to the business calculations of the international money markets—in other words, they must be all the more concerned with what this international financial and business world appreciates. So it comes that all countries—not only since then, but since then without alternatives—also make an effort to advertise the country and its people to the international business world and to offer, among other things, a job market where you can get the best work performance for little money. And in order to remedy this situation, all countries have since then been in the process of imposing all sorts of expenses, be it for social costs or for innovations, on people's salaries and, as a precaution, of deducting such costs from their salaries without this part falling into the hands of the wage earners, who own the money and who use it for expenses according to their own priorities.[20]

Even after this side of the conquest of slips of paper with wealth entitlements, not only what you can buy with them, but also how much of them you get as a salary when you work for getting them, is a variable that depends very much on the international haggling over the value of these slips of paper, a haggling on which far more depends what you really get for your performance in the end than on how hard you struggle to work. The bottom line is that a salary, at least in most cases, is always not much more than a little

---

[20] Incidentally, it is this model of financing state policy via the international financial market that is the basis of the social science ideology of the subjugation of states to the interests of capital, in which the division of labor between the two is clouded as the subjugation of the state to the point of disappearing state sovereignty, and which, by labelling state policy as "neoliberalism", certifies even to capital, which has been so scolded, the priority of its economic interests in state policy, as a deviation from its actually very philanthropic nature, which violates this philanthropic nature of a "social market economy" in this shabby variant of neoliberalism.

more than what you get when you don't work—a small difference that no one but the state determines with the instruments of its social policy and regularly readjusts it so that the option of not offering one's work on the labor market to the business world does not become an alternative.

It is therefore one of the most audacious stupidities of politics and economics to present money as a service to the inhabitants of a society reproduced by the market economy, with the purpose of providing the inhabitants of these citizen societies with the necessary things in life. Nothing challenges this idea of a supply of the necessities of life by money more than the very global nature of money and the subordination of the whole world to the regime of its multiplication in the hands of those who do not work for it but make others work for them; and it is in this global nature of money that lies the rational core of all the false debates which, under the concept of "globalization", obscure the real purposes of the regime of the world under the command of money.

In any case, the majority of all inhabitants experience anything but that money provides them with the necessary things in life: For one must first have the money, and apart from the very few where the much money they have is not only reproduced but somehow even multiplied, it is true for most citizens of nation-states and their capitalist economy, whose well-being these states take care of as the exclusive basis of their citizens' livelihood, that they only get money, those share of wealth slips, if they can sell their work, and this is only possible if it pays off for the other side, i.e. if it multiplies their money. Other ways to get the wealth share certificates or what one can buy with them than by work, if one does not have these certificates in abundance anyway, and these certificates multiply by themselves completely without the own work, all these states categorically exclude by the highest law under the title of the protection of private property with the threat of juicy penalties. This is a law that all states have written into nothing less than their constitutions and have refined it in the Declaration of Human Rights of the global assembly of states, the United Nations, with the cynicism of a generous mercy for those who get no work, i.e., have no access to money, into a human right for which one can buy zero. And indeed, citizens who are not even offered work are the vast majority of citizens in the world. Their life looks therefore accordingly: no paid work is rewarded with absolute poverty struggling to survive.

That with those who get work, the conquest of money by work leads to the fact that they always get only so much of this wealth that it forces the man living by work all his life to have to conquer share of wealth slips by his work, that is, the life of these people consists of nothing else but the conquest of these share of wealth slips, that is, a life of work, is because the supreme purpose of the reason of state of all these states is the crazy aim of not using economics as a means to an end, but as the supreme purpose of their reason of state, and to subordinate all social and individual aims to the purpose governing this economy, to increase this wealth, measured in increases in money, so that states, the political organization of these citizen societies, prove to be nothing else but the political arm of the people, who make the ordinary citizens who live from work, work for the increase of their mountains of money, and who must see to it that this is the supreme purpose of these citizen societies, lived by all.

The wealth-share-coupons promise, with the state guarantee for the quantity of the shares of wealth, to exchange these for useful goods which they number, namely also that these can be acquired at all only under the condition that the economy, with the support of the state authority, succeeds in producing a wealth which is not measured at all by the production of all these useful things which this sort of economy produces, but by the fact that all these things increase the wealth which can be counted and counted in the growth of these share-coupons of wealth. Abstruse as it sounds, it is exactly so: the measure of all things in this sort of economy, including all the useful things it produces, is like the complete why and wherefore of modern states, with all their interventions in the economy and in society, which in turn measure themselves by promoting its rule for this economy and its aims, the measure of all things of these societies under the regime of money are not the useful things, but is the multiplication of the quantity of these wealth shares themselves; only when production is reflected in the increase of these slips of paper, which measure the increase of wealth as the increase of money, this increase in a wealth to which the usefulness of things is only a means to this end, and which exists only when it is effected in the increase of money, only then and only then do these societies operate, and to this end, to which the useful things only mean something when they mean the increase of money, to this end the political power of this society subjects the action of all its members by means of its political power. Growth is the treacherous term governing these societies, and that is why this sort of social model is called capitalism, a society in which the growth of money is at stake, and which subordinates to this growth everything, truly everything, and in which all the useful things, which people could produce and use well, but thanks to this way of balancing the economy do not receive, because all the money not put into this economy for this purpose is deducted from the monetary settlements of its results, and this is also true for the work which this sort has to generate. So there is only as much for the food of the citizens as is necessary for them to work out all monetary balanced products of this economy for these balances.

The beautiful appearance of the wealth of these societies with all the useful things it produces is therefore deceptive, and all the social science thinkers like to confirm this appearance in the ideals of their knowledge rather than reveal what it really is: It is indeed so, there are all the useful things that can make life pleasant, but they do not exist at all for that reason, and certainly not for that purpose, and that is not so difficult to recognize; they exist just then and only for multiplying the value labels in the hands of those who have plenty of them, and not even for these value label multipliers to consume their beautiful benefits; and that these slips of paper are never enough for those who acquire them with labor to buy all the useful things is not a failure of this sort of politics and economics, as the scientific prosecutors would like us believe, but their best lever to ensure this purpose of multiplying the wealth share slips of the value slip collectors with a well-adjusted poverty of the actual wealth producers, the citizens working for the acquisition of wealth share slips.

The truth about this sort of economy and politics is that what sounds so abstruse and unreasonable, to subject a society to its economy as to its political institutions, which does this in order to increase a wealth which it counts in a bare *more* among those who accumulate it in the first place only for the purpose of accumulating it, and in return to have this wealth produced by their society, which achieves this only by obtaining from this wealth, apart from a life of work, what it needs to be able to accomplish this life for work, and which, in large parts of the world where this calculation does not pay off, does not even grant this, that this abstruseness, which is hard to believe, but it is this, which is the ultimate purpose, the all-reigning yardstick of this sort of citizen societies, their politics and economy. Somehow everybody knows it, nobody may want to admit it, let alone put an end to this nonsense.

And then there are also two social actors of this sort economics and politics, who, with the orientation of politics and economics to this supreme goal of the production of this sort of wealth, which is liberated from all usefulness, in this sense measures wealth in a way that is as meaningless as it is excessive, in the pursuit of this strange goal of all political and economic activity in these societies, which get along with it excellently:

The first, the political controllers and masters of these goings-on, the politicians and the political elite of these societies, who, for the sake of the state, divert from it the shares of this wealth that its politics needs, and can thus obtain everything they need for their political program of enforcing this political and economic goings-on in their societies. And of course not only for that.

Secondly, the people who own and collect all the large quantities of these wealth share certificates, the collectors of value certificates, who are occupied with nothing else in their lives but how to simply make more of these, don't give a damn what this is and what this means for the world and for anything and anybody, the main thing is to get more of the abstract stuff and what these people have, who do not live from paid work, but for and from the propagation of this type wealth production, which they let others work for, incidentally also allows to shift a smaller part of these mountains of money towards all the useful nice things of a x-fold great life. The delicate agony of having to multiply their shares, because otherwise they would go away in consumption, is the lesser agony for people who, with the help of their friends in politics and their means of power, impose such an economy with these as crazy as misanthropic aims of the whole world as a way of life as—as they report—may not be the most perfect but in any case the best of all possible worlds.

The greater torment of practicing this economic mischief as the life purpose of a society, which is imposed upon the whole world with an unprecedented apparatus of power, for which vast sums of this wealth are spent, is borne by those for whom this gigantic apparatus of power is needed. These is needed for those, and this is the vast majority of the people in these societies of state and market economy, who spend their lifetimes earning for the economy for the increase of the wealth share of those collectors, and who are at the service of the state in all that these states must have in order to keep this economic and political folly going, with all its attendant crises, its attendant poverty, and its wars with other states of the same kind of raison d'être. For without these people nothing can be done, and it is these same people for whom it is the great art of the discreet cooperation of political and economic leaders to always adjust their share in the production of wealth in such a way that they may always not refuse, as a matter of their existence, to offer such services to the state for the growth of its economy.

With the blackmail of the existential need of the have-nots, to not reach their parts for living other than for the services of the increasing the wealth of the rich of this world on the wealth produced by themselves, which are enough to spend one's life with these services—provided one belongs to those, to whom such services are offered at all—,the states of this world make the population of this world of states hostages of the business world courted by them.

Nothing less than with the punishment of the existence of the citizens of this world of states, with the guarantee of private properties secured by their political power, this world population of citizens is used for this purpose, and its existence is made dependent on whether its commitment for the rich of this world, rich in this kind of boundless wealth, pays off in money quanta measured as their increase in wealth, an increase in wealth, for which, as the events on the world's stock exchanges document daily, the useful content of the money supply is completely exchangeable and is exchanged, and which, with this exchangeability and the exchange of products, places of production and their producers all over the world with their friends in politics, determines the course of the world in this world of states. Today in oil in the Arab world, tomorrow in the USA, or in soya in Latin America, the day after tomorrow in steel in India, or better than in steel telephone services, in any case in this and that, depending on where and with what most money can be made, antibiotics are no longer attractive, a pandemic promises new business opportunities, weapons always work well— this kind of economy shapes its economic reproduction according to the criteria that governs this society, the citizens of these societies and with them nature are the tools of these economic operations, which in this back and forth of its products and its places of production documents all its arbitrariness, including that of the food needed by its members of society, starting with what people need to eat, their dwellings, where they spend their free time, everything, but also everything exists or does not exist, exists here or does not exist, depending on whether it is worthwhile for the money-holders to invest in any agricultural products or in anything else. Those who determine the course of this economy don't care about what people need to live.

That the business world, which considers and treats all states and citizens as material for its business calculations, and that the individual states regard their sovereignty over their respective citizens as leverage to jockey with other states over which states and citizens have something more promising to offer for the "markets", as this economic subject ruling the world is so strangely objectifiedly called, for their wealth accumulation in the business spheres that are heralded for growth, and which do not, is only not indifferent to the part of the population of all these states which is committed to a life of and for work, only because it really depends on their respective political masters how much they succeed not least with the offer of a profit-promising working population to provide for the offers of work, without which in fact nothing is possible, because they have made any existence of these people dependent on such services to the wealth of the rich and do everything to prepare these citizens for the changing needs of the "markets". But they do only not care about this as long as they engage in this blackmail they share with the same people of other states, who therefore—and only so long—can cheerfully play their political people off against each other.

And since this blackmail with which the states force their citizens to only access any of the wealth, without which nothing is possible at all in these societies and which is only enough to carry out one's life as these services—given that one belongs at all to those citizen societies to which these services are at all offered—if they produce with any such services an increase of the wealth of those who own it all, since these services are organized as a wrangling about different levels of payment, all at the level of peanuts, for these services, the service providers wrangle among themselves about these differences, supported and organized by their accordingly organized trade unions. In this way, all states can be excellently governed by their political and economic leaders and can therefore devote themselves undisturbed to the task of providing and offering their populations, who are obliged to work for wealth-sharing certificates, as profit-making service providers better than other states in the global business world.

Conflicts between states, which treat the whole otherworld of states, including the economy of other states, as a business field for their capital, which pays off as an increase of capital in their respective national currencies, and which thus appropriate the wealth of the world of states abroad at the expense of other states, implying that all states dispute each other's economic basis as constantly as the values of their national money slips, conflicts between states are pre-programmed in this wrangling in the battle about the preferences of the global business world up to questioning the sovereign power over land and people—war. Wars are thus an inevitable ingredient of a world consisting of capitalist societies.

Then, while they are in wars, states no longer tolerate the nonsense about the conditional relationship between state and citizens, as which citizens like to see them as if state-constructed life was nothing more than a politically set condition for realizing their personal life plans, a nonsense in which states otherwise like their subjects to believe in, and then, in war periods, make their existence as states a condition of existence not only for their working citizens, by *forcing* their citizens into wars with other states over the question of which power has the say in the world of states, and open with a peace regulated by the winners a new round of their economic squabbling over the national currencies in which they preferably invest for the increase of their wealth which then allow those who need these slips of paper for their sheer necessities of life to earn their little merits for their services for the growth of capital again, for a growth their states find other sovereign states as an obstacle ... etc. etc.

In a world which, without exception, consists of essentially the same citizen societies, all societies in which money, i.e. the disposal of state-monopolized shares of wealth, is established as the exclusive access to the results of the economy, the exclusion of producers from this wealth is guaranteed as a permanent condition for an economy with state power and thus as the basis of life for this society, societies whose purpose is the increase of these titles of wealth and in which, therefore, the consumption of useful things which the producers of this wealth need in order to live is a deduction from this wealth for its increase, this purpose of increasing this kind of wealth is the all-dominant interest of sovereign state rule, *the* state mission of these societies committed to their economies.

To require from a society to obtain such wealth titles only in return for the service of increasing the wealth of others only makes sense if this business is profitable for one party only, and does so only if the producing service providers do not receive what they have produced but are fobbed off with just enough to ensure that their dependence on this service for the propagation of the wealth of others, which they already have in abundance and let them multiply through the work of those who urgently need them as food, if this coercion is thus ensured as a permanent institution, and it is only so if the exclusion of the producers from the wealth of money they produce is their permanently established basis of life, and as this is permanently ensured. That, ensuring the permanent exclusion of the producers of wealth from this wealth, an exclusion of the producers from what they produce through their payment with a share of wealth that fixes it at the same level of a minimum needed for existing as such producers of this kind of wealth, this exclusion is the job of the political power of these societies with the right to private property. And this kind of politically well-balanced exclusion from the wealth that the citizens of these states produce as the property of those who collect such wealth, this kind of poverty is the poverty that citizens are allowed to work for.

The majority of the citizens in this this world of citizen societies are indeed not even offered the opportunity to acquire any share of the wealth through their work for the wealth-producing nations. There, as everywhere else, only the possession of money allows the citizens of these citizen societies access to the means of existence, but they are not even offered the opportunity to acquire this money by working for the business world. Knowing well that this is not a temporary phenomenon, but applies to the majority of states and their citizens, the assembled world of states in its global association called the United Nations has established exclusion from wealth in this world of states in a way other than paid work for the world's profiteers to obtain the necessary things in life, with the cynicism inherent in these political powers as nothing less than a human right.

The fact that, on the other side of this relative and absolute poverty that rules so worldwide, i.e. on the side of the few who let their wealth titles be multiplied, enough titles can be diverted into a luxurious life, testifies not only to the absurdity of a worldwide socially enforced purpose of obliging all societies of the world with their state-implemented principles of the multiplication of private property to produce the inherently boundless multiplication of wealth titles to wealth as their wealth. The flip side of the exclusion of wealth of most of its members, who spend their lives crooked and reproduce nothing but their misery in the face of the wealth they produce, is no less idiotic than having bank accounts whose numbers could no longer be translated into any desirable objects, even the most abstruse luxury splendor.

It is no coincidence that in this logic of an economy of a boundless excess to this kind of wealth, one recognizes the wealth of societies in which the congenial need for state sovereignty, which can never be satisfied, is a need for state sovereignty in a world of states which mutually dispute their sovereignty, in which the other sovereign is always the sting in one's own sovereignty. If no other interest, such as that in useful products, this need for ruling sovereignty, both internally and externally, and the means of power required for it, the abstractly measured wealth serves this need just as congenially via the access to this type of wealth produced by means of state share certificates.

Societies in which not only in their economic department everything is geared to the disposal of wealth titles, money, but in which by political force in all areas of life the realization of all concerns is made a question of the disposal of money, all areas of life and all concerns are subordinated to the superior concern of the availability of money. By no means is money a means of life: Life in societies that have materialized in money the purpose of this society, as if it were the law of a thing, life as a service to the never-satisfiable need for more of this kind of wealth, established and organized worldwide as a mutual contest between sovereign states and their societies in the global struggle for access to this kind of wealth, these are not only abstruse but also very hostile goals of a world of citizen societies, hostile for these citizens, a world in which the enduring poverty of these societies is complemented by the enduring misery of warlike violence between these states.

And the social sciences, what do they let us know about the life of a global state-constructed way of life and its creatures? The social sciences accomplish the mental feat of making states and their societies think of themselves without the world of states, which makes them into nation states in the first place, already in their sheer demarcation of a *national* sovereignty, and imagine their reason of state as if it were not their negative reference to the world of states, i.e. their sovereignty over land and people vis-à-vis other states and their sovereignty, a negative reference which already with this tells what the essential content of their reason of state is and what matters to them in their sovereignty over land and people.

All the state constructions, citizens, families, students, workers, capitalists, pensioners, teachers, genders, children or politicians, for social science thinking they are creatures that spring from human nature, and the nation state for this thinking across all disciplines is a repair store freed from its reasons of state and its world political agenda, states which struggle with nothing but the weaknesses of a human nature up to and including war, for which this thinking sees its state-made nature, its means of state sovereignty over other states, as nothing more than a reaction to all kind of too human weaknesses, even though it is not that difficult to notice that the construction principle of all these state made creatures is to be suitable for the sovereigns and their disputes with each other.

It must obviously be a concern of social science thinking that, in a world of states that grant each other sovereignty in their mutual recognition, i.e. sometimes also deny it, and thus express that in the other sovereignty they detect the limits of their political will, they do not want to recognize in this granted acknowledgement of the will of other sovereigns over their country and their people, that the recognition of the exclusive validity of the state's will in its territory also means, conversely, that any country and the people over whom that state has granted itself sovereignty exercise that sovereignty as the unrestricted validity of its rule over the country and the people in its territory without restriction by any other will. Sovereignty over the country and the people does not come into the mind of social science thinking as the unrestricted rule of the state over their people; sovereignty cannot be a rule inwardly, but only the protection of the country and the people against other evil sovereignties always outwardly, because they absolutely believe that the state is there to serve its people, to avert harm from them, etc., as every state writes in their constitutions.

That the best service to the people is to enable them, thanks to the unlimited power of the state, to prove themselves in imperial conflicts with sovereigns against other people from other states, by strengthening the sovereignty of their state in the struggle between states over the wheeling and dealing in their national currencies on the "markets" of the world, is something which a critical social scientist could still follow; that for this enablement of the people as the service for the state and his concerns for the markets makes the majority of citizens lives dependent on the standards of the global "markets", the political representatives of these sovereigns like to present as the indomitable necessities of that subjectless "globalization", whose makers they conceal because they are these makers, this is unthinkable for thinkers for whom the state is the a service for providing with—mostly bad—but in any case conditions for people to pursue their live agendas.

Not even this simple hypocrisy can be seen through by social science thinkers, who place globalization in an elusive interplay of all sorts of factors, because it simply does not fit in with their thinking of the state as a servant of its subjects, to see the state as the subject that not only sets up and serves all these constraints of the world of states and their global economy so that it itself, and not other states, is the winner of sovereignty over other sovereigns in the dispute over it, who finally benefits most from the use of the success of the "markets", because he is best able to customize his people for these markets, because this interpretation of sovereignty over the people does not want to go along with what they want to see underneath all state reality—unswervingly through every view and experience, inspired by their ideas about democracy—serving the satisfaction of the deeply human need of people for sociality, free of any content and purpose, for social sciences the most fundamental desire of humans.

That there is therefore, for dominating the world of states and using their people for this purpose, not a single sphere of life within these sovereign states which is not politically shaped by and for the purpose of promoting the sovereignty of states in the world of states in all directions in order to move the business of the global "markets" into business in their own national currency, and which can all only be understood from this orientation of politics inwards for politics outwards, is an insight which is hardly accessible to social science thinking, which, for its belief in state sovereignty as a service to the citizens, thinks away everything which does not go hand in hand with this ideal.

State sovereignty and the life of citizens under this sovereignty is therefore misunderstood by this thinking as an idea of the social, which takes place completely independently of the dealings of states with each other, so that these dealings of states and their meaning for social live in states do not occur in this thinking as an object of reflection on the social live, even where one thinks they are impossible to not notice them,—for example in international comparisons of states—and cannot even be overlooked by the naked eye, even in these studies of these disputes and the preparation of national societies for these disputes—the world of states is theorized away, as if the social inside the states had nothing to do with these disputes between states, to thus construct the object and the way of looking at the world's citizen societies, their states and their economies in accordance with the scientific nationalism of how globalized thinking wants to see the world of nation states.

2. The Final Worldwide Enforcement of the Social Science of the Citizen Society through Its "De-colonization"

With the worldwide enforcement of the US model of a nation state in all nation states, namely that of financing it via the capital market, and the transformation of the colonized countries of the world into—just such—nation states, forced by the USA with its Vietnam War, which thus turns the whole world into a world of citizen societies and their states, this social science thinking discovers a scientific paradox, a historical anachronism. Social science thinking, which creates its theories of national citizen societies through the very perspective from which citizen societies, their social subjects and their concerns view these societies, has generated its knowledge of the social world as knowledge of the societies of the imperial world of states, imperial states which, under the leadership of the USA, have made the world a world of such citizen societies with their nation states and with their market economies.

The fact, that this forced transition of the colonies into citizen societies along the lines of the citizen societies of the old colonial states is taken for most normal, just as if it was most natural, it is not at all: That the new citizen societies of the former colonies, by adopting precisely the model of society that during colonialism have denied the very materialism that was constitutive for these citizen societies and granted to the members of these societies by their political powers with the emergence of state-constituted, post-feudal societies, i.e. societies which constitutes these post-feudal societies and distinguishes them from feudal societies, that these very post-feudal societies during colonialism denied to the people of the colonized world subjected by them and have conquered and treated the nature and people of these regions of the world, as if they were their feudal dominions, so that, with their exclusive and unrestricted availability over them, they could fight among themselves the world domination claims of competing imperial states, this adoption by the former colonies of a model of society which can obviously very well reconcile its post-feudal achievements with the feudal subjugation of the rest of the world, and did so also until finally, in the second of their world wars for domination within the world of imperial states, one of these states succeeded, to subjugate all the rest, and to rise to become the chief imperialist of all imperialist states, and on the basis of his world domination of the entire world of states, subjected the colonized parts of the world under the rule of these U.S.-led imperial states as post-colonialism, i.e. now made all former colonies as new members of the world of states as states making these former colonies the same type of societies as those of the former colonial masters, enforcing this transformation towards the society system of the colonizers with the help of the exemplary US-war against a former colony, Vietnam, this transformation of the colonial parts of the world into just that model of society of the imperial nation-state societies, including their thus worldwide completed enslavement of humanity of the entire globe for the production of capitalist wealth, which these imperial states ensure with a state-regulated poverty of the members of the societies of the world of states as a lever for this wealth, this is everything else but natural, but is probably rather an unprecedented historical madness, which is celebrated with the complacency inherent in this world of states as "free world", and with this "de-colonization", coining this subordination the final subordination of the whole world's mankind under this free world and by this celebrating this via this very coining as its "de-colonization", i.e. as its liberation from colonization, and does this while it documents its nature in the globalization of war and poverty prevailing the world since then, including the continuation of treating the now de-colonized world as if they practically were still their feudal dominions—this is anything else but a most natural way of transforming the colonized world to anything beyond colonialism, since it is a way of perpetuating it in new and even more exploitive ways, not to mention the new types of the world's mankind poverty.

And this is not even the whole drama of what goes on under the neat notion of de-colonization: That this transformation of the colonized parts of the world into the social model of the old colonial power, their model of citizen societies, their nation-state and their market economies, that this is happening in a historical world situation in which, next to the social model of the colonial states, capitalism, in the form of the Soviet Union, existed another society model in nothing less than the other part of the world, which saw itself as a counter-model to capitalism and its state model and yet, this anti-capitalist Soviet Union with a very peculiar policy, was more concerned with obtaining political-diplomatic support for itself as a nation state in the "Cold War" of the US-led alliance of states from the old colonies that had mutated into nation states with a market economy, instead to support the anti-capitalist movements that certainly existed in the anti-colonial wars, a policy of this anti-capitalistic Soviet Union, in which many anti-capitalist movements in the former colonies were sacrificed to the goal of recognizing the SU as a state, is probably one of the strangest events in recent world history, thanks to a very strange interpretation of an anti-capitalist model of society, which does not want to know anything about its own anti-capitalism elsewhere in the world and without which, in any case, the transformation of all colonies into precisely the social model of the colonial states, capitalism, could not come about as this so self-evident, just as if there were, despite of the existence of the SU as an alternative society model, no other society models than that of the colonialists. Transforming the colonies into independent nation states with market economies and interpreting the national independency of these new capitalist societies adjusted to the society system of the colonialists as a victory over colonialism, this is one of the oddest oddities of modern history.

The only exceptions, Cuba and North Korea, obviously could not and cannot shake the generally accepted view that the liberation of the colonies from colonialism can of course only consist in the adoption of the colonial masters' model of society, which is why such convinced state apologists never ever are able to comprehend, that the "arguments" of a war, which the U.S. presented to Vietnam, are the one and only way to create nation states. A colony which was striving for national independence, supported for this aim of national independence by the Soviet Union, a political rationale that identified national independency from the capitalist colonial world with an opposition against capitalism, therefore accused as communism, this project of national independency beyond the sub-ordination under the rule of the US and their Western allies, this was enough to be destructed as an option for all colonies via their very purposefully most brutal war against Vietnam, a lecture for all the colonies that were also striving for national independence beyond the Western imperialists. And it was this war that was after all the really ultimate reason why the colonized world adopted the colonialists' model of society, such as any citizen society with their now independent nation states are all the result of wars.

2.1 The adoption of the knowledge concept of social sciences in the former colonized world through the critique of "Eurocentrism"

That this transformation of the former colonized world into the very society system of the colonizers happens under the title of a de-colonization, presenting the incorporation of the colonized parts of the world into the now worldwide ruling capitalism as freeing the colonies from colonial oppression, this is an irony of modern political history. That then the adjustment of theorizing about this world of capitalism with the adaption of the former colonial societies to the science approach of the sciences of the imperial world happens under the same glorifying title as a de-colonization of theorizing, this already announces another historical irony, now in the world of social thought, as will be shown in this chapter. To grasp a bit of this irony of this de-colonization of theorizing before discussing why it is a historic irony, it is enough to remember that this de-colonization called development of theorizing departed from theorizing that not only in the former colonized societies, but also in the West itself, was characterized by all kind of critiques of capitalism.

Indeed, with the adoption of the colonial masters' model of society forced by war, and the transformation of the colonial world into citizen societies and their political power, including their commitments to the production of capitalist wealth, these states also take over not only their institutional system of knowledge, i.e. the separation in these societies between scientific knowledge and knowledge for work and the delegation of scientific knowledge to professional thinkers, but also their way of scientific theorizing about these societies, social science thinking, including the disciplinary science guilds, which in their theories for the formerly "uncivilized" people of the colonized world had and still have its own theory, anthropology, and which knew and still know such "uncivilized" people, and, because of this approach to social thought of these citizen societies and their particular way of reflecting on themselves, this thinking encounters an anachronism in this kind of thinking,—but only if one omits from this way of theorizing its insistence on objectivity in order to newly define scientific knowledge as done via this debate that knowledge in a de-colonized theory creation about societies must from now on be understood as a product of its—politically defined—"contexts", that means if one takes for granted the very way of nationalistic theorizing, the very way of theorizing which in the world of the former colonialist societies has been created thanks to its "globalization".

This formation of theories through their context, this arch-social science idea of thinking trough an abstract relatedness, through which this thinking opens up the freedom to think of anything and everything as a suitable context of the thing under study, however it suits the thinker, and to assert this context related thinking as a commandment of reality, this formation of theories mostly presented by the masterminds of de-colonized thinking as thinking through *place* as a source of theory formation, this depoliticized paraphrase of thinking, the place, meaning a view of the world differentiated according to the nation-state affiliation of the thinker, this invention of a kind of thinking committed to the self-representations of nation states, characterizes the content of scientific theory and, through this, the concern of a discourse, which, in the discourse of a "de-colonization" of thought, especially in the social sciences of the new states, with the equally false and universally accepted proof of a necessarily locally conditioned knowledge, detects a monopoly of this nationalistic thinking theories of the established world of states, which violates the worldwide pluralism of local, i.e. nationalist theories cultivated by the social sciences. And with its criticism of a theory monopoly—not the critique of any of its theories—no less than the social-scientific form of theory-building is thus purged of any form of objectivity, as a way of looking at their national citizen societies, which from now on will always be individual national-state views, as a new form of theory-building in this world of nation states and thus of that form of theory-building, which were first acquired by the state-constructed societies in the colonial states of Europe. With this criticism of their claim of objective, i.e. context-free knowledge, that is a supranational-national-state knowledge, from now on, thanks to this cleaning of social science theory formation from objective, from context-free knowledge, called "de-colonization", any theories are nation-state contextualized theories, which in the old colonial states as well as in theory formation in the new nation-state societies of the former colonies, are thus united in the pluralism of the committed subjectivism of contextualized, theories, all contextualized, the epistemological phrase with which social science thinking, through a pre-modelled reality, by this concept of contextualized thinking claims also the existing reality of those locations as the measure of its knowledge, contextualized knowledge, this is the de-colonized knowledge, a concept of scientific knowledge, in which this knowledge is constructed as the product of those politically defined locations, i.e. of its local scientific nationalism. And, one should draw attention to this, this, the introduction of space as a contextual resource of thinking and with this arguing for a worldwide nationalistic thinking, this is a project of the critics of colonialism as they show in coining this thinking through a multiplicity of nationalisms the de-colonization of social sciences.

The critics of the society system and their social theories under the nation of de-colonizing social theories advocating theory formation through nationalism? Have the intellectuals in the former colonized world not always been anti-capitalist and anti-imperialist thinkers and now they become nationalists just like those thinkers in the imperialist world, they so far radically opposed?

As always in the history of nation-states, in which the idealistic overall capitalist must be forced by his victims to secure his own livelihood, such as the creation of the so called "welfare-state", it was also in the social sciences that the opposition to the imperial states and their sciences had to discover the anachronism of creating their theories through nation-state views of the world of the social, and of claiming the theories of science in the imperial states as the theories of the entire world of states, and that with the elimination of this anachronism of social-scientific theory-building, a global monopoly of nationalist theory-building, the final enforcement of this form of theory-building from the imperial states as a now globally benevolent form of scientific theorizing, thus also in the former colonized societies, with its opposition to the sciences in the imperial state world, an opposition that has given this adaptation to the sciences of the old colonialist science, the smell of criticism, has been completed and thus has become the source of all sorts of presupposed theory formation about what this de-colonization of science is in the substance of its theories, the advocation of a multiplicity of politically presupposed theories, epistemologically advocated via thinking through the context of space.

And not only that: with this worldwide assertion of the form of social science theory-building and its discourse forms, it brings, through the necessary transformation of this science from theorizing through the viewpoint of state subjects to theorizing through individual nation-state inspired views, the relativism of a theory-building that always generates its theories through some disciplinary pre-assumptions and the model theories selected for them, in a sense down to what this thinking essentially is, expels from science its already only formal claim to objectivity and ends in the worldwide enforcement of the model of citizen societies with a pluralism of knowledge differentiated according to individual nation-state views of the world, which, with the expulsion of even the last formal forms of objectivity, gives up its distinction from the arbitrariness of mere opinions.

Not at all coincidentally, the social science thinkers from the former colonies, who had received their scientific training in the social sciences of the imperial world and usually earned their scientific laurels in their institutions, were needed to take on the role of the protagonists in the staging of the historical scientific tragedy, and to argue that by pointing on the paradox that all the "local" knowledge, i.e. all the nationally inspired knowledge also in the new nation states were theories from the sciences, all of which originate from "contexts" of the nation-state societies of the imperial world, so that these therein "hegemonic sciences"—this abstruse idea of theories to rule other theories, as if knowledge was power over other, deviant knowledge and rule it, forcing it to think what the "hegemonic" theories think—must be overcome and that social science thinking worldwide must be further developed further towards a multiplicity of nationally constructed theories, towards a multiplicity of locally valid knowledge by means of a worldwide "provincialization" of scientific knowledge.[21]

The result of this "decolonization" of the "imperial" social sciences is the elimination of what scientific knowledge in the social sciences, despite their relativism, once constituted as a critique of religious thought, the elimination of scientific knowledge aiming at objectivity, replaced by the strange idea of a worldwide "local" relative, i.e., worldwide nationalistically created knowledge.

---

21   Regarding the epistemological debates, which justify this dissolution of objective knowledge towards arbitrary opinions via a critique of the natural sciences, also look at volume II, "The nature of the social sciences of the citizen society—Notes for a Critique."

The central arguments of the post-colonial critique of social science thinking, its methodological objections, as the consequences of this critique for social science thinking, and not least the argumentative feats of now no longer only advocating the objective necessity of relative objectivity but the objective necessity of non-objective science, can best be presented along the arguments of the criticism of a "Eurocentrism", a criticism, which founds and directs the de-colonization of social science theorizing and which is meanwhile a globally shared criticism of the sciences in the former colonial states, shared not only among the thinkers of thinkers in the post-colonial parts of world, but worldwide.

The criticism of "Eurocentrism" was, before it was adopted by the debate about the social sciences and their de-colonization, initially a political critique, and this political criticism from the new, de-colonized states of the imperial states' view of the world is strange enough after its original critique of capitalism has not only been eliminated by this debate about de-colonization, but this critique of capitalism—the criticism of "Eurocentrism" by its founder Amin[22] was all about—has been made itself an object of critique by the contemporary interpretations of "Eurocentrism" in these discourses about de-colonization with their critique of Marxism, i.e. the critique of capitalism, as another variation of "Eurocentrism". And with this elimination of anti-capitalism from the notion of "Eurocentrism" and the interpretation of Marxism, resp. anti-capitalism as itself a case of "Eurocentrism" the political critique of "Eurocentrism" became more than bizarre.

To argue against the imperial states in Europe their economic and political relations with their former colonies, which are ruinous for the societies in the former colonies, this destruction of their economic, natural and social foundations was due to a lack of understanding on the part of the political leaders of the imperial states for the lifestyles in the former colonized societies, which are different from those of European societies, is more a sign that the political elites in the new states have a rather euphemistic view of the imperial states and their political and economic purposes. The accusation that points to the destructive effects of imperial profiteers and their political handlers and attributes this to their ignorance of the

---

22 Amin, Samir (1989), Eurocentrism, Modernity, Religion and Democracy, A Critique of Eurocentrism and Culturalism, Monthly Review Press, New York.

nature of the former colonial societies, an ignorance that is said to stem from an inappropriate transfer of the interpretations of state and economy practiced in the imperial states to the societies of the former colonies, and wants to say that it is this false image of the old colonial societies that is responsible for their destruction by the imperial states, testifies to a strange philanthropic good faith about the purposes of state and capital and their dealings with other states. The accusation that the businessmen and their political leaders could not really want the ruination of all livelihoods in the former colonies, and to interpret the progress of the ruination of the societies in the new states after the decolonization by the old colonial states as the result of false comparisons with the European societies and therefore as impossible to refrain from doing so in the future, bears witness to the philanthropic ideas about state and market economy that the political elites in the new states obviously cultivate.

The transfer of this critique of a "Eurocentrism", i.e. the accusation of interpreting societies in the former colonies through views of societies gained from the observation of European societies and—wrongly—transferring these notions to them, and to misjudge in this wrong transfer and therefore not being able to understand these societies and then to apply this philanthropic, political critique to science, gives an idea of the part played by the sciences in the former colonies, which argue in this way, in the formation of such strangely gullible notions of imperialism cultivated among the political elites, and that no enlightenment on what is going on in the imperial world of states can be expected from this science, let alone a critique of the social science theories when they are accused of a "Euro-centrism".

To anticipate it: The critique of "Eurocentrism" is the proclamation of social science thought as a pluralism of theories, which are all supposed to consist of individual, state-inspired views of the world, a multiplicity of nationalistically motivated worldviews, which, with this redefinition of theories into self-portraits of state societies, are winning their place for social science theories in the entire world of states, that worldview of a worldwide provincialized thinking.

As a critique in science, the accusation of "Eurocentrism", i.e. a rejected view of theories, in the discourses about de-colonizing thinking is even stranger than in political debate, because with it, theories for their insights fixed on only one point of view, namely the European, more precisely the insights gained from the observation of European societies, are rejected as one-sided, euro-centrist insights that are unsuitable for explaining other societies, because—as the following example from Arabic Studies shows—these eurocentric theories are, as they phrase it, "not suitable" for theorizing about societies beyond European societies. In other words, for European societies these theories may be "suitable" for understanding these societies, but not for others, here the Arab societies.

But how is it possible to have theories that "suit" here and not there, if one may assume that the object of theory formation is identical here and there, that it is not simply thinking about two different objects of thought? And how do you recognize that knowledge "suits" to the object of thinking? When one knows what a thing is? A theory "suits" when one has gained knowledge about a thing and knows what it is? And if you know what it is, then you also know that it does not suit? How is that possible, theories that suit?

Are theories images that one creates from a thing and then compares with a thing and asks oneself if the image created is the image of the thing that this thing creates about oneself? Only, if this were so, couldn't one then omit all thinking, if a thing creates what it is? And what is this concept of knowledge that suits or not? Suitable for what? To the object of thinking? The theory that the sun revolves around the earth is not the image that the sun and earth produce about themselves and that does suit, but this theory suits to the images one makes of the mere sight of the sun and the earth, but it is known to be simply wrong. And a theory that ascribes properties to Arab societies that they do not have is not an unsuitable theory, but simply a wrong theory, like the one about the sun revolving around the earth, even though this theory suits to the image of itself exactly. But wrong or right theories are obviously not the criterion by which suitable and unsuitable theories differ. Suitable theories can fit here and not there, as the accusation against theories that they are "Eurocentric" claims.

The example of a theory on Arab societies that is not affected by this "eurocentric" view, a post-colonial theory from sociology, which is said to "suit" to these societies differently from the "eurocentric" one, shows what this criticism is about—and the theoretical mistakes that must be made in order to establish such "locally" appropriate thinking in epistemological terms, what this "locally" appropriate knowledge identifies as appropriate knowledge, and what all this thus says about what distinguishes a "de-colonized" social science theory formation.

> "Sociology is most commonly classified in the West into two trends, depending on the starting point: the individual or society, the partial or the whole. This classification is confusing to many Arab researchers who have not found mature European individualism in their societies or coherent nations made up of Western-like stratified societies from which they can start their research. Maybe that is why Arab sociologists believe "Western" sociology is not suitable for their societies and resort to the Arab-Islamic heritage to come up with a "local" sociology. (Ali al-Wardi's work is an example that we will later discuss in detail). A new Arab proposal in this regard is gaining prominence; it calls for a new classification of sociology into two trends: balance and conflict."[23]

One wonders first of all why, when the Arab scholars cited here reflect on the societies in the Arab world, they do not simply deal with the peculiarities of these societies, but instead go on to investigate what makes them special, using a theory they already have, so, they approach the Arab societies with a comparison of theories they already have before they have understood what they are, before they can even know what they are comparing with what, and then come to the strange conclusion that the picture they had formed of them through the theories of European societies does not match what they are. And, one wonders further, since they obviously already have a theory on Arab societies for this comparison, if they know the differences between them and European societies and reject European theories as "Eurocentric" and therefore as unsuitable for Arab societies, why they do not simply create their theories on Arab societies without resorting to the theories of other, European societies, and why they do not simply put aside these "Eurocentric" theories for their theories. Then one could still, but only after the analysis of the local society, find out what these theories have in common and what not. So what is the point of this strange tour, to first put a theory about the European societies like a mirror image on the Arab societies, only to find that the Arab societies do not reflect the same as the image of the European societies, and are therefore unsuitable for their study? What is the point of this strange operation

---

23   Faleh Abdel-Jabbar, Insights into the Topic: Arabs and Sociology, Epistemological and Ideological, Characteristic and Seclusion, Synthesis and Openness, unpublished paper.

of finding out that a theory is not a theory about what one theorizes about?—Exactly that, to find out not what the nature of something is, in this case the Arab Society, but to find out that a theory does not fit; only this finding out is not a discussion of an object and a theory about it at all, but a kind of intentional epistemological hypocrisy, like when you put the theory into the world, the sun turns around the earth, only to find out that this theory "does not fit" the relationship between sun and earth.

Yet this very sociologically thinking social scientist somehow notices in his considerations that there is something irritating about the juxtaposition or confrontation of individual and society in this "Eurocentric" theory. With his assessment that this "Western" sociological dualism is "not appropriate" for understanding the societies in the Arab world, this critic of European social scientists not only proves to be their very learned student, but also replicates, despite all the inconsistencies of this primordial sociological theorem, all the assumptions and theoretical errors that are peculiar to it.

To reject a theory as "not suitable" for the insight of any phenomenon, treacherously does not even try to explore what causes the irritations of this theory, because it is decidedly aimed at something else, namely a very own theory. Such a rejection of a theory as inappropriate to explain something here does not even notice that the juxtaposition of individual and society, and even more so the juxtaposition of individual and society, contains all kinds of insinuations that are in great need of explanation. Why never the society of individuals? Why their juxtaposition as well as their juxtaposition with the discrete insinuation operates all too clearly by means of a pronounced or unspoken "and" with an opposition as somehow a quasi natural opposition between the two, between individual and society, which is none at all, if both, individual and society, share and unite in the same goal, this question does not occur to a thinker who marks out this "Eurocentric" theory in the consistency of its thoughts, because he wants to say that it fits there "in the West" already, but not here.

Why this dualism at all? Do individuals actually exist without society?[24] All this is swept aside and thus ignored by the reference

---

24 For all those who no longer know: It is this identity of a society of individuals, who regard society as their society, which constitutes the rational core of the decision of the social sciences in the former Soviet Union to ban sociology as the science of capitalist societies from their nomenclatura of social sciences.

to societies elsewhere, i.e. a reversal of the exoticization of societies "in the West", and by this ignorance of the criticized theory with the disinterest in whether this irritating theory is less irritating elsewhere and has an explanatory value there, this rejected theory is left to a strange indifference, which also does not want to know how it can be that a theory is supposed to be suitable for explanation there, but not here, with the consequence that the question of whether the comparison of these theories is actually about the same phenomena is no longer in focus. Such reviews of theories rejected as inappropriate come as little into the mind of the criticism of a theory rejected as "Eurocentric" as the methodological oddities of having to know them before and for the insights into a social phenomenon in order to investigate them with an appropriate theory. Whatever the reason for having to investigate something that one already knows about the matter as the means of this investigation by means of a suitable theory, even this methodological somersault does not strike the critics of a "Eurocentric" theory critique and proves these critics to be erudite users of the social scientific way of the European scientific tradition to create theories that actually proceed in the same way as the critic of "Eurocentric" theories.

According to their way of theorizing, it is essential that, in order to generate knowledge about whatever, one must take a theoretical "approach", that is, first with the view of a social science discipline and then with any theory of that discipline, to go out to its object of investigation through which one can understand, or better interpret it. That this kind of knowledge generation through a preselected viewpoint, such as that of sociology here, i.e. to explain everything social through the parameters of a relationship between individual and society, must lead to obviously pre-occupied theories, does not even occur to a thinker who does not want to reject such a way of theorizing because he considers it pre-occupied theorizing, but who wants to do precisely that, pre-occupied theories with his pre-made interpretations of his phenomenon to be explained, to interpret it through such pre-assumptions, but not by this rejected "approach", but by another, as he says, by a locally "fitting" theoretical preliminary construction, of which he thanks to his knowledge of how his society is not constituted knows, that it, the Arab society, is not one of educated individualists, and for him from his knowledge that it is not like European societies, he concludes that because he knows what this Arab society is not, that he therefore knows how this society is and by which preliminary interpretations it must therefore be explained. Can we go on with more theoretical nonsense?

And these pre-interpretations are, one can almost guess it, when one wants to deduce from knowledge knowing what a society not is, i.e. does not know anything positive about it, by which theoretical assumptions one wants to interpret for the formation of knowledge about it just like the European sciences, but reject their interpretation model as unsuitable, that this "non-eurocentric" interpretation model suitable for the unknown Arab societies is—exactly the same as the unsuitable, "eurocentric" one: *"Balance and conflict"* are in fact nothing else than the processual translation of the static counterpart of society and individuals. Balance and conflict translates the dichotomy of individual and society into the dichotomy of the dynamics of their in both dichotomies assumed antagonisms, whose dichotomous sides, individual and society, are somewhat hidden behind the observation of their to and for, around the same, now dynamized, dichotomy of both, i.e. the same now as the "locally" fitting sociologically constructed prejudice of the same pair of thoughts, a pair of thought which constitutes any sociological thinking and without which not a single sociological thought can come into being, to then present this now not a "Euro-centric" but an Arab-centric sociological model of thinking *"from which they could start their research."* Operation succeeded, one would like to note for a thought operation, to which all arguments are right, if they are then suitable to tinker an own Arab view of the Arab societies for the Arab research then born with it, a research thus, which admits itself by its national attribute "Arab" to its interest in an openly nationalistically colored view, a post-colonial way of Arab theorizing is thereby constructed.

And what is that theoretical nonsense all about? Exactly that, a nationalist view, and that is why this very targeted thinking does not care in the least what judgements and arguments they accept with their so constructed justification of a local theory formation, for the achievement of this goal all theoretical salti mortali are welcome. Do social science thinkers really need to be made aware that the manner of speaking of a pronounced individualism not to be found in Arab societies, such as that of Europeans, *'many Arab researchers who have not found mature European individualism in their societies',* is first of all based on a confrontation between the individual and society, in which the social constructs of citizen societies are presented as quasi natural, ahistorical conflicts of every form of sociality, not only has nothing to complain about this, but manages without any hesitation to transform the historical form of the subject of citizen society, i.e. the citizen as an individual, into the ideology of a desirable social form of life, and celebrates that very "individualism" in the imperialist world which this imperial world glorifies as its proof for the superiority of its societies , and must one indeed remind these "Eurocentrist" critics that this form of the subject of capitalist societies as an "individualist", which is homed as a profoundly human form of life, is secondly a quite common stereotype of the very European self-portrait of the European about himself, and that the same stupid and equally pretentious abstraction about the Arab and, as if this was not enough centrism, that then also the next thought, to present this Arab as not yet quite "matured" individualist European, like the first one about "the European", that all these are pretty awful racisms about both, Europeans and Arabs? The European an individualist, the Arab a still immature European? Who is actually measuring people here with his criticism of a "Euro-centric" way of thinking by what he means, what the European is and thinks, and then describes the Arab as an immature European? Or does the critique of a "Euro-centrism" of thought not get along without such secret or openly expressed nationalistically defined racisms as those of "the Europeans" and "the Arabs", if it aims at a way of theorizing that wants to be explicitly nationalistic?

So what does this critical objection of a "Eurocentric" knowledge, which may "fit" there, in Europe—needless to say, none of these critical scientists is interested in examining any of those theories "fitting" there in Europe, but beyond it certainly "do not fit". Is it perhaps not at all about the same societies, whose distinction is both admonished here without any problem, as well as in their comparison, the Arabs as unfinished Europeans, as the same are claimed—this is also not a question that the critic of "Eurocentric" knowledge may ask himself, but who can obviously imagine, or better, wants to see knowledge about the same thing to be knowledge there, but not here. How is that supposed to work? What does a critique that does know knowledge as fitting there and here not actually understand by knowledge? Are theories, is knowledge a kind of intellectual trying out of the fit of images, in which one tries out which knowledge "fits" for what where? How does one know whether it "fits" or "does not fit", what is that supposed to be, "suitable" knowledge? What should it be suitable for, the "locally" suitable thinking? If one understands theories as mere suppositions and then realizes that the thing is as the supposition assumed it to be, then every supposition is right and proper? Thinking as trial and error, so one must be allowed to try what can be done? Isn't it precisely this kind of knowledge generation, in which one, guided by the theoretical, alternative "approaches" of one's discipline, chooses an "approach" from this disciplinary pool and then sets off with its views of the world, which in the criticized "Eurocentric" science creates those modelled theories in this way, about which the critics of this view, in view of their explanatory value for their societies, ask themselves what these theories actually have to do with reality, in order not to question this kind of theory-building, the imposition of any disciplinary models on the world, but to draw the conclusion from the arbitrariness of such thinking that they should then build their own model theories themselves: instead of individual and society, let's go for balance and conflict! And how do we even know that the assumption rejected as "Eurocentric" is the way things are or not, if we have nothing but our own assumptions about the thing and try to go back and forth with various assumptions? How and when do we know when and, above all, for what such constructed knowledge is "suitable"?

Obviously for what the critique of a locally biased, the critique of "Eurocentrist" thinking, with its critique of "Eurocentrism", wants to get at in its arguments as single-mindedly as arbitrarily, namely to be allowed to do the same in one's own place as the local centrists elsewhere in Europe and to use one's own mode of interpretation, serving one's own national identity, i.e. one's own theoretical nationalism, to interpret the established modes of interpretation of the same sort of pre-occupied sciences from European science as one's own nationalistically inspired, pre-occupied model-knowledge in order to add and maintain an interpretative model of the same kind of European science with the same theoretical questions in this so criticized scientific scene "dominated" by theories of European provenance, representing in this European science world the own "local" nationalism. Instead of the "hegemony" of one patriotically inspired view of the world, namely that of those "Eurocentrists" up to now, to counter the pluralism of a multitude of nationally inspired, scientifically pepped-up world views, i.e., exactly what the inventor of the term "Eurocentrism"—Said—suspected as a false consequence still being criticized by him and what he warned against?

The result of this just as wrong as interested criticism called Eurocentrism thus achieves the worldwide spread of social scientific thought and its methodological relativism into the new nation-state societies of the de-colonized world, a relativism that, after all, up to this turn towards theorizing freed from Eurocentrism, was still formally based on objectivity, i.e. the necessity of provability of its knowledge as a sign of scientific knowledge, and which now, by means of the elimination of what constitutes scientific knowledge, relativizes and thus radicalizes its relativism by replacing its methodological relativism with the relativism of a knowledge freed from any objectivity in the concept of spatial, i.e. according to the political affiliation of the thinking subjects to political entities created for this purpose, such as "northern theories". It is not only the state affiliation of theorists and their theories to a nation-state grown view that knows this kind of locally inspired thinking as the last source of locally contextualized knowledge, the invention of new scientific entities such as a "global south" replaces, what scientific thinking, even in its methodological relativism, still holds to social scientific thinking by a form of science of locally determined knowledge that denies any objectivity, and thus creates a scientific world that consists of the unmediatable coexistence of locally, i.e. nationalistically inspired theories, whose insights can only be opened up to thinking that is connected with "place" thanks to its nationalism.

To reproach the European social sciences for overlooking the locally determined relativity of their knowledge is thus an as obvious as pretentious misunderstanding of social science thinking, which only well-trained thinkers in these social sciences can create and who have learned from them that social science thinking is thinking that creates knowledge through and by the view of nation-state constructs. Only those who define knowledge in this way, and who do not want to reject the bias of knowledge that is thus given, but rather well trained in this very sort of thinking want to accept it, can come up with the idea of accusing the knowledge of the European sciences of ignoring, with their claim to the locally independent validity of their knowledge, the determination of their knowledge by the national occurrences of the object of thought and thus the local relativity of the validity of their theories, in order to use this staged memory of the local relativity of knowledge, which this knowledge did by then not know at all, at least not until its "globalization", to demand that their knowledge of their new states, interpreted in the same way as their local relative theories about and through their societies, as a contribution to this kind of post-colonial social science thinking and to have it recognized by theses social sciences as its complementary theories from the de-colonized world, in order to then, on the basis of this recognition, enter into the dispute about which nation-state inspired view of the world with its theories is capable of imposing its local theories as model theories for worldwide theory creations.

2.2 The place of thinking as the "contextual" source of knowledge

The European social sciences' own view of constructing their theories through the practical concerns of a citizen society, for whose spheres of life, separated into private, political and economic, their sciences, separated into the corresponding scientific disciplines, provide their models of interpretation and thus create their relative knowledge, this methodological relativism of disciplinary theorizing radicalizes this opposition of the post-colonial discourse to European science with its concept of a validity of knowledge dependent on the place of theory formation, i.e., the denial of the objectivity of knowledge in general, and this as a science-theoretically founded nature of knowledge, its always only locally relativized validity.

This opposition to the meaning of Merton's proclamatory idea, boldly reinterpreted in retrospect, after the transformation of the world into a world of nation-states, to the idea that science is universal, in Merton's view meaning that science knows no exclusions of knowledge and science knows no other than scientific criteria, to the claim of an equally retrospectively redefined meaning of universally valid knowledge, according to which universal knowledge is reinterpreted as knowledge that claims validity regardless of the location of its object of knowledge, and with this retrospective interpretation of the idea of Merton's scientific universalism, this opposition against the knowledge of the European social sciences, led under the criticism of Eurocentrism, with its demand for a multiplicity of a locally limited knowledge validity, for which the not coincidentally leading theorists of the very European social sciences, such as, to name but one, Foucault with his rebellion against objective knowledge, provide the scientific-theoretical justifications,[25] this opposition eliminates the last rational moments of social scientific thinking, its insistence on the at least formally objective form of a nevertheless relative knowledge and sacrifices this least formal objectivity of relative knowledge to the absurdity of a conditionally relative knowledge, in which the place of its generation constitutes this conditionality, i.e. the absurdity of knowledge about one and the same thing, which is supposed to be here knowledge and not there.

As if not all knowledge were knowledge about an object that is always any *where*, in one place, and as if knowledge about this object were not always valid everywhere, regardless of whether it exists everywhere, the concept of local knowledge is used to claim the abstruseness that "Eurocentric" knowledge is knowledge in Europe but not elsewhere, and this with the equally abstruse justification that the object is both the same and not the same. In other words, because there are different things in two places, knowledge about a thing, even if it is the same, is not valid in both places. This headnut must be created in order to attach to this recognition, by means of the where of the objects of recognition, which has been elevated to the status of an epistemological authority, the political interest to take away the scientific monopoly of interpretation of the world from the old colonial societies of Europe and to grant the societies of each citizen society of the decolonized world of states as a whole the claim to their own national view of this world.

The "place" is the seemingly innocent epistemological lever used to reject the idea of a universalism, re-interpreted only for this purpose, with which never any location-independent validity of knowledge has been asserted, which only the theoreticians of the place have attributed to this idea of a scientific universalism and this only in order to give their proclamation of the epistemological performance of the place the appearance of a criticism, by criticizing this interpretation of its proclamation, only they made up for this

---

25 See also "The Social Science of the Citizen Society, Volume 2, The Nature of the Social Sciences—Outlines of a Critique."

construction of a criticism: it is the place as source of knowledge that is opposed to this interpretation of universal knowledge as knowledge without place, which has never been asserted by anyone and which is only asserted by the inventors of place as an instance of knowledge, and which, with its geographical innocence, must justify the less innocent concern to prove the idea of national homelands as a cognitive resource of all thinking, inherent to the nature of any theorizing.

The construction of the chimera of a scientific universalism, according to which knowledge is universally valid knowledge regardless of the question whether the objects of knowledge exist somewhere at all, only this proof of the necessity of place as a knowledge instance invents in order to present its idea of place as a knowledge instance in the form of a critique of this so reckoned idea of a scientific universalism and thus the idea of place as an epistemological instance of thinking as a progress of scientific thinking, as overcoming a concept of knowledge of the old colonial world by decolonized scientific thinking, in order to give the political concern of the sciences in the new state societies the appearance of liberating scientific thought from a false dogma of science theory that has always been wrong through the history of the social sciences and thus to give its political, nationalist ambitions of theoretical nationalisms to which everyone is entitled the beautiful appearance of an epistemological progress of science.

The fact that this de-colonization of the sciences, presented as a progress in scientific thinking, is performed as a liberation of scientific knowledge from objectivity, i.e. as a liberation from what distinguishes scientific knowledge from other forms of judgment in the first place, and as such constitutes scientific thinking, thus making science indistinguishable from the arbitrariness of opinions, is one of the ironic spectacles without which the worldwide assertion of citizen societies and their form of their social science thinking cannot be had.

Supported by the philosophical gurus in the imperial world, it was once again the privilege of the learned critical students of European social sciences from the old colonized societies, especially its science theory departments, to derive from science theory this step towards a science freed of all objectivity as a knowledge ascribed to the place of its generation that represents nothing more than the politically opportune local opinion, to bury with this critique of the

European social sciences their historical achievements in their dissociation from the idealisms of classical philosophy of a knowledge directed to the real world and aiming for objectivity, which they had conquered with their—false—critique of classical philosophy as a founding idea of social sciences, not only without noticing this funeral, but as support for their de-colonization with contributions from their philosophical departments giving this funeral of their founding ideas the higher philosophical blessing.[26]

And it must probably be due to the achieved state of theoretical undemanding social-scientific thinking, a science that now considers the mere gawking of the world with its supply of data to be theories, that it does not cause this kind of thinking any headache at all, if science-theoretical de-colonizers of the social sciences can unquestioningly claim that a theory about the same thing in two places cannot be the same simply because the same thing is found in two different places, to use this argument, that a dog in place B cannot be a dog, if a dog in A has been identified as a dog, to substantiate their de-colonized theory about the cognitive power of place in this absurd way, and that such theoretical nonsense, with which one succeeds in giving the transparent concern to give local patriotic views of the world the appearance of a scientifically founded, objectively grounded necessity, actually succeeds in expelling from this science even its last foundation, the certainty about its concepts, as subjectivity bound to place, i.e. to the nation-state.

In the most recent variant of social science thought, in theorizing through the location of thinking, the mysticism of the teleological idealism of classical philosophy, in which the world was presented as the realization of ideas and which social science theorizing had replaced as the formation of theories about the world, experiences a strange renaissance in the idea of place as a catalyst for thoughts about it, an idea according to which the world consists of a multitude of politically constructed unique places, which constitute the "context" through which social science thinking articulates its theories as a multiplicity of parochial thoughts, born from a mystical connection to the place of thought accessible only to local thinking, the idea of a scientifically blessed nationalism that interprets its affiliation to its nation-state as a quasi natural mission of its scientific

---

26 See about this the more elaborated reflections in: "The Social Science of the Citizen Society, Volume 2, The Nature of the Social Sciences—Outlines of a Critique."

mission to create knowledge as nation state-connected worldviews freed from any objectivity.

The statement that knowledge is the result of the thinking of a thinking subject that is in a place and thinks upon an object that is in a place would be more than banal and theoretically only ridiculous if this banality in the most modern version of a post-colonially purified thinking was not the entry into a science-theoretical reasoning that establishes the place as a source and as a spiritual force for cognition:

> "... the proposition that thought is related to places is central to my project provincializing Europe."[27]

Thanks to the postcolonial version of the globalized form of social science theory-building, what one thinks is decided by where one is, which is why de-colonized thinking is characterized above all by the distinction of the places of knowledge and characterizes them by corresponding local attributes of knowledge: Thus, in this kind of theory-building there are local and global, very cleverly "glocal", national and international knowledge, and also theoretical monsters like "Southern Theories" in contrast to the, well, "Northern Theories", in short, all kinds of locally constructed dichotomies of knowledge types, which, by indicating a place, signal their belonging to knowledge shaped by these places.

And since such theoretical nonsense of a decolonized thinking freed from colonial thinking about thinking qua place is not rejected as pre-scientific, mystical, monstrous and an anti-critical hyper-determinism, but rather considered as evidence of a particularly critical form of thinking in this post-colonial debate, one must take the trouble to trace the intellectual steps that construct this nonsense epistemologically.

Undoubtedly, the place of an object of knowledge is of a significance, if highly banal, but of a meaning. For there are phenomena with which thinking is concerned, which exist here but not elsewhere, so that some people here and there do not know them. Such things exist. Thinkers from here and there think about such phenomena and share their theories, the results of their thinking, with other thinkers from here and there. So much and so little could be

---

27 Chakrabarty, D., (2000) *Postcolonial Thought and Historical Difference*, Princeton University Press, p. xiii.

said about the place of the object of thought and the place of the thinker, as well as about the time of the object and the thinker—if not in the science-theoretical foundation of a theory formation inspired by place, which therein presents the science-theoretical basis for the "de-colonization" of the social sciences after the transformation of the world into a world of states with a market economy, if it were not for this justification of the "de-colonization" of social science theory formation that place is not one—of many other—properties of the object one thinks about, just as time is, but rather that place must be regarded as a knowledge-generating force that leads the thinker to the content of knowledge that a thinker has about the thing being thought about. In other words, the place of thought and the place of the object of thought, those places usually politically defined in the de-colonization debate, in the manner of speech of that idea of "provincializing" the European social sciences by introducing the place as a knowledge-generating force, is not directed in this manner of speech against the European tradition of science, but accuses it of not having recognized the place of generation of its theories, Europe, as a knowledge-generating force and therefore of having created theories, which, without realizing it, reproduce the place of Europe thanks to its cognition-forming power, but—so the accusation—also consider their theories to be valid theories beyond this place, which cannot be, because the place of cognition decides what one thinks about its object, i.e. theories cannot be valid beyond Europe, if and because the place about which one theory is created is another, i.e. no theory created in Europe can be valid beyond Europe.

In the case of one of the masterminds for the cognitive performance of the place, Chakrabarty, this argumentation sounds like this:

> "To 'provincialize' Europe was precisely to find out how and in what sense European ideas that were universal were also, at one and the same time, drawn from very particular intellectual and historical traditions that could not claim any universal validity. It was to ask the question about how thought was related to place. Can thought transcend places of their origin? Or do places leave their imprint on thought in such ways as to call into question the idea of purely abstract categories?"[28]

If one straight forwardly formulates one's scientific question in such a way that one asks oneself how one can achieve the purpose aimed at with it, the "provincialization" of Europe, and how one can derive

---

28 D. Chakrabarty, (2000) Postcolonial ... p. xiii.

this purpose as a conclusion from the knowledge of the relationship between place and knowledge, then thinking is certainly creative enough to do the thinker this favor through his thoughts top achieve what he wants to achieve. Chakrabarty does himself this favor first of all by putting aside theoretical troublemakers for this thought construction he is striving for, that the place "imprints thoughts", and in return denies thinking what every thinking takes as its precondition and as its result, i.e. what thinking is all about, that is the concepts it creates and in which it materializes its insights: The question how it is possible that knowledge of the same thing, when the same thing is elsewhere, is probably the same thing, but that knowledge of it is not to be the same, because it is exactly that which he wants to establish, i.e. it is the place where the same thing is, as he expresses himself, that shapes knowledge of the same thing at another place differently, this post-colonial thinker, who argues completely detached from any place, proves this with no more and no less than questioning what scientific thinking is, namely the formation of and certainty about concepts, i.e. the shared knowledge on which scientific thinking is based and with which this thinker naturally also operates when he justifies why he wants to take them out of circulation. As well as the concepts, like the concept of an abstract category, with which he operates unmoved in the certainty that everybody knows and shares what an abstract category is, in order to deny in the certainty of knowledge of these epistemological categories to every knowledge the certainty about any concept as basis of all thinking, in order to use this argument of arbitrariness of concepts, to prepare the field for asserting knowledge as a subjective articulation of an associative state of mind, freed of all objectivity, which the place as a local national view of this thing that the thinker associates with this place, and which this view, which is then attributed to the place, "imprints" this thinker as his scientific knowledge into it.

It is quite remarkable with what audacious mental escapades of all things, or should one say better, who else, social science thinkers, who are occupied their whole life with using their brains to create knowledge about the world—and this not only since Chakrabarty—have been pursuing the doubt about knowledge as an upscale science and also possess the audacity of scientific activity, which they operate as a social privilege, to deny the elementary foundations of any thinking, not in order to stop science once and for all, no, if they want to prove that this science is anyway not different from the likes of a 10-year-old, they just prove that what is knowledge cannot be knowledge at all, and claim this cheekily as a deep scientific insight into what knowledge is. This is what all the post-colonial thinkers have learned from their provincial European gurus, well-behaved and completely free of any localities, when they are obsessed with the thought of trying to prove that knowledge is a sheer effect of the world on their brain and that it is not the thinker but the world that "imprints" the thought products into their brain. For this, any kind of stupid humbug is just right for them. And this, of all things, by scientists from regions of the world where misery would give all reasons to think about why this is so, to gain knowledge about it, so that one can do something about it; no, this thinker denies, like all his Eurocentrist science-scepticist predecessors, that in thinking anything clever can come out with which one could intervene in the course of things.

And why then, when the world imprints the thought products of thinking into the mind of the thinker, why then think and not simply take the rap, when the place is the true thinker anyway? Because thinking gets nothing imprinted from anywhere, except that one turns on one's intellect, no insights are called by any reality to the ignorant, or otherwise reveal themselves to the thinking, it is probably better here too, in the discussion of thoughts about the place as source of insights, not to wait for the imprinting whispers of a place about the mysterious relationship between place and cognition, which would eliminate his lack of understanding of such connections, but to rely on thinking and to examine what has been imprinted as insight by this postcolonial thinker from a where about what this where about thinking about the where, to this thinker as insight.

What, then, are such insights that some place has imprinted to this protagonist of the place as a source of knowledge?

> "Until I arrived in Australia, I had never seriously entertained the implications of the fact that an abstract and universal idea characteristic of political modernity everywhere—the idea of equality, say, or of democracy or even of the dignity of human being—could look utterly different in different historical contexts. Australia, like India, is a thriving electoral democracy, but Election Day there does not have anything of the atmosphere of festivity that I was used to it in India."[29]

---

29 Chakrabarty, ... p. xii.

There can be no more unequivocal statement as to what disturbs these thinkers, who liberate social science thinking from its imprisonment in universally (here in place-directed thinking simply means "everywhere") abstract concepts, about abstract concepts that do not want to bow to their relativization by the place of their use: What disturbs this science-theoretical thinker about science is that knowledge materialized to terms is knowledge that does not allow to express with its terms what the thinker subjectively wants to see the objects of thinking as.

For that is what the social scientific thinking of citizen societies has really achieved, after all, despite its idealizations of the world as a civilization progress for thinking about the world, namely, that the released free will of the state subjects of citizen society, who set their own goals, must make their world their own in thought, and that they must know how this world works in order to achieve their goals. That it is the same state power that concedes this freedom to him, in order to immediately regain it with its subordination to that which defines this power as goals, in order to direct this freedom of its citizens into paths that are useful to it, means all the more that these citizens must know how things are in the state-constructed world, which is why the same state makes science its task and orders its citizens to acquire knowledge that will enable them to understand their world as citizens with all its curiosities, such as the fact that one produces wealth all one's life and hardly gets anything out of it, as a society model that is not perfect but in principle somehow quite reasonable. The social sciences are there to critically ascribe to the world its actually reasonable goals and to measure it critically against them, so that one can at least make a plausible rhyme for all these curiosities, and create this kind of knowledge, which interprets this world through all kinds of preconfigured thought constructs, but also has at least to prove this as provable knowledge.

It is precisely this, proving knowledge, that annoys the thinker who considers proving knowledge, proving a theory that the world is as his knowledge claims it to be, the validity of theories to be a shackle to his need to see the world simply as he wants to see it. In order to free knowledge from the barrier that, in order for it to claim to be knowledge, it must prove that it is knowledge, i.e., that it cannot be dissolved into any arbitrary state of being, this thinker invents the place as a hitherto unconsidered moment of the formation of knowledge and attributes to it the property that no place has of whispering its knowledge to the thinker. What Chakrabarty reveals to us about his visit to a place as a source of knowledge, which, because of the place where it is conceived, must always be locally relative knowledge about the same things, i.e. objective knowledge cannot exist at all, is that all the crude efforts to present the place as a relativizing source for the critique of a knowledge independent of place dissolve into the fact that there are different, no, not different judgments about the same thing, in his example elections, but different subjective appreciations of elections.

People in India, he says, celebrate elections like a festival, while in Australia voting is more routine. From which we should draw and share the conclusion that knowledge is conditioned by—forget about the place—no, conditioned by the fact that the thing about which the knowledge is about, some find it great here, others less so elsewhere, so from this, from the variety of subjective appreciations of elections, we should conclude that elections, i.e., knowledge about elections, is not the same here and there, because it receives different subjective appreciations here and there.

No way, the place imprints knowledge: The place that this epistemological attack against knowledge tries to make its argument appear—that's the way it is with science, even if you want to prove that objective knowledge cannot exist, you have to prove that as well—as if it was a reasoned, instead of simply saying, because I want to be able to see things/elections the way the people in India see them, that is I want to find them positive, the place that has been striven for in the theory of science dissolves into nothing else but the likes he likes, the bare personal, political appreciations of elections, and because he finds these appreciations of elections shared by others in one place, he attributes to this place the abilities to imprint his like to him. And when he then returns to Australia, does this place imprint the opposite judgment about elections to him? What kind of knowledge, imprinted from what place, does the post-colonial thinker have about his subject, here about elections? The knowledge Australia or the knowledge India imprints for him?

The whole associative hullabaloo with place as a source of knowledge is presented by this scientific-theoretical mastermind of a post-colonially liberated science, because what bothers him about science is that it does not allow him to claim as knowledge any personal appreciations of things, especially political convictions, which post-colonial thinkers would like to see attributed to a nation state as a viewpoint, and therefore argues that knowledge should simply be interpreted as such a subjective, political appreciation.

Mind you, the plea, with all its as inflated as abstruse nonsense about the place of thought and the object of thought and the mystical imprints between the two, does not want to advocate that everyone should be allowed to find that the world is like one finds it is. To proclaim the pure subjective opinion about anything, this is not his plea, the advocates of post-colonial thinkers are scientists and advocate a way of scientific thinking. What Chakrabarty argues for with all his nonsense about place and thinking, is to justify, why any subjective prejudice has to be regarded as well-founded scientific knowledge. Because people in India think elections are great, and he wants to see this view of elections as the national view of India, and because he wants to see this national view as the scientific contribution of India in India's post-colonial discourse on elections, he attacks any concept of knowledge based on objective reasoning with his critique of the objectivity of concepts, that is why one cannot say what elections are, but must be allowed to find elections great in India, because people there see it that way, because this national view of elections, by liberating knowledge from the objectivity of concepts, serves him as an example of knowledge of a concept of decolonized thinking that destroys the foundations of all knowledge.

The radical subjectivity of knowledge, its dissolution into the arbitrariness of political sensitivities about the world, especially knowledge, not to leave it as what it is, as a political opinion, but to elevate these political opinions to postcolonial scientific knowledge, is the scientific-theoretical concern of this thinker liberating knowledge from its colonialism by liberating it from its nature as knowledge.

But this is not all, the reclamation of the place as a judgement forming cognitive instance of knowledge, in order to justify political opinions as knowledge, goes a step further, and attacks not only science, but the basis of all thinking, the concepts formed by thinking, without which all thinking and argumentation is impossible, and with which therefore all thinking operates, and which are all the more the precondition and not least the object and result of all scientific theory formation.

Concepts are the insights into the essential nature of the objects of thought, generalizations about their essential properties that make these objects essentially different from others, abstractions that refrain from variations of the same thing and describe its essential nature and, as these abstractions, are the basis of thinking and theoretical discussions about the world, not least about concepts. Science, whatever its specific historical form of theorizing, is not only the instance that creates concepts, but also the instance that therefore examines whether these abstractions capture the essential, the central features of the distinctions they make from other things. The critique of concepts is therefore the central task of science, and in an approach to science which, in its scientific-theoretical reflections on what knowledge is, claims that knowledge is by nature always relative, relative to the theories and their categories used in the process of cognition, one must also, and even more so, expect that the critical examination of concepts is the task of science. It would be better to say that it should be the task of science, because it is already the theoretical misery of the methodological relativism of the social sciences of these citizen societies to let these debates with their concepts die in the no-man's-land of their relativism. All the more reason to reflect on the terms used by this relative theorizing, without ever really examining them to see whether the judgments about the nature of things generalized in them are correct generalizations, would be the task of a science that has every reason not to trust such a relativism commandment, if only because with this relativism commandment it blocks and immunizes every theory as well as its terms against its critique. And reason for criticism, also of those concepts that are the basis for the theorizing in the "Eurocentric" sciences, is more than enough provided by this science with its theories and, even more so, by the politics of its nation states towards the societies of the former colonies. The dualism individual/society discussed above, constitutive for sociological thinking, would be such a case for reflecting on the conceptual basis of sociological thinking, but the de-colonized science does not criticize any concepts or theories, but copies and varies it.

The theoretical considerations that propagate a place-bound formation of knowledge, relativized by its respective local, i.e. political context, and that do not refute any single concept of the opposed "Eurocentric" theories, i.e. attack them as false abstractions, this post-colonial thinking does the opposite of a critique of concepts; instead of criticizing concepts, this thinking attacks the foundation of all concept formation, abstraction itself; it does the sheer opposite of a critique of concepts by not criticizing just any concept, but by attacking abstraction itself as what distinguishes knowledge, finding out the nature of the objects of thought and solidifying them in concepts.

That it is the nature of abstractions to refrain from characteristics of things not characterizing their essential nature, because it falsifies the insights into its essential qualities, which distinguish this thing from others, it is exactly this falsification of insights by the deliberate mixing of essential and incidental things, to which the attack on—once again, not the content of any concept and its abstractions—is aimed, but at this distinction between essential and incidental aspects of things, that is, at abstraction, that is, what thinking is all about. In order to pave the way for every subjective state of mind about the world, especially for politically inspired judgments about the world, against and vis-à-vis al scientific knowledge—paradoxically, into the world of scientific judgements—the attack on what distinguishes concepts, abstractions that make well-founded distinctions to fathom the nature of things, attacks this, what distinguishes scientific knowledge and with this propagates knowledge itself and thus—the return of—the irrational arbitrariness of opinions before any knowledge, the replacement of well-founded judgements and of decisions derived from them, thus verifiable and only with this as disputable decisions as the renaissance of, not only the regime of subjective appreciations as scientific judgements, but also of despotism in the practical handling of the world.

And indeed, since then the world has been full of terms from this kind of science, which—preferably—turns expressions of disapproval, one might even say vulgar bleating, into terms exported by science into everyday language. "Inequality", the stilted form of articulation of the desire for an equality that nobody strives for, otherwise called "unfair" in the form of everyday grumbling, is such a new de-colonized term, which, simply because it wants to take a difference negatively as a deviation from its desire for indistinctness into a lawsuit, encounters grammatical and linguistic obstacles and thus, in the grammatical linguistic world of the German language, took a few years to overcome the resistance of its mere pronunciation. Nothing would be more distant to post-colonially liberated thinkers than to criticize the nonsense of a term that describes a thing as the absence of a desire, because nothing is more distant to these critics of abstractions, of what knowledge is, than to criticize any knowledge. Rather than spelling out its transparent logic to such wishful thinking as a linguistic monster of the concept of "inequality", they want to be able to criticize abstractions by pointing out that abstractions disregard aspects of things because they only distort what they are, such as judging what voting is, does not care about what voters might appreciate about elections, appreciations a Chakrabarty observes on election day in India, and, because be shares these appreciations, wants to see them as a scientific judgment about them; instead of objective concepts the critics of concepts want the concept of elections to express—as here in the example of elections—the positive political assessment of elections by Indian voters, which he obviously shares, such subjective assessments of elections as knowledge about elections.

But such a thing, to grasp subjective appreciation as knowledge, does not work with knowledge, and certainly not its basis, its concepts. Elections in India are, according to Chakrabarty, a highly valued thing in India; what they are, knowledge about what elections are, what concepts are, is what disturbs them, that they are not suitable for articulating the political positions cultivated in a country on anything, here the homage of elections, because concepts refrain from such appreciations of positive and negative nature by abstraction as a moment not essential to the thing, thus abstracted, for the purpose of what they are. And this for a good reason, because knowledge of anything, before its evaluation of how to find the thing, wants to have certainty about what it is and aims at, and how in it the concerns of the knower are or are not.

Undoubtedly, the need to want to use knowledge as a carrier of political value judgements of places, that is, of states that want to interfere in the world of states and their judgement of the world inside and outside, blocks both that which distinguishes a concept and, a fortiori, that which is knowledge, and this itself in the residuals of formal objectivity, which social scientific thinking cultivates in its regularities of obtaining knowledge, with which it creates and justifies its relatively objective knowledge. And it is precisely this residue of formal objectivity that is too much objectivity for the post-colonial social science theorists, which is why they attack concepts as the basis of knowledge and argue for being allowed to add their nationally inspired political worldviews—ironically—as a contribution to this—opposed—social science knowledge and this as acknowledged by these opposed sciences as well-founded in the theory of these very social sciences.

That they themselves make their own attacks on what constitutes knowledge, on the abstractions made in concepts, which know how to distinguish the essential characteristics from trivialities, ultimately an absurdity and expose their argumentation against what distinguishes not only knowledge but also arguing with and about knowledge in science as a politically motivated science-theoretical farce, is just unavoidable, just as all the proofs, that you cannot prove anything, if you want to prove, as here with the abstractions of concepts, that concepts are exactly those abstractions, which they too must strive to discredit concepts as "tabula rasa",[30] i.e. as nothing meaningful, because they do not convey the knowledge on which they are keen on, their locally patriotic, politically biased appreciations of any things. Because, with their argumentation against the meaningless concepts, they do not simply want to communicate that, compared to scientific statements with their meaningless, empty abstractions, they prefer to simply say nothing well-founded and to simply show off their local patriotism, but rather to reason, why such local patriotism is the only meaningful form of knowledge, by equating abstract—falsely—with meaningless for this assertion, in order not to be stupid enough, to mobilize exactly for this not only the very concepts defamed by them as meaningless=contentless for their proofs—what else, if one wants to prove something—, but they then also rise to the assertion that their evidence against a knowledge that is not locally relativized, that thinking that by its nature is always to be locally inspired thinking and that produces that provincial knowledge, those local patriotisms, that this thinking propagated by them as articulation of local patriotisms is of course an objective and universal—in their interpretation of universal as the independence of knowledge from place that they criticize—that this an epistemological necessity, an objective epistemological thought about theorizing that is valid independent of place and valid worldwide.

> "If this argument is true for India, then it is true of any other place as well, including, of course, Europe or, broadly, the West."[31]

---

30 Ibid.
31 Chakrabarty, ... p. xiii.

So let us cross out everything that has been said about place as the source of knowledge bound to place because of it and about concepts as abstractions empty of content that stand in its way, and take exactly this statement in order to prove its validity with its opposite, which is independent of any place, the universal validity of the theorem of a place-bound validity of knowledge, which thus asserts its smooth opposite, in order to prove its validity with it. So what the heck, theories are there to substantiate what one likes, we have heard that before. And all that pompous science-theoretical talk about concepts that block taste judgments; who cares; and those who find the science-theoretical nonsense perhaps a little odd, such nonsense, which, as well learned, only the tabula rasa concepts do, cannot not question the intentions, that the social science thinkers in the new states must be allowed to bring theories onto the science market that enrich with their own provincial political views, those "Eurocentric" sciences that have been set up as provincial knowledge in a post-colonial debate that was instigated only for this very purpose: To each state and its science its nationalist view of things, that is all that wanted to be said.

Also no surprise: with their criticism of colonial thought, with their criticism of concepts as empty statements and their universal validity, met with repentant insight from the scolded theorists in the old colonial states, because the social science theory formation there, thanks to its "globalization" with its meanwhile matured national political eagerness to practice science as policy advise could no longer be distinguished from post-colonial science and its desire to further develop science towards the national identity formation, and this not only in the new states with their science committed to their places, so that the science-theoretical fuss about knowledge and places for all busy social-science data seekers became anyway science philosophy of any exotics. That is the way it is: whoever equates the abolition of colonialism with the imitation of states and the science of colonialists must also prove that he knows how a science works that such states maintain in order to complete the worldwide enforcement of this very science with a farcical criticism. The overcoming of an "incompleteness of science" is therefore the name of this positively turned critical mission in the language of the discourse on a de-colonized science.

With its attack on the objectivity of concepts, i.e. on what characterizes the nature of thinking itself, this attack propagates nothing less but a regression behind the civilizing merits of social science thinking, this attack on concepts as the last resort the nature of thinking and criticism, neither the very state powers and also not the knowledge concept of relatively objective knowledge of the social sciences could drive thinking out of, thinking aiming at knowledge, this is what these masterminds of science liberating science from colonial thinking, want to drive out in order to conquer for their new states the freedom to be able to introduce every political, explicitly pre-scientific judgment cultivated in these states as a scientific theory into the world of a pluralism of theories, in this very sense all universally provincialized.

The accusation consisting of this nonsense about a way of thinking, which is conceded to have its validity in Europe but not elsewhere, not because the object does not exist there at all, but because the same thing is elsewhere, is the as nonsensical as transparent reasoning that every knowledge is always only locally correct knowledge, i.e. must be different everywhere, even if it is knowledge about the same thing, with which the transformation of knowledge not only of the European social sciences into a science consisting of a multitude of locally valid knowledge is pursued; with this de-colonization of science, not only is a concept of knowledge established, with which under the title of its "provincialization" the political, i.e. nation-state definition of the places of knowledge production is circumscribed, but with which the transformation of all knowledge into a multiplicity of locally benign knowledge methodically redefines social science thinking both in the old colonial states and in the new states of the former colonies as a variety of nation-state induced knowledge enforced into the world of nation states as the globally valid form of scientific knowledge.

To concede to the European social sciences in this way that their theories, which declared violence against the people in the colonies as well as their economic exploitation, on which the economies of the imperial states based and continue to base their wealth, in former times before their de-colonization as dealing with their uncivilized nature and today, decolonized, to help solve their economic problems, that these theories justifying their imperialism towards the new states are one possible, but only one possible, view of the former colonial societies that is not criticized, because the propagated subjectivism of such theories excludes any criticism, but rather contrasts it with other, as equally possible subjective theories, this achievement of criticizing "Eurocentric" thinking achieves one thing above all: with its relativism adapted from social science thinking and its radicalization against any objectivity of concepts and knowledge, it ruins every science and every knowledge that argues against the critical circumstances of life, not only in the former colonies, but everywhere, and opens the door to science as knowledge to all nationalistic and racist ideas. A look at the world of decolonized science, its knowledge and discourses documents the renaissance of the mystical and nationalist views for which decolonized science paved the way onto the stage of science.

All this, the rebirth of nationalism and its brother racism, would not be particularly noteworthy if they only spread in science as now scientifically recognized knowledge, if the scientific stage were not the place through which all these nationalisms, elevated to the state of knowledge, establish their recognition as well-founded notions in the world's citizen societies, and from there endow their politics with theories that can be best used for imperialisms of all kinds. A glance from the world of science into the world of politics is enough to notice the political harvest with which these theories feed their national ruling political dominion.

2.3 From the critique of capitalism to its anti-critique—from Marx to Heidegger

The irony of the whole de-colonization of science, with its attacks on what constitutes science and the science-theoretical circus mobilized for this purpose about thinking places and ignorant concepts, in order to demand the relativization of the knowledge of the "Eurocentrists", is that they could actually have spared themselves all this, at least as a criticism of the "Eurocentrists", because the "Eurocentrists" have been preaching and practicing this relativism for 200 years, just as they have made the affairs of nation states and their societies their own in their theories.

And not only that: The critics of a "Eurocentrism", who, by propagating their concept of locally contextualized knowledge, demand the recognition of their local patriotic knowledge, are the ones who are in favor of this critique of a "Eurocentric" knowledge of the European sciences, a critique the thus scolded European sciences generously concede, and it is these critics of "Eurocentrism" who are the only ones in this discourse on the de-colonization of the social sciences who actually have to really change something and this is to completely abandon the scientific theories they used to justify their arguments with the colonial states in their fight against colonialism in order to be today recognized as a contribution to the decolonized sciences of social sciences in the new states. The only ones who really revise their theories in this discourse of decolonization are indeed only the critics of "Eurocentrism" itself. And this self-criticism implies historically shifts in worldwide theorizing and is much more than this epistemological opera about a universally relative objectivity, and this is a shift not only for the social sciences in the old colonized societies but worldwide.

What is actually demanded of the sciences in the former colonial states? That, following the relativism of knowledge, which they themselves justified as a scientific necessity, they should apply their theory of science theory to their own knowledge and "provincialize" their knowledge. That they thus recognize that, in addition to their theories whose worldwide validity has been enforced not scientifically, but by force, there was and is a different view of the colonized world and its post-colonial states in the sciences of the former colonized world, and that the colonized part of humanity may now, after its transformation into the same citizen as those of the former colonial world, be considered citizens by the former colonial world. That they thereby recognize, after more than 50 years of the transformation of the colonial world into the social system of the colonial powers, that the states of the colonial powers then, during colonialism, not the same states today, had oppressed the colonies with their means of violence and exploited their riches. That today, after the colonized world has taken over its own social system, they abandon their theories of "uncivilized" people and recognize that these too must now be regarded as social science thinking tends to view the creatures of nation-state societies with its theoretical racism, now all of them as people to whom all the characteristics they have acquired from this social system must be regarded as if they were their human nature, that is, all of them now "civilized" people. This is the easiest exercise that these scientists accused of "Eurocentrism" can concede, because their postcolonial purification demands nothing more than that the sciences from the former colonies be allowed to do exactly what their former scientific colonial masters have always done and are still doing, to abandon their persistent colonial contempt for the now equally civilized and to recognize that they had, not now, but in the past, maltreated these people during the colonial period, and their views on these drudgeries as not sufficient for their understanding of scientific knowledge, because "indigenous" knowledge, and with the rejection of this "indigenous knowledge" as knowledge not meeting scientific demands, have rejected any discussion of this "indigenous" knowledge, without having to waste a single thought on this criticism with all the arrogance of master science.

An arbitrary example, here from criminology, may shed light on what is demanded of this master science by the de-colonization of the social sciences—and what is not:

> "Decolonization Criminology does not assume that indigenous societies were a paradise of tranquillity before they were conquered and colonized nor that decolonization would usher in a crime-free society. Rather, decolonization is a matter of social justice under the assumption that the invasion, kidnapping, enslavement, and mass murder of Indigenous peoples represent organized crimes against humanity and so, decolonization should be at the core of criminological theory rather than be ignored, excluded or relegated to the margins. I argue that it is in the interest of humanity and of criminologists to decolonize the entire world and the discipline of criminology because it is dangerous for any discipline to evade major developments that are relevant to the core subjects of the discipline especially when we are talking about threats to humanity."[32]

Those parts of humanity, which are responsible for "invasion, kidnapping, enslavement, and mass murder of indigenous peoples" with their orders, will certainly gladly accept the offer of this critic to at least in hindsight take sides with humanity, to hide themselves and their deeds in the great monotony of the moral monotony called humanity, and in return for this appropriation in an invented subject called humanity and its invented morality shared by all human beings, and in return for this appropriation into humanity to concede to their victims, not that they were and continue to be the perpetrators, but that these victims—somehow, not exactly, one does not know about the perpetrators—simply existed, but actually should not have existed. This art of arguing with the ideals of a mankind, to which one only comes because one does not want to have

---

32 Biko Agozino, Humanifesto of the Decolonization of Criminology and Justice, in: Decolonization of Criminology and Justice 1(1), 5–28.

true what is true, in order to demand, with the great embrace of mankind, to be allowed to belong to this great invented moral subject, thus to give up all opposition to the perpetrators of the victims, in so far as the perpetrators concede to the victims that today they are allowed to regard themselves as victims of then, this art of critical devotism is one that the followers of a de-colonization of the sciences have obviously learned admirably from the scientific guardians of the European idea of humanism, with which they have always accompanied colonialism and its deeds like those of its more modern variant after the colonies were incorporated into the social system of the colonial masters.

De-colonization—not de-capitalization or even simply "no more victims"—is therefore not by chance the name of this neo-humanist purification program of science: The demand to be allowed to name the victims of colonialism as victims in the name of humanity buys this critique with its subsequent appropriation of the makers of colonialism into the big picture of human morality, not only with the withdrawal of the critique of its makers and the analysis of their concerns and deeds; De-colonization is the name of this endeavor especially because this way of seeing things as a de-colonization has distanced itself from the critique of the social system, capitalism, that is responsible for colonialism and on whose economic power their continued imperialism is based today and a society system with which the same states with this economic power gained from colonialism not only continue their exploitation of the de-colonized world today with other means, but intensify it today, because from all this critique the critique of de-colonizing thinking has distanced itself from the critique of what all caused and causes all this in the past and today; and de-colonization is the name of this anti-critical program above all because this critique of a way of thinking that allows the victims of colonialism to finally say that they were victims of colonialism proves today how little this science, not least the European science, has to reproach itself for in dealing with de-colonized societies today.

With the mea culpa of the European sciences about the colonial period, wrested from the sciences in the old colonial societies after 50 years, this European science is given the opportunity to prove how critically enlightened this European science thinks about the world today and how critical science in the new state societies is when it demands the kowtow of the European sciences about their yesterday's thinking. No wonder, then, that European social science does not miss out on this offer and is remorsefully happy to let itself be decolonized by this criticism with the cheap admission of guilt about what used to be in the past, and that the social sciences from the new, now decolonized societies, are happy to decolonize their critical world view with their criticism, no, not in the misery of the now decolonized societies of the former colonies, but with their criticism of the old colonial exploiters and their sciences, in this cheap way, in which nothing and nobody is criticized today for what is happening and thought today, can be used today as an identification of their critical thinking.

On top of that: The accompanying new reinterpretation of "indigenous" knowledge, which had denied with its adjective this knowledge, its character as knowledge, not only requires nothing more than to classify this adjective with the reference to a special kind of knowledge, and with this classification to continue stigmatizing everything that is said with it, beyond any critique of what is said, and having already refuted it in it, and to now regard this knowledge as, admittedly, still unscientific, but as a now respected view of people who are not capable of making distinguished judgments of social science provenance, generously define it nevertheless as a contribution to science, for whose integration into the theories of social science this science, with its de-colonization, has been driven out of its claim to scientific knowledge anyway.

With the decolonization of their science, everything remains for the European social sciences, except for the cheap mea culpa, as before, from decolonized criminology with the reverse confession that criminals also exist in indigenous societies, that is, that they were no better than the societies of the colonialists, bought, expensively bought, because with this deal, you admit, we admit, it buries every criticism of colonialism underhand. The offer of the de-colonization advocate, which is as chumming up as it is stupid, that there are bad people in your society as there were in ours, simply sweeps aside all differences between the societies of the colonialists and the colonized in the face of today's shared social system for the submissive begging after being appropriated by the criticized sciences from the old colonial societies. The fact that decolonized criminology, just like its correspondingly constructed social science discipline, has thus quite fittingly ticked off the complete rule of law principle of the states of citizen societies as somehow identical for all forms of society, and thus just as marginally declared itself to be the most humane in the world with regard to the construction principles of the societies of the colonial powers, may not be clear to him, but it signals to his "Eurocentric" criminologists that their post-colonial critic, has adopted the social system of the old colonialists, including its moral departments, and has zero criticism of this social system any longer, the very social system—one would like to remind him of what he said two lines earlier—which was after all responsible for "the invasions, abductions, enslavements and the mass murder of indigenous people" and which social science thinkers from the colonized societies had recently branded as proof of the brutality of this social system, also they then called capitalism.

This criticism and any connection between the colonialists' social system and their "mass murder of indigenous people" was obviously packed in by the decolonized criminologist in the interest of his promotion of decolonized thinking among social science theorists from the old colonial states, and with the remark in indigenous societies, too, there are criminals who have made themselves so common with them that the commitment to the atrocities of those ancient times, which is demanded of them, expects nothing more from them than a commitment to the shared morality offered beyond the earlier actions of the colonial countries. The critic from the formerly colonized world has thus left behind quite different critical views for the de-colonization of his guild as a criminologist than the cheap commitment to morality, namely no less than his criticism of the colonialists' social system and the "mass murder of indigenous people" for which this social system is responsible.

The true addressees, exorcising scientific thought its basis, the objectivity of their concepts and with them their critique of the colonialist and the same imperialists today, are therefore not those Eurocentrists at all, but only these critics themselves. It is not the criticized "Eurocentrist" thinkers who have to change their theories with their de-colonization, but rather the critics of a "Eurocentrism" who, in order to prepare for this post-colonial sort of criticism of a one-sided view of the European sciences, which does not want to take into account the local conditions beyond European societies, fundamentally criticize their own previous views of the colonial world, such as those of the colonial powers and their imperialist extensions, as well as their own view of the theories of the European sciences and their theoretical justifications of both.

With this criticism, the critics of Eurocentrism are not only taking for granted that they are adapting the entire social system of the old colonial masters, i.e. that which is responsible for the "mass murder of the indigenous people", and with it its entire scientific system, including the disciplinary sciences, their theories, and with them their entire methodology and their concepts of theory-building and their discourse practices, against which the thinkers in the former colonized societies had previously opposed as apologists of the colonial masters' social system. Certainly, not all thinkers of the anti-colonialist movements may have been fundamental opponents of the colonial masters' society system, of capitalism, but the political opposition in the former colonies to the colonization of the world drew the justifications for their opposition and for their goals in all parts of the colonized world from Africa, through Latin America, in India and Asia from the critique of the colonialists' social system, called capitalism.

To then argue with the accusation of a "Eurocentrism" for the recognition of his criticism of theories, all of which are based on the science of this capitalist society, by the recognition of this criticism by the criticized theories as a possible point of view approved by them, this criticism presupposes not only to have abandoned his criticism of the colonialists' social system, of capitalism, but also to have adapted his theory formation about the world in the old colonies and vis-à-vis the colonialists to the theory formation of these colonialists, because they had continued their science with and after the de-colonization of the world just as they had done during colonialism. And in order to arrive at this critique of the Western sciences, which had been tolerated by their critics and which had thus worked its way from the critique of their social system and their theories as affirmations of this social system to the critique of a unilaterally biased view, these critics, who were now welcome in capitalist societies, would first have to exorcise their critique of capitalism.

That these critics are then also welcomed as witnesses to the fact that any substantial criticism of the unchanged society system of the old colonialists and new imperialists must be sorted out of the canon of knowledge of decolonized science and its provincialized theories, even if it is already well-founded in the theory of science, in order to serve as witnesses to it, the fact that any form of society other than capitalism is now self-critically denied its scientific validity by the former scientific critics of capitalism in the colonized world is only a welcome side effect of a critique that has replaced its opposition to the European social sciences with a critique of a one-sided view, that accusation of "Eurocentrism", with a complaint for permission to participate in this very science.

And not only that. While the "Eurocentric" theories thus criticized are conceded by their critics with this criticism from the old colonial states as a possible view that European thinkers may have of the world, the critics of "Eurocentrism" are buying the recognition of their alternative views—by withdrawing their fundamental criticism not only of their society system, but also of the theories of science of the colonial powers. The theories whose recognition is won in order to respect one's own criticism of the theories attacked as "Eurocentrist" are not just any theory of anything about which one has a different view. The criticism of theories that one withdraws with the accusation of "Eurocentrism" by granting these theories their validity in Europe and thus accepting them, and thus demanding one's own criticism of these theories in turn to be seen from a different perspective that is acceptable to Europeans, is nothing less than theories that have as their content the fundamental theoretical attack on the incompatibility of the colonial powers' society system with the vital interests of the societies in the old colonies. In order to win the respect of the critique of the "unsuitable" Eurocentric theories of science in the colonial powers by the same criticized theories as a possible point of view, science from the former colonies with this kind of critique accepts these theories not only as a valid point of view for the societies in Europe.

The critique the critics of "Eurocentrism" bury with this criticism in order to win recognition of their theories as alternative views by relativizing their critique thus revises nothing less than their theories of the contradictions between the colonial societies and the colonized societies and, by transforming them into the same society systems of states and market economy, turns its theoretical opposition to the society system of the colonialists into a now only deviant knowledge of the same kind of science that thus buries nothing less but its fundamental opposition to the society system of capitalism in this way.

And that is a scientific achievement that has to be done first. For it is nothing less than the systemic criticism that critics from the former colonies are taking back and redefining the hitherto contradictory theories about the colonial powers and their colonial policies into mere differences of mutually respected views of the same kind of theory formation. The opposition to science in the colonial powers is thus purifying itself into alternative views of the same science, which claims its participation in this science of the colonial states and which since then has been characterized by nothing more than its status of meaning within the same science, a mere difference in meaning of the same kind of theories, which is reflected in the gradual distinction between "center" and "peripheries" that has been discussed since then, a difference, in which the old theoretical opposites have been transformed into variations of the same kind of theorizing to the critique of the locally misplaced theories of European social science theories, and which state that theories that determine this thinking with their meta-theories are, as before, created in the old centers of European science and indigenous knowledge with its insistence on the victims of colonialism is created in the sciences of the former colonial societies.

Thus, while in this post-colonial scientific world, the theorists accused of "Euro-centrism" continue to produce their theories exactly as they have always done, their critics have to transform their theories from their fundamental critique of the colonial powers' social system to nothing less but to their critical apologists. In order to work their way from the critique of the society system of the old colonial powers to the same idealization of their new society and state, which are the same as in the colonial states, an idealization the theorists of the colonial states formerly were criticized for this as a principle of their theory formation, the theoretical achievement of the former opponents of the social system of the colonial states and of their scientific idealisms of the theories of the colonial societies consists in expelling their old system-critical thoughts about the state and its citizen society, their Marxism. And this transition is a substantial shift, since it consists not only of nothing less than moving away from the critique of the state and capitalism to its constructive design but, with their idea of the state and the market economy as locally contextualized knowledge, of their way of theorizing to the theoretical home of any thinking. This scientific exorcism from opposition to the critical acclamation of the society system, which until then had been held responsible for all the misery of the people in the colonized world and that of its now state-organized societies, is the real tragic farce of that de-colonization of science in post-war history, because it is nothing less than shifting thinking from the critique of state and capitalism to its idealization as the ideal home of mankind.

And how else than as a theoretical farce can the transformation of the critique of capitalism into the insistence on a national identity creating a new variant of a citizen societies with a locally highly individual capitalism be achieved than as a progress of knowledge in post-colonial thought? In fact, the meta-theoretical argument of attributing epistemological forces to the place of thought is not only the umpteenth warming up of the argument of reality as an instance that decides on knowledge, but in any case only the subsequent response to the actual challenge that the former opponents against colonialism had to overcome theoretically, after de-colonization ended in the transformation of the old colonized societies in the imitation of exactly the society systems that the colonialists practiced and still practice today: Nation states and market economy with their worldwide activities of imperialism.

And in order to make the self-representation issues of these replicas of the colonial states one of the tasks of the science committed to its local society and to interpret this state propaganda as a successful liberation from the misery of colonialism, one has to crack completely different brain nuts than the doctrinal repetition of the arguments for the foundation of a social science theory formation inescapably committed to its social interest, i.e., the necessity of relative objectivity.

It is no satire at all, but once again the reality that the advocates of the epistemological necessity of creating knowledge through place, i.e. a homeland connection of thinking, in their search to cite scientific authorships—as one does in this kind of science of relativized knowledge, if one wants to substantiate anything—which prove such mystical anchorings of knowledge in ones land in order to stand up for its "provincialization" vis-à-vis the European universalists, as witnesses for the scientific nature of their concern to discover for themselves the most homeland drunk of all homeland-bound—what else, of course, the most European—thinkers, the "blood and soil" fascist philosopher Heidegger.

Desolate but completely consistent: Obviously, as a fighter against colonialism, one must have always equated the political status of the colonies with the struggle against the living conditions of the people in the colonies and consequently the attainment of one's own state sovereignty with the elimination of these living conditions, or one must have even confused state rule over the land and people of the former colonies as now an independent state with the rule of the new citizens over the shaping of their living conditions, in other words, the de-colonization of the former colonial societies must have always been viewed from a very (state) political perspective, a perspective in which science does not have the task of making politically well-informed and well-founded decisions, but is an ideological instrument to provide otherwise made political decisions with the higher blessing of scientific substantiation, if one is a scientific actor of the historically double irony and with a right opposition to a wrong concept of social scientific theory formation, the "historical materialism", does not criticize its errors, but repeat them, and thus helps a concept of science to gain acceptance in the former colonies as well, which radicalizes the rightly criticized determinism of history by nothing less than the hyper-determinism of the given social reality, which comes into sciences via the innocent-seeming idea of a place that gives birth to knowledge.

How else but as a convinced follower of the very social scientific idea that science is ultimately always knowledge guided by interests, i.e. the ex post ideologization of decisions made elsewhere, which are decisions justified with, but not made by scientific knowledge, one can, in the name of the former colonies under the notion of the "historical materialism", an ideology which the Soviet Union opposed as a counter-model of science to the sciences in the imperialist Western world and therefore found its followers for its struggle against the imperialist world of states especially in the world of the former colonized world, how else can one first share and then reject such concepts of science because one accuses them now of not being suitable for the rather transparent political cause, just as one changes one's clothes according to the weather and for this purpose and in this way mutates from a critic of capitalisms to an advocate, from a Marxist to a follower of the fascist Heidegger.

Because "Historical Materialism" does not say the same thing as my new theory about place as a signal for the formation of theories that support the state, I break away from Marx and become a follower of Heidegger. That's how simple the transition is from a critique of capitalism to state propaganda for the new independent nation states in post-colonial thinking is. Only an opposition to approaches of science, which are adopted for reasons of political opportunism as well as rejected again for reasons of political expediency, to change any views not because of any kind of critique of their kind of thinking, is the way how thinkers of this kind of opposition succeed in articulating a correct point for a critique of the HistoMat without noticing it, only to then repeat the same mistake in a radicalized version.

For the idea of "historical materialism" is indeed an unspeakable dogma about a historical automatism of world courses, to which its inventors first of all did not adhere, and with their anti-capitalist program, before it could even establish and spread in the time after the Tsarist Empire, practically refuted this dogma as theoretical nonsense, a nonsense that pleased the anti-colonial thinkers and fighters on the one hand, because they shared their opposition to the imperial world with the Soviet Union, but that got in their way on the other hand, because this dogma called for passive toleration of their struggle against colonialism, all the more so when their struggle against the colonial powers became a plaything of Stalin's foreign policy doctrine, according to which anti-capitalist struggles were replaced by the pursuit of recognition of the SU by other states and the foreign supporters of anti-capitalist ideas in the colonies, who did not want to say goodbye to their criticism of capitalism in the colonies, were handed over to their enemies for the enforcement of the state recognition of the SU as the top priority of Stalin's anti-capitalism, as well as for their instruction as proof of the friendship of the SU with the ruling powers in the colonies.

And how can one justify the fact that the opposition to capitalism should be stamped out, because this society system, in the struggles against its actions during colonialism, is now to be taken over by the societies freed from colonialism, and this very society system is to be interpreted as their liberation from their misery— the job of post-colonial theorizing? How can one find the appropriate theoretical justification for the fact that the USA with its napalm example Vietnam left the colonized societies no other choice but to adopt their society model?

One already suspects the solution: as with all the theories accused of Eurocentrism, all of them, whether critique of European societies (see Marx) or apologists of the same, because simply all of them are from *there*, because they are there, in this way, beyond and completely unmoved by their content, they are all stirred into the same pot, because simply all of them are from there, their critique follows the same pattern, they are there okay, here the local is missed. The application of the postcolonial logic of denying the validity of theories because they ignore local differences of the same thing to Marx's critique of capitalism and the examination of the question of whether Marx actually discussed such differences between capitalism in Europe and in the colonies or not can therefore be neglected, since the purposes of this operation are too transparent; finding about missing any local particularities is anyway not about a criticism of any theory, and certainly not about the criticism of a theory of capitalism; and, because the colonies were not capitalism at all, something will be easily found there that can be held against a theory that deals with capitalism as a typically Eurocentric disregard of the colonies; because anyway: Whoever rejects a theory because it does not deal with differences of the same thing, in order to use peculiarities of the same thing as an argument not only against the judgment common to all peculiarities, but also to reject generalizations in general, wants to use this humbug only to demonstrate his intention to stand up for his local peculiarities beyond and against all knowledge of what distinguishes them as peculiarities; whether Marx therefore in his critique of Capitalism thematized differences in the countries of Europe and in the colonies to pursue this question—anyone who knows it not only from the textbooks of ideological exercises in "Historical Materialism" for quick readers knows he has, and has done so in the context of his remarks on original accumulation, i.e. the theft of wealth from the colonies, which is the reason for the private wealth of the colonial states and which is explained there, as it is expressly not done according to the rules of capitalist accumulation in the capitalist societies of Europe—is superfluous, because someone who has been accused of the need to supplement this criticism with other local peculiarities of capitalism in the colonies, or to correct it in whatever way, anyone who rejects criticism of capitalism at all with this argument, because it is locally too undifferentiated, is only looking for the cheap semblance of a different justification for his political decision to purify himself from a critic of capitalism towards a nation-state inspired thinker of his new nation state, for this simple political intention to theoretically use his theoretical work for celebrating his nation state, because his colony is now a nation state and this seems to him to be an obviously welcome affair and to dress up himself as a great post-colonial scientist for this simple political agenda; and because this nation-state, like all states, is in one form or another a market-economy state, and the U.S. has allowed post-colonial states only this kind of society on pain of extinction, the criticism of capitalism that now disturbs this celebration must be eliminated in welcoming the nation-state and its inherent capitalist economy.

And also for this greeting of the nation state, the HistoMat provided the colonialism critics with the appropriate perspective and theoretical preliminary work for the period of their critique of capitalism up to the achievement of independent nation statehood, in order to then dispose of it as a disturbing ideology with the achievement of nation statehood: The other great idea of this Soviet-Unionist interpretation of the critique of capitalism, with the practical transformation of Soviet power into that of a Soviet state, was to reinterpret materialism, i.e. the material interests of life, increasingly as morally reprehensible and the political goals of the state as the heroic goals of life of true Marxists. Nothing suited the indigenization theorists of the new nation-states better for their project of idealizing their conquered nation-state than the discrediting of all material things and the ennoblement of all political things, for which the Soviet Marxists, with their celebration of their state, did the best preparatory work to get rid of its remaining component critical of capitalism by achieving an independent nation-state and with this the market economy that was part of it as an ideology that was now disturbing.

Somehow, it seems the post war II history shows, the Soviet-Marxist masterminds of the old anti-colonial movements, with their distancing from Soviet Marxism and their discovery of the colonialists' model of society as the better model of rule, were a little ahead of the Soviet Marxists of the post-colonial thinkers and their departure from an alternative model of society back to capitalism.

This, the theoretical purification of the critics of colonialism away from Soviet Marxism to a theoretical welcome to the nation-state, the colonialists' model of society, which the "free world" had 'suggested' to the colonial states to adopt with the bombing of Vietnam, this is in any case the core of all the debates about the whole science-theoretical wiggle of a locally particular against a universally general, against objective knowledge, about the distancing from Marxism in the version of historical materialism and the whole science-theoretically exaggerated nonsense about the place as an epistemological instance. Because Marx did not see the difference between capitalism in Europe and in the colonies, his critique of capitalism is no longer a critique, at least not for these Marx critics—with this ghostly logic the Marxist, thus purified by his critique, turns to a patriotic and profoundly European philosopher and convicted fascist as an appeal instance for the place=state as the source of decolonized social science, Heidegger, whose Eurocentric view is not even a little too patriotic even for the Eurocentrists, but is just right for the local thinkers of the new state societies as witnesses of their self-criticism as Marxists. Even if a Heidegger does not have the best reputation in Europe because of his affinity to the homeland-connected Nazis, with their criticism of Marxism, the critics of Eurocentrism do, however, come up against the Eurocentrists' likeminded revision of their system-critical thoughts, which European thinkers also regard as theoretically refuted by the end of an alternative social system in the Soviet Union.

No wonder, then, that such theories, which replace system-critical thinking with home-grown self-portraits of their new state societies, meet with the approval of all Eurocentrists. After all, the social science thinkers in the West have also come to terms with the odd end of the SU[33]—odd because their political elite must have let

---

[33] That the state is not a political institution usable for any political purpose, but the agency of the society of private owners, which establishes and keeps it running in all its departments, from the freedom of private owners to democracy in the selection of its leading personnel to its monopoly of violence, all this was known to people like Lenin, who therefore also worked towards the "withering away of the state" with the implementation of their anti-capitalist project in the SU. Their strange idea of an automatism of history, which had prophesied the end of capitalism and its state at some point, in which they themselves obviously did not believe, but which they cultivated as a theory about capitalism and its state, and which then, in view of the war with Germany, came to the opposite conclusion, to entrust their revolutionary goals, including the death of the state, to their automatism of history and instead to the building and expansion of a state of socialist design, as the supreme goal of their political program, including their dealings with the anti-colonial movements—until, from the point of view of the needs of domination of their state, which was as a winner of the war successfully involved in the battles among all imperial world of states, they decided to replace their socialist reason of state with the one that was simply more useful for these purposes from the point of view of the tussle between the states, this is the equally tragic-comical and consistent punch line of HistoMat. Nothing collapsed there; three or four leading people in the political elite simply no longer knew what the revolutionary state philosophy was actually about and good for and therefore decided to

themselves be whispered through their ear to the history of their place that capitalism is ultimately more suitable, in order to play a role as a state in the world of states, and have transformed their project of a state capitalism, as elsewhere, into the division of labor between state and economy—their criticism of capitalism, because from now on it was the only thing that existed, found to be refuted, not to mention their theories about their critically revered state, so that other Eurocentrists, with the end of the power of history attributed to it by Historical Materialism, could proclaim its variant from the old pro-capitalist camp, immediately the end of history, i.e. state and capitalism as the product of an incorrigible human nature. From then on, the social sciences around the world, purified by their criticism of capitalism,[34] transformed their criticism of capitalism into a practical constraint reigning in all states around the world, which ultimately struggles with the weaknesses of human nature, for whose problems they provide critical advice to the state.

For the scientific care of the consideration of national localities, purged of all abstract categories, the department of social science thought, which had set up an extra theory department for the formerly uncivilized people in the colonies with anthropology in the colonies, is transformed into a viewpoint that is now the same for human beings worldwide, in which all old and new state subjects, after their integration into the social order appropriate to human nature, are now interpreted as bearers of a domestic culture protected from any critique of any abstract category such as state or capitalism, domestic cultures whose peculiarities are only accessible to the thinking united with these cultures and which assure the impoverished part of the state-administered world population that nobody and nothing, especially no science with any objective knowledge about the world of state societies, knowledge about their wars and their poverty, can rob them of all possible things the need to eat, but never ever of their precious cultural identity.

---

dispose of it and return to the social system that helps all the other successful imperial states achieve their imperial power, a nation state with a market economy. As could be seen, the transition from the workers' and peasants' state with the state as owner to the state-organized ownership of the capitalists was not a collapse either, but went remarkably smoothly as nothing less than a transformation of a social order hostile to capitalism into its opposite.

34 It must be said: the strange disappearance of all Marxists is strange because one could think that it is not the SU that has disappeared, but capitalism, the object of their critique.

3. Indigenous Knowledge— Contributions to the Ideological Armament of States

3.1 State self-portraits of indigenous knowledge

The theoretical making of nationalist theories beyond the "Eurocentric" theories of the ruling world powers is their indigenization, namely in the former colonized world.

To argue that the knowledge created by science must always be local relative knowledge, a knowledge that is breathed into the thinker by local circumstances, this odd argumentation is not possible without all the argumentative nonsense that postcolonial thinkers create in their interest to attach to the epistemological nature of all scientific thought that this consists in the creation of self-portraits of citizen societies about themselves. The creation of such self-portraits of national citizen societies in the societies of the former colonies, which create political identity, under the motto of an "indigenization" of science, prolongs the scientific nonsense of its quasi-ontological foundation to the point of ideologically arming the new states with self-portraits of their own state for the purpose of differentiating themselves from other states.

Political nationalisms, that is, the celebration of one's state without any justification, are silly enough, silly because citizens of a state must perform the trick of wanting, against all mere experience, to attach to their state as its most natural concern, that this state is there for nothing else but their own good, and this simply because it is their state. For what then the state needs its power monopoly over the citizens, this question must not be put to a nationalist, because for nationalists, nationalism belongs to the nature of every man. When asked, the nationalist can prove his view by saying that this is so because without his state he would be nothing—which is somewhat true if one equates his existence as a citizen with his existence, but which only reveals about this citizenship the extent to which citizens are creatures made existentially dependent on states.

Indigenized knowledge

Therefore, reasoning political national identity scientifically, reasoning something that relies on self-evidence, that belongs to the nature of humans and thus cannot be reasoned cannot do this without even stranger constructions of thought than the justifications that the construction of political identity is the natural task of scientific thought.

> "In social sciences Zahra Al Zeera critically reviews the conventional positivist paradigms in the west. She finds that emergent paradigms of post-positivism, critical theory and constructivism have provided some space for alternative ways of thinking and understanding. She suggests that they are nevertheless connected by an 'invisible string' to Aristotelian principle of 'either/or', which holds that every proposition must be either true or false. This principle fails to integrate the material, intellectual and spiritual dimensions of life ... This is where Chinese traditions of unity, harmony and oneness can play a role. Potentially Chinese efforts to indigenize its social research can make important contributions to a re-balancing of Western and Eastern patterns of knowledge ... In social research indigenization means to integrate one's reflections on the local culture and/or society and/or history. ... Chinese researchers need to develop their unique perspectives and values based on their rich local experience, an awareness of their local society and culture ... Chinese social researchers need to respond to the momentous challenge, rather than taking the rationality and progressiveness of science as an obvious fact."[35]

What is it and how does it work this *indigenization* of social science knowledge?

The annoying contradiction of presenting the peculiarities of what characterizes the indigenization of knowledge as an intellectual product that is distinct from the Aristotelian principle of false or right knowledge and wants to be associated more en passant with another Eurocentrism by referring to this Greek thinker, and in doing so has to build exactly on it, i.e. that all these statements only convince all the followers of an indigenization, if they are reasonable, the advocate of an indigenization only enters into this contradiction because indigenized ideas, which are expressly not to obey the laws of science, those "principles" of "true or false", are to be presented and reasoned as scientific insights. As pure nationalism,

---

35 Yang, Rui, Indigenised while Internationalised?, Tensions and Dilemmas in China's Modern Transformation of Social Sciences in an Age of Globalisation, in: Kuhn, M., Okamoto, K., *Spatial Social Thought, Local Knowledge in Global Science Encounters*, Stuttgart 2013, p. 55/56.

not presented as scientific insight, the discussion about the indigenization of knowledge, which does not want to know anything about knowledge, would get along without this annoying contradictory justification; as a product of scientific intellectual activity, the reasoning of indigenized science is not possible without this theoretical contradiction, and already with this contradictions indicates what the real concern of indigenized knowledge is all about: the creation of political self-portraits of nation states, which deny being reasoned presented as well reasoned theories; the idea of an indigenization of knowledge, which distances itself from scientifically founded knowledge and which nevertheless propagates nation-state self-portraits as the mission of indigenized science, is indeed obvious scientific nonsense, but it gives the stupidities of nationalism the appearance of a sound reasoning, that reasoning, which Wallerstein attacks precisely for this reason as the cause of all evil of any "universalisms", the very "scientism,"[36] which the indigenists of a de-colonized science completely in line with the very "western" thinker Wallerstein have identified as a Eurocentric trick to make the formation of "nationalisms" of the new state society impossible. All this knowledge of what constitutes national identity, the knowledge of all indigenous people, does not work through and with, but, as the scientist knows, only without science, whose most important activities, therefore, is to eliminate, in the interest of national identity formation by means of this science, everything scientific in science, so that all the irrational that constitutes identity is given free rein.

In contrast to all the scientific-theoretical, innocently looking concepts such as context, place, culture, or indigenousness itself, which present the project of indigenization as a liberation of thinking from misconceptions about thinking and as progress in science, the propagandists of an indigenization of Chinese social science openly and unambiguously profess this, that all these concepts of philosophy of science are about nothing else than the political intention to create national self-portraits, which are only to be glossed over with the magic of justifications of philosophy of science, and make no more hide from the fact that all this is about states and their self-portraits in demarcation to other states.

---

36 "Scientism has been the most subtle mode of ideological justification of the powerful." Wallerstein, I., (2006) European Universalism: The Rhetoric of Power, The New Press, New York, p. 77.

The fact that the foundation of identity as a task of indigenization of science is about national identity, i.e., the creation of nationalisms in the new state societies, is, as can be seen here, not at all worth a question mark for de-colonized science. It is about, here, China and about a science that, quite clearly, thinks, shall we say, creates, in thinking about the world of social theories, which reflects a Chinese national view of the world. That an indigenization of science is not about indigenization beyond national identities like such nice de-subjectified subjects like those of an innocent apolitical "place", but that indigenization of science is always the indigenization of a nation-state science, here just the Chinese, is not worth a question for fans of indigenization: nationalism as guiding idea of science? What else could be indigenization! And yet, in order to be able to distinguish as a scientific thinker his theory formation and his nationalist ideas from such political nationalism and to present them as scientific knowledge, all explanations of how the indigenization of science works and what distinguishes indigenized knowledge cannot avoid reproducing their theoretical salto mortali over and over again.

This begins with the fact that the critics of the European sciences and humanities, with their criticism of "Eurocentrism" and their propagation of the state model of society in their theories, have anything else to do but to criticize the refinement of national state societies in Europe in humanistic world missions, at least in this, that the self-portrait of the European state societies ruling in these societies for the concerns of these European nations is exactly the national spirit with which these European states used to cover the colonial societies with violence and misery as colonialists, and with which these European states today, with the same self-portraits and values, have to save the whole world with their business and military power from what—exactly, from other evil moral values. And this, thanks to the type of opposition under the notion of "Eurocentrism" not critiquing any of their theories is taking revenge.

For not only that, not only does indigenized science not criticize the transfiguration of European self-portraits and their states in benefits for humanity, but preferably indigenizers from Africa are characterized by the fact that they present these values of Europeans, rejected as Eurocentric, with their Christian-inspired spirit, as their own values developed with the help of their indigenized science as the only true representatives of those European values.

Thus, Arab indigenous thinkers do not realize that their insistence that Kaldoun said the same thing in the 14th century as the modern European sociologists do today, but did this even earlier, that they are thus endowing their indigenized self-portraits with the same content as those from which they so strongly wish to distinguish themselves for the sake of their own identity. But what else: the self-portrayals of the higher values of citizen societies and their state are the same values in any state, because they are all the same citizen societies and nation states, and that is why everywhere, after it is discovered that the alternative state self-portraits are endowed with the same values as those of the opposing others, there is a fierce dispute about the fact that Kaldoun is the better one, the better European theorist, because he is the earlier European thinker, and that Lao Tzu is the better Goethe, etc., etc., etc. And, also not surprisingly, all these indigenous thinkers do not realize that with this dispute they are again underlining the identity of their indigenized world views, while they want to prove their difference.

The other way around: non-patriotic people such as Marx and his ilk are, at least after the end of the Soviet Union, protected from being quoted as idols of any state self-portraits by any indigenizer of any state, because they give nothing for their homage thanks to their criticism of the society system to be celebrated, and are therefore already sorted out of indigenized science as a source of the contents of such self-portraits and do not belong to the treasure trove of scientific state value-seekers—unless they too are reinterpreted as followers of the idealizations of state and market economy, as for example in China.

The concern to contrast in the interest of the own nation-state one's own values for the equally nation-state constructed societies with those of the Europeans, thus generously ignores the criticism of European values and, because of the essential identity of all those societies that already cultivate such a national identity or, as new citizen societies, are still searching for one, ends up, albeit ironically, with the same construction principles of national identities as with the same sources—and thus with the same national identities. What else. Nothing interests the indigenizers, less but what all the societies for which they are seeking national self-portraits have in common—they are, after all, determined, when looking at the world for the project of their indigenization of thought, to find differences and therefore do not realize that all these state societies have a great deal in common, with regard to the peculiarities of all as citizen societies, including their very dominant mode of economy, but also not that their sciences everywhere, just like themselves, not only share this need for a representation of their peculiarity with which they want to differ unconditionally from all others, but also that this search for differences of the same fundamentally identical societies follows an identical pattern everywhere. What the Chinese scientists say about this search for the indigenization of Chinese science is exactly the blueprint for all indigenization projects in all states and their sciences.

What indigenized knowledge is and must accomplish is shared by all indigenization projects in a strange universalism which they all consider to be the cause of all scientific evil and which makes them all indigenizers of their sciences. And so they also share what the sources of indigenized theories are for the creation of unique state images, this too is also completely part of the universal indigenization know-how, this is what all the indigenizers in all the unique places with all their identical citizen societies see exactly identical.

State values must first and foremost be worthless, immaterial values, indeed—one knows what really matters in these societies in terms of values—values, but higher values, because the common sharing of material values of all members of state societies is not possible, because these societies do not share their material values, but are in conflict over these values. Poor and rich in real values, these divisions of their societies know all these value-oriented societies, so that the indigenous values shared by all are otherworldly values, in any case beyond what really counts in these societies.

As can be seen, the first requirement for the scientific creation of an image of a state subject that identifies itself with a state, that unites this all citizens "we", consists in eliminating that which distinguishes science, thinking about reality, for the creation of this "we". For that is true: *"This principle fails to integrate the material, intellectual and spiritual dimensions of life ...,"* if only because reasons for whatever, reasoning has the annoying quality of offering a "why" and because every "why" opens up some for and against, it creates difference instead of integration, and so the scientific creation of a national "we" by integrating the material, intellectual and spiritual dimensions of life again only stands in the way of this integration project searching for the uniting "we". And that in all three fields—"*the material, intellectual and spiritual dimensions*" all possible conflicts slumber when they are penetrated with thought, the social-scientific connoisseurs know so well that their integration into the aspired great whole, the great we of a citizen society, would fail because of this knowledge, so that the great whole, the great common "we," must be produced with other intellectual achievements. And since they have confused their rejection of their—false—criticism of capitalism with the help of their HistoMat as a rejection of all materialism, which they found reprehensible, and the heroization of all political, they now know that the national search for identity must find what it seeks for in the sphere of political moralisms.

All the seekers of indigenized knowledge for nationally differentiated knowledge, which presents the same citizen societies as profoundly different, therefore agree that the sources of this knowledge are to be found in the products of the cultural creators of these societies. Indigenized knowledge therefore generates this knowledge by abstracting from the real social conditions of life beyond what is real and what is really valid in these societies, and therefore gains this knowledge from worldly wisdom about an invented life, life in general, that life in itself, worldly wisdom about man in general, that world of culture that disregards all social realities by mystifying this reality as variations of the same human nature, of imaginations beyond any real life.[37]

This mystified human nature has via this abstraction from reality to any world beyond reality been opened for any imaginary ideas indigenizing thinking implants into the world, preferably with any goals only this society's exclusively has with which one proves oneself in such a way that, despite the unpleasant reality with all its discord, one has done well with one's state, so that one's national identity lies quasi one's nature, but of course not in any human nature but exclusively in that of the citizen of this very state. It does not matter that no one chooses or even considers which state he chooses as his own but confirming in this way one's belonging to a nation one can pretend that one's own state affiliation is one's own individual identity.

---

37 The contribution to these creations of legends created by ordinary social sciences that are not at all indigenized is the subject of Book II, "The Social Science of Citizen Society, The Nature of the Social Sciences—Sketches for a Theory".

For the same reason that the indigenist digs in the world of the all-too-human abstracted from the real society, all scientists searching for sources of knowledge that create identity also know that they cannot find in the presence of today's society and in its present living conditions, thus also not in the present culture of society, but best of all in the history of culture, i.e., in its cultural past. For the art of finding sources that create identity of state communities, it is therefore better to look away from the present of these societies into their past, preferably back so far that nothing reminds one of the present, but is seen by the present society all the better as a currently shared cultural past. Looking back into the past culture is best suited to the swindle, all—in our example Chinese—share the same life and would allow themselves to be fundamentally demarcated from all the "Westerners".

In order to ensure that this look back for the creation of national identities for today's citizen societies actually ignores contemporary societies, the indigenist's inquiring gaze moves back into societies in which all the disturbing elements that form national identity and that characterize the nature of contemporary citizen societies do not exist. So, the gaze goes back to other, pre-state, pre-capitalist society systems.

The scientific look back into the culture of past society systems is suitable because there, at least in the look controlled by this search for national identities, in the memory of the feudal societies and their cultural life, it is easier to mystify what is today by a heroization of feudal societies, because although most citizens, such as also Chinese were not at all what they are today, citizens, but all poor hungry peasants, who in their lives would not have thought to take an interest in what their national identity as national citizens is, because only in citizen societies citizens have to show their identity with their state through their self-representation as servants of their state concerns, but from this pre-citizen time one knows people transfigured into heroes, wise, mostly men as cultural workers, which the ruling feudal lords and their little squeamish rule, with which they have made their subjects their subjects by pure force, tend to exalt in all their submissiveness as the spawn of lordly wisdom, wisdom, mostly about totalitarian rulers, which can be much better exploited for the mystification of the relationship between states and their citizens, because in this comparison with the ways of ruling feudal societies they make their rule as nation states appear as a merciful self-relativization of their power for the concerns of their citizens.[38]

And because these worldly wisdoms are the surest sources of national self-portraits, poets and other far-sighted creators of cultural goods, the older the better, about such ahistorical worldly wisdoms about everything all-too-human, are the most fertile sources of indigenized knowledge generation, so to speak, the inspirers of a nationally-minded view of indigenized science on the world.

So it is no coincidence that although it is social scientists who resonate a lot about the indigenization of their science, the inventors of the idea of creating images representing national identity are not scientists at all, but other intellectuals, above all poets who are closer to their beloved homeland.

Even the very idea itself of searching for an indigenization of the science of the new citizen societies, with which the whole indigenization project of science against science starts, that idea of a Eurocentrism of European culture and only after that of a Eurocentrism of European science, is originally not an idea of science, but an idea of political debates against political colonialism, which was only in the course of and through this political debate, e.g. for the Arab world, further interpreted by people like Said on the topic for science, and in this way and only in this way did it come into the field of vision of science through this political debate and could enter science only thanks to the very political mission of science in its indigenization agenda. Here, too, the social sciences are the ex post commissioners to give political concerns the appearance of being scientifically substantiated. What a Goethe is to Germans and their national self-image, other intellectuals before the emergence of citizen societies are to their state self-portraits: From pre-scientific thinkers, the indigenizers in the Arab world made Kaldoun the first

---

38 In the real difference between the ways the political powers of feudal societies and of citizen societies rule their sub-ordinated subjects, the indigenization of theorizing is not interested, because this would only disturb the instrumentalization of the heroization oft the past for constructing the identity of rulers and ruled today. The appearance of the power monopoly of nation states compared to the absolutism of feudal reigns as a relativated power results from the fact, that nation state power obeys constitutional laws, assuring that nation states commit their policies to the nation power objectives and not to any individual interest of any ruling subjects executing the power monopoly. This distinction is unknown to the ways feudal societies are ruled.

social scientist even before there were social sciences; the Central Asian countries also like to quote their poets (Rizal) as the source of their indigenized world view, the Chinese indigenizers their thinkers about feudal China (Lao Tse) or Japanese indigenizers right away take their tenno, who has survived through the ages, as the divine creator of culturally inspired national identity.[39]

So, this is how one can imagine the self-portraits of citizen societies and their state that indigenous knowledge excavates from the archives of local cultures. Which ruler, whether feudal tyrant, colonialist exploiter, or democratic statesman, would not like to invite a poet to serenade him, who, like Rizal, for example, rejects that the inhabitants of the Philippines, in contrast to the insults of their colonial masters, are not lazy at all.

Indigenized Science

And indigenized science, how does it indigenize itself? After mobilizing the preferably pre-state feudal culture and its spiritual products for the self-portraits of post-feudal citizen societies about their nation states, indigenized science takes the next somehow consistent step away from the intellectual products of thinking about the real world by tapping religion as a source of indigenous thought, be it only for the needs of this real world for national self-portraits for the self-portrayal of states, towards the intellectual products of a finally completely spun world and mobilizes with the mythologism of religions as a source of cultural self-portraits the intellectual products of the suppression of science as the next pioneer of indigenized knowledge: Religious thought, once the reason for the emergence of the scientific thought of classical philosophy through

---

39   Examples of wisdom from feudal Asian thinkers:

  Lao-tzu: "The best leader is the one whose existence is not even noticed, the second best the one who is honoured and praised, the next best the one who is feared and the worst the one who is hated. When the work of the best leader is done, people say, "We did that ourselves.""—Chapter 17
  https://wq-de.wikideck.com/Laotse

  Confucius: "The ruler should be like the pole star. He remains in one place while all the stars revolve around him."—2.1 "He who loses daily will conquer eternally."—"13,34"
  https://wq-de.wikideck.com/Konfuzius

  Jose Rizal: "Filipinos don't realize that victory is the child of struggle, that joy blossoms from suffering, and redemption is a product of sacrifice."
  https://www.azquotes.com/author/12414-Jose_Rizal

the criticism of its mythologization of the world, and then that of the social sciences, whose enlightened knowledge was (and still is) a condition of life for citizen subjects, this mythological thinking of religions thus not only paves the way for a return to the world of citizen societies thanks to the indigenous social sciences, but it is these indigenous sciences that bring back into the circle of scientific knowledge acquisition in post-colonial societies those irrational spinning mills that were once fought by the social sciences as intellectual products of feudal bondage, such as the Christian or Islamic sciences, which have thus been newly included in the circle of indigenized sciences.[40]

The former critique of the irrational transfiguration of the world by the feudal mythologies of religious thought giving birth to social sciences, indigenized social sciences mobilize these irrationalisms for the creation of authentic self-images of post-colonial citizen societies about their nation states against this "enlightened" criticism and its birth of science, thus radicalizing the irrationalities of the demarcations of state world views against each other.

Instead of their poverty beyond states and religions all citizens really share, in their religiously indigenized self-portraits citizens share the exclusivity of their unmediated, pre-scientific mythologies, unmediated because religious knowledge, unlike scientific knowledge, presupposes itself, that is, that form of handling conflicting interests in citizen societies mediated via knowledge is withdrawn, a form of mediating conflicts which first constitutes citizenship existence in the form of reproducible knowledge and conflicting interests which, with the monopolization of violence in the hands of their state power, deprives these societies of their members in domesticating these conflicts in their practical implementation, a domestication vis-à-vis all other identities within these citizen societies as well as vis-à-vis the nation states of other citizen societies, a domestication which surrenders the religious knowledge of a religious state identity and its dealings with other religious state identities to the arbitrariness of the irrationality of social identities that presuppose themselves, identities which cannot be substantiated, including their practice thus handing the demarcation of these

---

40 Ahktar, SA.W. (n.d.), The Islam concept of Science, part 1, Al-Tahawid, A Journal of Islamic Thought and Culture, 12, no. 3.

irrational political identities to the excesses of violence between religions now fueled with the power capacities of nation states. As already mentioned, the return of religious thought and its elevation to the status of intellectual achievements of state, i.e., post-feudal societies that create social identity is not the product of religious zealots, but of the science of post-colonial societies in their efforts to construct nation-state identity. Murder and manslaughter all around the world in a world of states, worse than in the Middle Ages, because these religious excesses of violence are now carried out with the means of violence of citizen societies and their state monopolies of violence, bear witness to the successes of indigenized thought, thanks to whose intellectual achievements religiously motivated conflicts are now being fought out internally and externally with the means of the monopoly of violence of states in the post-colonial world.

This elevation of religious thought into the state of indigenized science is a very special one and reveals all the violence that lurks in indigenized knowledge. In fact, one also learns here from what indigenization of science is about, and this is important, that such a scientific self-portrait as a national citizen must be "unique". Uniqueness here is of course not a question of aesthetics, but of the distinction from other state self-portraits of the same kind. State self-portraits are only state self-portraits if they can not only be distinguished from the self-portraits of other states, but can also be demarcated from them, i.e., if they do not consist of identical self-portraits of different citizen societies derived from identification with the same culture, but must be self-portraits that are fed by identification with the local society and culture so that they serve to demarcate the self-portraits between the states of citizen societies.

For exactly this reason, the idea that Chinese indigenous science is a contribution to the indigenization of the science of knowledge patterns of the "East" must be supplemented by the fact that this Chinese indigenous knowledge must not be confused with any other indigenized knowledge of the "East", because otherwise it is not uniquely Chinese. The fact that indigenous knowledge is knowledge that serves to demarcate it from the indigenized knowledge of other nation-states and their societies does not create any hesitation about this indigenization project for these scientific thinkers in their search for national self-images.

This uniqueness of national self-portraits insists not only on differentiation from others, but on the inferiority of all those who—of course—can only be unique because not all can be unique; we alone are unique, and the demarcation lurking therein from others who claim the same of themselves is this demarcation, as is well known, what is always blamed on the national identity of others, all uniqueness, to which their hostility toward others is inherent, until it is released when politically opportune—and sometimes lets off steam without orders from above. This kind of argumentation that national identity presupposes its uniqueness and that it is always the national identity claiming the other uniqueness that is blamed for its demarcation and the violence lurking therein, this kind of blame is known from the blame attributions, which are then tried when the violence lurking in them is released against others, and which are then released in the violence lurking in this post-colonial world of all the indigenous citizens, when their states call up these indigenous self-portraits of their citizens for their conflicts between the post-colonial states for these conflicts.

The fact that for such demarcation achievements of indigenous knowledge, science itself is first of all the greatest obstacle and must be removed, and that this is necessary to mobilize all kinds of irrationalisms and with them social violence against other nationalisms, and that the mobilization of imagined demarcations from practiced violence is prepared with the help of science, does not disturb the indigenizers in their mission of the foundation of national identities either. They know very well what violence-impregnated images they are talking about when they mobilize their national cultures for their national uniqueness, and their theoretical back and forth in the knowledge of this dormant violence therefore consists in always both creating identity for demarcation, in order to slow it down in the same way in promoting understanding for the other identities that they themselves produce and mobilize with their indigenous knowledge project. In this, too, all indigenizers are the same well-educated citizens, that they all know, across all demarcations, that a good citizen leaves it to his state to decide for what and when and to whom their images of identity with their demarcations are given the order to make them practical.

So one must sum up that indigenized science does not only create self-portraits, which, like Rizal, for example, should make any ruler of any kind, be it a feudal tyrant, a colonial exploiter or a democratic statesman, rejoice as a self-portrait of his society. The de-colonization of the social sciences has led to a radicalization of the relativity of social science knowledge, which derives its relativity from the knowledge constructed by meta-theories, with which it produces its findings as presupposed and therein relative knowledge. The indigenized of knowledge no longer takes its starting point in knowledge, but draws the knowledge content of its theories from the history of mythologies of pre-state societies for the mystification of the very present states of these very present citizens societies, and sacrifices for the scientific creation of such mystifications of the states of citizen societies the really only progress that the social sciences had achieved with their criticism of classical philosophy, that is, to free scientific thinking from drawing the goals of its teleological thinking not from mythologies but from the practical concerns of citizen societies.

Why such a national identity cannot be shared with any other national identity, even though all the other state societies are the same as one's own, namely also national citizen societies, and why, because of this identity, in the search for an identity, it must be suitable for demarcating the same nation-state societies from one another, is explained later in the following Chapter4, about *"The final scientific highlights of the masterminds of globalized post-colonial thinking"* by the scientific experts from the old colonial and now imperial states, which were successful in asserting themselves against other states, states in which this process of finding identity has not only been long and successfully completed, but which have also used these national images of identity just as successfully, and which no longer have the agony of creating national identity in the first place, and this even with science, and therefore, with all of this, in the typical serene complacency, they know all the better what national identities of citizen societies are ultimately good for: for mobilizing people for their wars.

3.2 Indigenized Knowledge in global discourse

Just like indigenized science with its state self-portraits reproduces the theories of the European social sciences content wise, also science itself, which indigenizes its thinking, reproduces exactly the kind of science in terms of how it creates theories it accuses as the

Eurocentric science of the Europeans. And this is no wonder: whoever not only copies the complete social sciences including their construction of a disciplinary theory formation, creates with the complete categorical framework of this disciplinary science also with his indigenized theories of this disciplinary science variations of the theories of this disciplinary theorizing. The previously discussed example of a theory from the Arab science scene is only one example of how theorizing for theories adapted to local societies through the categorical framework of disciplines, here sociology, results in the variation of essential sociological theorems.

The following considerations of a Japanese sociologist make no bones about the fact that the indigenization of these Eurocentric theories consists in nothing other than linguistic tricks of interpretation of the same sociological concepts and make no secret of the fact that the dispute over these variations of the same sociological terms does not, of course, decide which theory or which term is correct, but rather which national-language variant of the same theory or the same term conquers the position of ruling the worldwide theory formation.

The concept of truth as the goal of the dispute over knowledge may be considered a little religiously colored and a matter of concern for science, or rather the discourse between its theories, which is anyway only in the way of the project of indigenized theory-building. But even if instead of truth one spoke of correct knowledge, one would say how little the indigenized knowledge of decolonized science has to do with knowledge, truth or no truth, and every kind of rationality, logic or plausibility of the indigenization of science is not only something that stands in its way, but simply disturbs its discourse on knowledge and would be a downright absurd idea of indigenized science, to assume their discourse as a distinction between the correct knowledge of the sciences from the former colonial societies and the false knowledge of the colonialists, this can be clearly seen from the peculiarities of the discourse on indigenized theories and it can be also seen what the dispute within all the indigenized sciences and their theories is then about, if not about correct theories. The example of a Japanese social scientist, who deals with the question, "Are Asian Sociologies possible,"[41] discusses this question with the following problematization, which illuminates

---

41 Sato, Y. (2010) Are Asian Sociologies possible? Universalism versus Particularism, in M. Burawoy, m. Chang and F. Hsieh (eds.), Facing an Unequal World: Challenges for Global Sociology, Vol. 2, Asia. pp 192–200, Taiwan.

not only what the dispute between indigenous theories is about, but also what their real problem is:

> "Why is social capital, rather than aidagara and en, popular among sociologists worldwide, even though the terms are similar?"[42]

To the criticism with which the indigenization of science is justified, namely that the concepts of Eurocentric science are concepts that are images of European societies and are therefore unsuitable for describing other societies beyond European societies, this Japanese expert on the indigenization of Japanese science certifies that this criticism is pure hypocrisy and that the indigenization of science is for quite different concerns than that of a criticism of theories, i.e. that all the questions that have been pepped up in epistemology are nothing but the pretense of a scientific problem for the pursuit of a simple political concern. And whoever believes that science is about finding out what the world is like and that scientists then argue about their different judgments about who is right will be taught by indigenous scientists a better lesson. Knowing what the world is like and arguing about what knowledge provides knowledge about the world and what doesn't, that doesn't interest the indigenous knowledge experts in the least, they are interested in how to construct knowledge in such a way that in the dispute about indigenized knowledge one can get other indigenous thinkers to share one's own theory, no matter what it says about the world, or more precisely, how to construct the theories in such a way that others adapt them, whereby others means for indigenized thinking—and this goes without saying—thinkers with another nationality. In indigenous theorizing, knowledge and arguing about knowledge are upside down. Here, the dispute about knowledge is not a means for knowledge, but knowledge is an argumentative means to decide which category has the say in the dispute among nationally defined thinkers.

The Japanese terms *aidagara* and *en*, as we learn here from the Japanese indigenized methodological thinker, say more or less the same as the European term "social capital", so that the whole difference on which indigenized knowledge so insists turns out to be the political interest, to say the same as the terms of Eurocentric science, to use their Japanese version, not because it says something that only the indigenous version can say, but because the use of an

---

42 Ibid., p. 193.

indigenized term, in this case a Japanese one, is to dispute the European version of the same statement, which means, as this scientist puts it, is to question that it is this European term that is popular in the international scientific scene. The difference between indigenized science and "Eurocentric" science is thus the pure linguistic variation of different national languages, which in terms of content say more or less the same thing, and the whole indigenization project, as we learn here, aims only to strengthen the nationalism of the scientists of a nation-state by means of the nation-state language of a country, here of Japan, in comparison with other sciences of other national languages, and with the boosted popularity of the use of a term in the Japanese language, to promote the scientific rank of this country as a scientific leader nation in the struggle of nation-states in the world of nation-states for their political position in relation to other states in the world of states. The project of indigenization here professes to have no other purpose than to serve this nationalist cause through theories, so that the whole epistemological criticism of the necessity of indigenized science is nothing other than to use indigenized science to contribute to the national self-representation of the nation-states and their self-representation in the sciences of other states, that is, to serve their imperialism.

This purpose of indigenized knowledge, with the international rank of nationalized science to polish up the imperial greatness of nation-states, leads this kind of science to consider how such science must be constructed so that it can be made more assertive in the struggle for its international ranking in the battle about the popularity of terms in national languages.

The Japanese-indigenized scientist also knows how to do this, and has two options for this:

Option 1 consists in inventing indigenized terms that are used everywhere in the world of science because they are so meaningless that they fit everything everywhere, that is, they can be applied to anything and everything, no matter what it is, as an appropriate term.

> "I would argue that thin concepts spread faster among sociologists than thick concepts, which are loaded with local meanings. This is because when individuals are exposed to a concept and try to understand it, a thin concept has lighter cognitive burdens on its receivers than a thick concept."[43]

---

43 Sato 2010: 197.

After the introduction of geography as a cognition-stimulating element of decolonized science, the reflections on the art of creating indigenous knowledge enrich science with geometry as a property of knowledge and offer the postcolonial strategic thinker the distinction between thin and thick terms for his indigenization project. Less astonishing than the irritation about the characteristics of the results of knowledge, which are linked to the distinction into terms according to how meaningful they are in terms of the question of their reception, in order to find out which terms become a shared category, less astonishing is the kind of 'blatant instrumentalism' that is documented in the products of this scientific craft constructing terms for representing nationality. For this science, concepts are not the result of thinking about the world, but rather the result of politically motivated scientific handicraft, theoretical tools for the production of theories, which this science understands without question as the self-representation of nation-state societies in their struggle to distinguish themselves in a world of nation-state societies for their global propaganda wars, and which therefore itself lacks any reminder that science could be about understanding this world. For the artisan professionals of indigenized conceptual constructions, a completely absurd idea that science could be about understanding this world.

The art of scientific term carving for indigenized knowledge with such terms as thick and thin, therefore, consists first in option 1 in the creation of thin, i.e., meaningless Japanese terms. These are, so the thought goes, so prima facie meaningless that, although no one really knows what they say, and for this very reason, they tempt to be used everywhere in the world for anything and everything by the social-scientific thinkers, whose des-interests in knowledge they serve best, and thus carry the fame of Japanese science around the world.

The silly thing about this option, however, is that by means of these thin terms the fame of Japanese-induced thinking is faked with the all too obvious meaninglessness of these thin Japanese terms and thus also thin their nationalism. Nevertheless, such considerations of buying their popularity with the lack of content of thoughts are not the considerations that the strategists of the indigenization of science pursue and lead to the rejection of this option. The silly thing about this option for the aims of the indigenization of science is that with the meaninglessness of the thin terms also their whole Japanese identity is diluted, i.e., exactly that which matters in the procurement of internationally popular terms, the concern to make the nation popular, this concern which cannot be applied thickly enough, itself dilutes with the thin terms.

Because option 1 has this mentioned hook, the indigenization expert knows another option, which he likes better.

> "The second strategy is a particularism-to-universalism-to-particularism strategy. Using this strategy, the Japanese sociologist would invent a broad concept that covers both Japanese and the Western types of social relations, as well as the Chinese type. The Japanese sociologists could then derive local concepts such as aidagara and guanxi from the more general concept. Generally, this is an authentic scientific strategy and is, therefore, preferable."[44]

One could already guess what the problem is in the idea of thin concepts for the nationalist thinker who wants to sell his national view of the world as a view in his thin concepts, and then worries that the necessary lack of content of the thin concepts will, with this lack of content, also lose their function as carriers of nationalism.

Instead, the idea of a broad instead of a thin concept of social relations allows this carved concept to construct concepts from the particular, that is, the Japanese national worldview, but these concepts must be broad enough to include other national worldviews of social relations, from which the Japanese element that was previously screwed into the universal concept can then be presented as local Japanese particularism, thanks to the thickness of the concept thus produced, as a concept derived from a universal concept. In other words, the strategy of broad concepts makes it possible to construct Japanese ideas about social relations in such a way that one incorporates the whole of the rest of the scientific world as a subset of the Japanese view, while at the same time not dissolving and thus abandoning one's local nationalism in universal world views. The world is Japanese, Japan is the world. No wonder that this strategist of post-colonial theory formation likes his second idea with the broad concepts of social relations better, because it allows him to sell his nationalism as a global view in which all the others, at least the scientific world empires with which he, as a Japanese-safe indigenous scientist, would like to be compared, namely the assembled West, i.e. Europe and the USA, and China, can be presented as sub-cases of a Japanese sociology, and this is therefore a scientific strategy

---

44   Ibid., p. 199.

promising both national authenticity and international significance. Whoever it was, the surely famous conceptual composer may forgive it, someone has christened this conceptual carving of knowledge as a lever of thin national self-representation, with the thick term "glocal".[45]

Thus, the seemingly harmless considerations of the critique of "Eurocentrism" and the translation of this critique into an indigenization of local sciences end up in theoretical exercises on how to conduct science as the screwing together of imperial thought, a science that uninhibitedly ponders how the nationally inspired thinking of science of a national society subordinates itself to the national thinking of science not only of other national societies but of the whole world, and with its national interpretations imposes on the world of science with its thick nationalisms how the latter should think about the world. That the formation of theories could have anything to do with knowledge about the world, nothing is more absurd to such postcolonial thinking of indigenous science. That the creation of knowledge is all about the fact that this knowledge is first of all a national view of its national society, the view of national society through the eyes of the nation state, nothing is more self-evident to the post-colonial thinker, theory formation is a necessary process, as we know from the Chakrabartyian epistemological mastermind of thinking.

Accordingly, the discourse actually looks like among all the indigenized sciences and looks like the subjects of this discourse. The subjects of this discourse are imaginary scientific subjects that the post-colonial discourse community constructed for this dispute over the question of which self-image of which nation-state society succeeds in guiding and dominating global theory production with its concepts and theories. In this imaginary world of post-colonial

---

45   Whoever thinks that these reflections by a Japanese thinker on how to construct indigenized theories as a national view and how to foist this national view on the science of the world of states as shared by all are somehow outlandish nonsense from the fringes of science should be reminded of the current debates about Achill Mbembe in Germany, who has been banned from giving lectures on the murder of the Jews and has been told that he too must adopt the German view, which the same African figurehead of post-colonial thinking accepts as the German view, but which he wants to see complemented by another African view. Even this famous post-colonial thinker does not utter a word of criticism about what this most German of all German post-war creeds is saying about itself, but insists on a complementary other national perspective next to the German view, he accepts.

science, the world of science consists of a struggle of nation-state constructed political blocks of science for the global interpretative sovereignty of their world views, West, North, South, etc., all in the service of the global position of their nation-states assembled in these blocks of states. The inventors of these national or international "science communities", which exist nowhere in the world except in the imaginary world of globalized and post-colonial social sciences, recognize which theories belong to which of these imaginary scientific subjects by the—what else—nationality of the theorists, those local loudspeakers that represent the knowledge that their places breathe into them, and which, no matter what the content of their theories is, whether they like it or not, are assigned membership in such scientific "communities" thanks to their national affiliation.

That then, secondly, the discourse between these bearers of nationalistic self-portraits consists in imposing their national viewpoint as a view of the world on other theories of the same national construction is self-evident for pioneers of an indigenized science. The indigenized science scene is also discussing how to carry out this dispute and, above all, how to win it, with nationalisms of all kinds, including the squint of the scientific "communities" at their support for their ideological struggle in the sciences between those "science communities" through the struggle of the economic and political "communities" in their struggle for political and economic power, and this too without any hesitation in making themselves the fools of the imperialist ambitions of the states.

To settle the scientific dispute between all the indigenized and provincialized theories with the persuasive power of the insights of its knowledge and their reasonings, nothing is more absurd to the critics of "Eurocentrism" and the proponents of provincialized theories. And somehow they are right: How can one be expected to be right in a science in which every theory is recognized as a correct theory, whether this contradicts itself in its own insights or the insights of other theories, as it is already the case in the social sciences with its relative objectivism and then even more so in post-colonial science with its proclaimed subjectivism of theories and concepts with a nationalist touch, how is it to be decided in this science differently, which theory is now valid and which not, than by means of all possible criteria, which all must inevitably lie outside of knowledge, if the criteria, which science has, all are put out of force.

This, the search for which all relative knowledge is now knowledge that is considered knowledge, has already been decided in pre-postcolonial discourses, in which the social sciences, which knew the stronger political violence—formulated in social science terms, with the higher humanistic values of the civilized world—behind them were decided with this violence and with this ideological justification.

The postcolonial discourse of the indigenized sciences of all the now nation-state societies and their national self-representation sciences, freed from all models of society critical of capitalism and all essentially the same citizen societies, elevates the sciences, packaged in humanistic values about citizen societies and their nation-state, to the ontological basis of all social science thinking, so that these sciences, thanks to their post-colonial mission of nationally inspired thinking, carry out the dispute of relative knowledge of social science thinking, their discourse, as a struggle for the global interpretative dominance of the self-portraits of the world's national citizen societies.

In the best case, within this discourse between the indigenous sciences oner can articulate an interest in understanding the indigenous theory of the other side. But this discourse as a mere comprehension of an indigenized theory ends right at the point where one tries or even claims to have understood the theory of the other, because all these theories claim to be accessible only to the thinker who is part of that culture, nationality, that context. The one who presumes to comment on the indigenous theories of others, not to mention the idea of criticizing them, immediately proves to be an incorrigible old colonialist. Sharing the insights of indigenized theories prohibits their indigenousness.

For the fact that the de-colonized social science with its indigenized theories has nothing less to do with anything than knowledge about the world, that it could be shared, but that this science is concerned with the question of which of the world's state societies contribute to this with the scientific self-portraits provided by science, to use the ideological struggle of these world views to support the political conflicts between these states, this is shown by the "speculations", as this scientist of a formerly colonized society calls his thought, one of the most renowned social scientists worldwide for his decolonization activities, especially in the Arab scientific scene, but also worldwide:

"Here it would be interesting to speculate about how academic dependency may be affected by the shifts in the balance of economic power. It is not uncommon in Asia to hear optimistic views to the effect that if Asian economies overtake the West, Asian culture will become more dominant globally: . . . But, it is doubtful that any Asian nation or Asia as a whole would become dominant in the social sciences on a global scale. The case of Japan is instructive in this case. Japan is a world economy power but it is not a social science power by any means."[46]

The scientific experts of Asia are confident that the victory of the Asian business world over the "West" will lead to Asian culture dominating the culture of the whole world. The same applies to science, that is, that a victory of the Asian economic powers will also lead to the predominance of science, there the connoisseur of indigenous theory formation has his doubts and cites as proof for his doubts that Japan is an economic world power, but its scientific power is rather meager.

Even if the follower of indigenous thought does not reveal why he does not want to rely on the power of the economy as opposed to the power of culture for the power of science, the rejection of this hopeful speculation with reference to the fact that it is not so in the case of Japan is nevertheless informative.

First, it should be noted that indigenized science, not only in its theories provides knowledge to nationally defined subjects, but also operates with alliances of states, which this thinker uses for his speculations on how nation-state and national-economic power could hold its own against an enemy shared by science and even by those states and economies. For this purpose, rather hostilely opposed Asian states are spun together into an alliance of an "Asian economy", which, although it does not exist, this post-colonial thinker invents in his invented discourse between all the provincialized, post-colonialized "scientific powers" with the equally invented opposite side, the "West", just as fairly free-hand. In forging this alliance of states, the post-colonial, strategic thinker himself makes use of the invention of commonalities such as that of an "Asian culture", which otherwise the sciences from these Asian states rightly reject as racist inventions of that ignorant "Western" science. For the reflections on the discourse between all the indigenized self-

---

46 Alatas, S.F. (2003), Academic Dependency and the Global Division of Labour in the Social Sciences, Current Sociology 51: 605.

portraits of state societies, one ends up very consistently in the construction of a delusional struggle of "scientific powers", which cannot be constructed without the stupidest racisms of an identity of all the "gooks", racism, among which all Asians, who are working towards their difference with their indigenization projects, must now be united and be appropriated for the sake of a globally strategic post-colonial thinking about an invented scientific battle between the Asian and Western scientific powers.

The idea of a scientific power is the creature of the social sciences of the citizen society, in which its political and economic interests, endowed with power, use science according to these interests. And this and only this social science of this society,

- which, on the basis of and because of its dogma of relativity, which applies only to its social sciences, not to its natural sciences, can neither endure nor bear differences in its knowledge,
- which thus paralyzes the knowledge of these sciences also as a basis for decisions, thus justifying that the decision-making monopoly of society lies beyond its science on the side of political power,
- and which by this thus makes this relativism recognizable as a result of this decision-making monopoly rather than a scientific consideration,
- and which, because of its relativism within this science, in its social-scientific department the nevertheless unavoidable dispute about what this relative science regards as knowledge and what not,
- which can thus decide this dispute about its knowledge only with means beyond all those relativized judgments, hence, makes this dispute about this knowledge of social science a question of the recognition of knowledge by science. And which knowledge is considered recognized knowledge and which is not, this is presented on this epistemological basis, and only on this epistemological basis of the social sciences of the citizen societies in this world of citizen societies and thus of a scientific world of the social sciences in their indigenous theories in the discourse on these theories of decolonized science with their nationalistically constructed theories, this is presented as a matter of the national scientific power of those "scientific power" of national scientific

communities, of those "national science communities" in the global struggle for their scientific power over the meta-theories of social science theory formation. However, also in the science world of indigenized theories of the social sciences, in which meta-theories of disciplinary science that transcend all national theories and national science communities theoretically guide the formation of theories across all nationally defined sciences of indigenized theories, also in this science world this guidance has nothing to do with any scientific power, because these guiding meta-theories are only the result of the recognition of their theories by the world of science and this recognition of global meta-theories is not a question of power even for indigenous theorizing, because these meta-theories are also only knowledge, relative or not. That these theories are created by scientific subjects who are endowed with power, who may use them to use their theories as such meta-theories, even this power does not come from their knowledge, as, in other words, a completely un-indigenized other Chinese thinker knew somewhat tautologically, this power does not come from books, but from "gun barrels". And even this power impresses only the theorist if he who bows to this power that does not come from knowledge, mostly because, instead of once refuting this knowledge, he speculates on the help of such non-scientific powers.

But even this is of no use: even against knowledge, which, for whatever reason, does not suit one, there is no help in speculating on any powers or mighty ones, nor in inventing all sorts of scientific powers, there is no help in it, as it is with every kind of knowledge, only the refutation of these theories and their justifications, nothing else, otherwise all that remains is the critical lamentation against a dark scientific power, in which one would have nothing to criticize if only one had it oneself and could impose one's own indigenized theories on others as global meta-theories. But this option of refuting the theories of the "scientific imperialists" has been denied by post-colonial thought, thanks to its radicalization of the relativism of the European social sciences in the struggle for their recognition by the latter as being contrary to all the principles of indigenous knowledge.[47]

Post-colonial thinkers engaged in discourse about post-colonial theories have other concerns than arguing about theories. In their world, there are scientific subjects that exist only from the definitional viewpoint of the power of a state, for which and only for which all the theories, however different or conflicting, in the disciplinary departments of the social sciences in a country are irrelevant, but for science this is not the case, which is why science as science cannot be incorporated as a national scientific community, but sees itself as disciplinary constructed and therefore disciplinary organized knowledge and this across all state borders. Science does not know any members of a national science power defined by the nationality of scientists, that is an invention of the sociology of a "national science community", which only exists in the imagination of globalized and postcolonial thinking sociologists. This disciplinary science also recognizes its opponents not in the different nationalities of other theorists, but in the differences of their theories, in which nationality is completely irrelevant for the genuinely scientific discourse on theories—at least until the theory formation has been globalized or de-colonized after the transformation of the world into a world of citizen societies.

Only in the invention of indigenous, post-colonial science does define itself, with its ideological service to a nation state, as a nation-state subject, as those national "science communities", i.e. a subject which, in this idea of indigenous science, shares with this state its concerns and which, like other departments of state power, such as that of its economy, fights for power for the concerns of this state power vis-à-vis other state powers, i.e. a science which, because of these scientific concerns, produces state self-portraits, compares itself with the successes or failures of the other departments of state power and, on this basis, raises the question of whether the department of state ideology production benefits from the other departments of state economics and politics in its ability to assert itself against the "science communities" of other states, defined as competitors, or against alliances of states, whether these

---

47 See also Volume 2 "The Social Science of the Citizen Society—Sketches of a Theory". In this book it is also shown how and why theories in the social sciences become meta-theories through their recognition by science and why other theories do not.

are invented or not—as in this case the scientific communities of Asia compared to those of the "West"—or not, in the case of failures in these departments, if the ideology production suffers under their failures.

This interaction of the invented power department of science with the other, real departments of state power, an interaction in which the science of a country is regarded as part of the means of power of states in the competition for power, this view, which only really exists from the practical assessment of imperial means of political power, but not from the point of view of the intention to create knowledge, this false equation of science as a national means of power with that of a national economy, to reject this equation as an unscientific concern, is the last thing that would come to mind in this speculation on the interaction of the means of economic power with the power of science for the increase in power of science in the idea of a struggle of national scientific powers for global scientific power. Rejecting the speculation with reference to a world economic power in the case of Japan that economic power also leads to the power of science is not only anything else but the rejection of the idea that scientific power of a country results from the power of the economy of a country. To deny that this speculation in science, in contrast to culture, is successful does not reject the relying of national scientific power on the economic power of a nation power, but doubts the success of the effect of economic power on scientific power, and so may not rely on this connection, because the success seems doubtful.

To put it more colloquially: it would be great if a country's economic power, at least the one the indigenous thinker is fighting for, would help the national power of its science in the global struggle for scientific power, but it does not seem to be the case, as can be seen in the case of Japan. Even if he may not rule it out, as things stand, as an advocate of the global power of a national scientific power, one cannot rely on the help of the national economic power.

The advocates of indigenous science may find it difficult to resist the temptation to participate in these speculations with other, more hopeful assessments. It would be better to leave it alone and note that these speculations reveal the information that indigenous thinking is giving with these speculations about the idea of scientific power and about the connection between scientific and economic power, thus finally also revealing the concerns of indigenous science.

As if decolonized thinkers had a lot of catching up to do in terms of nationalism, this much-cited mastermind of decolonized theorizing speculates bluntly about how the imperial power of a state could support the "dominance" of sciences, which with its vocabulary borrowed from imperial politics "academic dependence" or vice versa "scientific hegemony", "social science powers" which are united unaffected by any content of knowledge thanks to their state-political classification of a scientist as "Western" or "Asian" science, and their the wrangling over the question of who in science, no, not who knows what, but who, with his avowedly ideologically nationally colored world views, is the opinion leader in this kind of world science—just as if scientists—whether they like it or not—were members of regional alliances of globally acting armies of science, who argue and ponder about the "social science power" whether these science soldiers can bet on how the use of imperial political power states could help science warfare with their real violence—and vice versa.

In its—speculative or not—betting on the violence of states for the—imaginary—violence of nationally defined armies of science against other national science soldiers, post-colonial critique shows the whole misery of this critique, which does not want to criticize the social system of colonial masters like that of modern post-colonial imperialism, but which wants to imitate the same social system and use it with the same means against the ruling imperial powers, i.e. wants nothing else than to use the same power and violence that this social system needs for its own purposes, for the same purposes of its national societies, and which, for this post-colonial concern, enriches social science thinking with genuinely imperial thinking. The strange lack of concern with which science here sees itself as a servant of the imperial interests of nation states must be due to the fact that the sciences of the former colonies define nation states and their citizen societies, i.e. exactly the model of society that harassed these former colonies, in their economy, i.e. in capital here and state society with state there, a division of the politics and the economy of this society system, the very division the incriminated European social sciences do in all their idealized finally good missions of states in their theory formation, just as if there were capital—ism without a state, just as if businessmen in the colonies had ever robbed land and people without the soldiers of a state and committed those mass murders the above cited post-colonial criminologist recalls, just as if the economic violence of exploitation was not the violence of a state, in the old colonial world as in the post-colonial world of states without the old colonies, a strange antagonism between the political and economic power sharing the same goals, a strange antagonism of business and politics, just as if this construction of an actually good state were intended to keep the evil business world clean of the state for the preservation of the wishes of its principally good intentions.

3.3 How the de-colonized social sciences view the world of science—and its ideological harvests

It takes a substantial degree of blindness by the idea,

- with the takeover of citizen societies, with their state, their market economy and their social sciences by the former colonized societies and their thinkers, that the very social science of the old colonial powers and of the new imperial states with all its particular forms of theory building, including its complete historical grown meta-theories,
- their methodological system and also their institutional apparatus, and in this including their concept of professional thinkers with all their hierarchies and career methods,
- with the borrowed power of state institutions of these scientific institutions and of their subjects,

to dream of the blossoming of their own national scientific scene with equally flourishing nationally impregnated, indigenized theories, to make with all these takeovers a deep reference to this scientific system with all its theoretical and institutional ingredients; and it then takes the same degree of blindness as of self-deception about the purposes of this science system, to then discover the consequences of this submission to the sciences of the old colonial powers, which this submission costs the thinkers of the former colonial world, namely to relegate them to the back ranks of the worldwide scientific hierarchies of this science, that is to notice this as the opposite of all the dreams of a flourishing national science, and then, for the sake of further participation in this science of the imperial world, which cannot be disconcerted by anything, to reckon this submission to this sort of science in a view of this science in such a way that one interprets this participation in this science as a fight against it.

Social science thinkers are true artists in the retrospective interpretation of politically intended and politically enforced events as a result of deep insights, which are only the result of nothing but of violence, of war. The epistemological necessity of a theory formation argued by their capricious steps justifying to distance itself from its critique of the capitalist society system, that then takes over its scientific system in order to commit itself to the self-representation of national societies, has the problem with the indigenization of their scientific self-portraits, that their political rulers by taking over the society system of the colonial states and with the adoption of their system of science and education, have also taken over the complete inventory of their social science theories and with them all those theories that are considered meta-theories of theory formation in this science system. It is not only because their states have taken over the science system including its theories from the society system of the former colonizers that the post-colonialist thinkers recognize their previous criticism of the colonialists' society system as a major theoretical error, because it does not allow them to glorify their new state they regard as a social gain, and invent the necessity of indigenizing social science thinking for the self-representation of their new national societies and present this political concern as a requirement for a revised way of theory-building as such.

The problem though is this: Since the formation of social science theories proceeds in such a way that the thinker trained in them views the world through these meta-theories, the science of the former colonies is confronted with the fact that their indigenous sciences, from the perspective of post-colonial thought, view the world through meta-theories that idealize the principles of nation-state societies, but to which those nationalistic self-images of individual nation-state societies are alien. And since post-colonial thinking closes the option of criticizing any theory other than by countering it with its own state-inspired, indigenized worldview, this post-colonial form of social science theory-building, freed from any claim to objectivity and thus from the refutation of other theories, creates a discourse form of science that is located entirely beyond the critical discussion of theories.

Postcolonial thought invents controversies whose object of dispute is not any content of theories, because it denies itself their critique by recognizing them as equally national theories about other national societies, but in which the object of dispute is the global recognition of their theories as their national views of the world—and it is these strange controversies beyond theories, which, in this dispute about the worldwide recognition of these state worldviews, constitute a "scientific imperialism", which consists in the fact that the national self-portraits of the sciences of the old and new states, which rule with their meta theories the world's theory formation, in this discourse among all those "provincialized" theories are not critiqued as theories, but as "dominating" science with their theories. The discourse of decolonized sciences argues about theories, but not about their content, but about the attention they receive in the global scientific scene. From this perspective of judging theories on the scale of attention, there are then "hegemonic sciences", a "scientific imperialism" etc. etc., i.e., the complaint that the great heads of the former colonial powers, with their meta-theories and their variations, are attracting greater attention in all kinds of theories and thus conversely suppressing the attention of the sciences from the former colonized societies.

It is true that the science of the imperial states in this kind of science and its 200-year-old scientific apparatus have the say in the world of science, if one understands by it the amount with which they fill the world of theory formation with masses of publications. Only, even in a science, the mass production of theories, no matter how large, cannot dictate the attention that theories still attract thanks to their interest in their content. To criticize these theories, despite all the quantitative dominance this is what anybody can do, but criticism of other theories, the advocates of the indigenization idea have forbidden themselves. Criticism of theory is not possible because every theory reflects only national views anyway, and where the content is not the concern and the resonance of theory mass is important, the rich countries with their scientific output are unbeatable. The idea of examining the plausibilities of these theories instead of those insults of a "scientific imperialists", dealing with theories as thought with plausibilities once can share or not, this way of examinations of thought cannot come to the mind of any post-colonial scientist with his commitment to thought as the self-representation of national societies, because this kind of critical examination of science is not able to take on the post-colonially purified kind of theory-building with the insight that objective knowledge cannot even exist, only to then complain all the more that only the theories which, thanks to their affinity to the political and economic powers of the world of states, have the say in this kind of science and are always the only ones given attention. Only, one must have engaged oneself with one's science in this strange battle for recognition by this science of the scientific hegemonic powers, to then accuse these scientific super powers as scientific imperialists in matters of theory output, the masses of theories they throw on the theory market.

Where the degree of attention of theories sets the standard for their evaluation, theories are born that deal with the question of what this popularity of theories depends on, just as the Japanese scientist already struggled with why his "aidagara" enjoys less popularity than the same meaning of the term "social capital". This problem has been called various names in decolonized science, "hegemonic science", "scientific imperialism" or less radically "academic dependence".

Dissatisfied with the popularity of social science theories from the countries of the so-called "Third World", decolonized thinkers know how to explain what is meant by academic dependence:

> "If we consider the parallels between economic dependence and academic dependence we may define the latter as a condition in which the social sciences of certain countries are conditioned by the development and growth of the social sciences of other countries to which the former is subjugated. The relations of interdependence between two or more social science communities, and between these and the global transactions in the social sciences, assumes the form of dependency when some social science communities (those located in the social science powers) can expand according to certain criteria of development and progress, while other social science communities (those in the Third World, for example) can only do this as a reflection of that expansion, which can have mixed effects (positive and negative) on their development according to the same criteria."[48]

Certainly, it seems inevitable that economists look at anything and everything with their input/output thinking and thus bend every object for their economic thinking. But the social science debates in the countries in question must have already done the groundwork for this economic approach of associating the phenomena of economics with those of science, in order to be able to compare problems of science in these countries as a question of the expansion of scientific communities with those of the expansion of their economies. To do so, one must first of all have brought into the world of

---

48 Dos Santos, Theotonio, (1970), *The Structure of Dependence*, American Economic Review, p. 603.

Indigenous Knowledge 171

theorizing the idea of national scientific communities, and one must have pre-transformed the question of what theories know about the world into the question of the quantity of theories created, and the scientific discourse of such theory masses into a question about the competition for the degree of growth of this quantity of theories. Then, and only then, does that "academic dependency" open up to the associative economic observer as the dependence of the growth of theories in the old colonial societies, which was discovered with a critical expression and eavesdropped on the economies, as a kind of theory production, dependent on the growth of theories in the "social sciences powers" he coins with the critical notion of a "scientific imperialism".

The desire, the simple adoption of scientific theory-building by the thinkers of the former colonized societies and its adaptation to the social science concept of knowledge of the old colonial societies and the present imperial states including their complete scientific system, the desires, not only the transformation of the former colonized societies into the society system of the old states and new states, those states who rule the world, to think that this adaptation to their society system including their approach to social theorizing about the world, to think this as liberation from their oppression, i.e. to want to imagine themselves as opposition to it, creates, on the basis of the process of this adaptation named de-colonization, the appropriate interpretation with an oppositional touch including the correspondingly the critical touch of the accordingly constructed subjects. The ennoblement of nation-state inspired theory formation to a form of liberation of social thought from a colonization of science, coined with the notion of a de-colonization of social thought, a liberation of social thought not only in the former colonized societies, but a liberation worldwide, creates the fiction of a global institutionalization of this form of science with the construction of imaginary national scientific communities to unite them forming those imaginary international scientific communities, such as the "North" and "South", and their discourse, presented as their battle about a global scientific hegemony, a battle carried out as a struggle under the notions of an "academic dependency" against a "scientific imperialism", a global battle of the "scientific addicts" against the "scientific imperialists".

This critique of a "scientific imperialism" is not only the opposite of a critique of imperial theories that resonate about state concerns vis-à-vis other states, such as those of their delimiting self-representations, but is, as can be already seen from their subjects, the international scientific communities, the world of the South against that of the North, itself originally imperial thought, which seeks to present the assertive power of invented, state-constructed international scientific communities, which fight for the global interpretative domination of state self-portraits, as the mission of a globalized science freed from colonial thinking. In their conviction that social thought, by its very nature, represents national views of the world in the form of its localization, these critical minds of the new world of states invent a world of these contending international scientific communities, which they interpret in their interest to understand their post-colonial theories adapted to the social sciences of the colonial societies as a continuation of their opposition, as their anti-imperial struggle of their own world of the "South" against the international scientific community of those scientific imperialists of the "North", and for this presentation of their adaptation of the social sciences to the social sciences of the old colonialists and actually ruling imperialist as an opposition create this image of a world of science, in which a "scientific imperialism" was ruling social thought.

If already the invention of national scientific communities is the child of the desire for a science which in its crude conception of wanting to understand science as an instrument of articulation of those national "places", this sociological invention of the post-colonial re-defined social sciences of post-colonial thinkers, then the nonsense of the invention of global scientific communities like South and North and their struggle for scientific domination over the world of science, both are deeply imperialist ideas that prolong this idea towards uniting those chimeras of national scientific communities into international scientific communities, which, absurdly enough, consist of nothing but those social sciences, which, with their mission of indigenization in their search for national identity, define themselves by their self-representations of their individual new national societies first and foremost from their demarcation from other social sciences of the same nature, and which therefore are constructed for anything else but to be united into scientific communities, thus denying what they are constructed for, their national identity.

These critical de-colonized thinkers accuse those invented "western" or "northern" international scientific communities of "dominating" all those scientific communities of all those indigenous demarcators of a "South". Oppressors and victims of this scientific imperialism, the inventors of this scientific imperialism naturally recognize, as always in post-colonial thought, beyond the content of any theory, in the national belonging of the invented national scientific communities of a global north, those states, grouped into global scientific communities, whose science system, including its theories, has been taken over by this global South and interprets itself now as an oppositional form of science presenting their alternative imperialist ideas as an anti-imperialist science in that it accuses the scientific communities of the North of denying international recognition to the South and its indigenized national identity images.

The inventors of this scientific imperialism, whose imaginary global scientific world brings together excluding theories in those politically constructed international scientific communities qua political classification, do not notice, thanks to their disinterest in the contents of any theories, that with their criticism of an invented global rule of knowledge communities, into which they incorporate, according to the principle "South=suppressed" and "North=imperialist", any theories qua national affiliation, that they thereby miss not only to oppose such theories which are actually imperial ideas, and thus, by critiquing what they say, reject these theories, wherever produced, as such imperial ideas, but instead supplement this actually existing imperially constructed body of thought with alternative, likewise imperial theories, i.e. with theories which, for their part, adopt the self-representation of states in their conflicts with other states in the world of states on the question of their sovereignty in the world of states, and which they use not only to enforce state programs internally, but also for their political ambitions in the world of states towards other states rearm them with imperial ideas for these foreign political ambitions ideologically—of course always for the good states, good because the others are the inferior states in the battles between states: With the consequence that in the international scientific communities on both sides of those good states, sciences come together in those imaginary communities that create the ideological ammunition for the political and economic conflicts between their new nation-states in the form not only of their individual identity images, but also, in their same refinement on all sides of all ideas that create national identity, such as ethnicity, culture and even religion, all exploited as the ammunition for the ideological battles between the nation states.

And then, when this world view is completed, all the indigenized scientists rush into the global competition of scientists for recognition, citation indices and for careers etc. etc. and similar insights pervading this world, only to be then outraged that the "scientific imperialists" are always the winners in this nonsense. The question whether this is perhaps due to the fact that, with all the consideration of state concerns raised by the supporters of indigenization to epistemological necessity, it is not surprising that it is then the states and their sciences which practice this way of theorizing since more than 200years are the winners in these knowledge races and "dominate" this kind of science; this observation is, of course, closed to scientists who have advocated to make reflections about the world through state perspectives to a scientific-theoretical necessity.

It is also not surprising that from this perspective, in which these invented international scientific communities and their tabular status become the criterion of good science in the societies of the new states, that in these former colonized societies, which are now troubled with the consequences of the takeover of the social system by the state and the market economy, their concerns about poverty and violence do not arouse any much interest in this view of what counts in this anti-hegemonic science in its struggle of South against North, committed to presenting any positive views about their good states.

One wonders what scientists, who, thanks to this kind of defeat in participating in this kind of science and who organize their kind of science as a global hunt for recognition, popularity and careers, who try to maintain their image of anti-imperialists by interpreting these defeats with their word-radical phrases, how they would see things if they were the winners of these races. Well, it is not difficult to guess ...

This approach, which scourges the winners of this invented scientific imperialism, not only defines theories as anti-imperialist by virtue of their national affiliation against those imperialist theories defined in the same way, but creates with this transfer of the category of a political power of the world of states on the world of science, called scientific imperialism, the ideological effect of not only presenting the states of the "South" and their rule inwardly as nothing but victims of that of the "North" and thus presenting the state rule of those states of the "South" inwardly over their own people as the rule of the "North", as if the national political elites and their states had nothing to do with it, thus freeing their own state rule from any criticism of what it does to its national citizens, but thus also allowing the very European idea to be ventilated that one's own state is only prevented from its own blessed intentions to care for the welfare of its own national population by the intervention of others, here that of the "North", in order to certify in this critical way its own state's own good intentions.

There is no question that the political rulers of the decolonized states draw their complete reason of state and their political programs from the old colonial as well as the new imperial states, whose imperial positions they fight among themselves and which are sometimes reordered, as after World War Two, through which the U.S. has become the superintendent of all imperial states and others, mainly European colonial states, such as Portugal, have relegated to the second tier of the imperial league of states. However, it is the states of the former colonies which execute the political programs of the imperial states with their state power against the citizens of their own states, and the portrayal of these states of the postcolonial world as nothing but victims does exactly what it does in the states of the imperial world by the same sort of blaming other worthy imperial states in the world of imperial states, by shifting the reason for poverty and violence from one's own state to other states, thus providing for one's own the image that it cannot carry out its own beneficial tasks on its own population only because of the other states.

Therefore, it is sometimes worthwhile not to dismiss theories that are at the forefront of the ideas of a truly globalized view and which argue about the best way of an imperial view on the world of states and to put them aside as the theories of the "scientific imperialists", but to take a closer look at what they say about the ideas and purpose of a globalized or de-colonized view of the world and to criticize what they say, instead of claiming to be allowed to create the same typed of alternative imperial thought as one's own theory and to stylize this as an act of anti-imperialist science. Then one can, for example learn from those "Western"—also always critical-thinking—world famous theorists, what they have to say about the meaning and purpose of imperial thought and who know without the cumbersome circus of an epistemologically derived nationalism of science called indigenization, that science about the world of citizen societies and nation-states cannot theorize about this world without nationalism, and that such theorizing guided by nationalism allows the construction of moral values and with them not only to interpret not only in retro respect imperial wars as help for their victims, but also to finally interpret wars as wars carried out on behalf of mankind without any moral concerns that disturb the national moral headaches of the imperial world when they initiate their wars.

Perhaps it is hard to believe that world-renowned theorists, who are world-renowned for their critical standpoints, who side with those de-colonization theorists with such theories and who also agree with those critics of a "scientific imperialism", that these theorists argue for morally clean wars? Nationalism as an instrument of cognition for creating social thought? Scientifically founded ethics finally freeing imperial wars from their moral hesitations? It's exactly this what these masterminds of globalized and de-colonized thinking of social science are telling us: one just has to study properly what these critical masterminds of that "Western" and protagonists of a decolonized science are saying, and then one can perhaps even avoid using all the radical phraseology a la scientific imperialism to then only imitate their theories, including all the ideological nonsense that is done with these imitations—and this not only in that "South" of the science world, but everywhere.

4. The Final Scientific Highlights of the Masterminds of Globalized Post-colonial Thinking

With the end of World War II and the subsequent transformation of the former colonized world called "de-colonization", the world is a world of citizen societies, their nation states and their market economies, in one word of capitalism, ruled by wars worldwide and with capitalistic produced poverty worldwide. Its practical critique by the Soviet Union with its alternative model of a state-regulated production of a very similar wealth, also measured in money, and its critique guided by humanist thought, which, instead of the end of a "working class" for the production of this kind of wealth and poverty, with its transformation into a state-controlled "workers and peasants state", has further developed its practical alternative to capitalism towards an alternative interpretation of this concept of state and its society as a true guardian of the humanistic ideals of the citizen society and of namely its state, and the alternative society model and state model practically put into action with this kind of wealth as the better citizen society has thanks to its final return to capitalism discredited any criticism of capitalism and all alternative models of society from then on as a moral as well as unworldly, incorrigible wish of dreamers. This practical critique and its celebration of the very ideals of the society it had entered to overcome and then revoked and corrected as an error with its return to the very society model from which its critique and alternative society model had departed, the de-colonization/indigenization of science on the basis of the new decolonized states with their imitations of the colonialists' society system with its exorcism of the HistoMat, that is its self-critique of its critique of the colonialists' social system, of capitalism, has further developed the rejection of any critique of capitalism from a wish of dreamers towards an epistemological violation of what the nature of social science theorizing is. With the new dogma of postcolonial thinking, social thought is by its nature the celebration of nationalism any critique of capitalism has become a violation of the nature of theorizing, detected by post-colonial thinking.

With the takeover of the colonialists' society system by the anti-colonial critics forced by the USA with its Vietnam example, with the discussion of the social sciences of this society model as the worldwide decolonization of science, this critique of every critique of this society system has once again after the war of the USA against alternatives to capitalism attested ex post facto the impossibility of alternatives to capitalism in the former colonies and with this anti-critique against the critique of capitalism for the worldwide assertion of the social science of the citizen society of capitalism, it has made its contribution to the ideological follow-up of this war of the USA against alternatives to capitalism.

And with and thanks to this anti-critique against the critique of capitalism it has gained access to the kind of social thought that this society system of a citizen society practices, their social sciences. Since then, this theoretical engaging in the concerns of individual nation states within all the national societies in their national affairs of their national states and in those of their national societies this globalized and decolonized social science of the citizen society has been made the worldwide shared mission of social theorizing, for the imperial wrangling of the world of states, this way thinking creates self-representations of state identities for its citizens. Since then, social science thinking routinely deals with the affairs of their national societies and their concerns, and with its images of national identities, which it elevates to the rank of cultural creations with its concept of culture, it provides the ideological material for the demarcations from other national societies.

What this kind of globalized post-colonial social sciences understand as their higher final mission and aims is explained by its critical masterminds, masterminds who, in addition to the routine everyday business that the social science professional thinkers deal with, all the unsolved problems they discover thanks their consulting sciences view on their societies, the master minds reflect on the fundaments of the social science theorizing and their final mission in the world of states.

This with the globalization and the de-colonization enforced ontologization of citizen societies, i.e., the consideration of the citizen society and its state as a society freed from any historical form of society in social science thinking, proven with the impossibility of the alternative form of society of the Soviet Union project, freed from any objectivity through their indigenization and spread worldwide through and as this de-colonized theory-building process, completes its global theory-building about the social world in its imperial theories in thinking about the world of states in a world of states, such as sociologists like Calhoun, for whom states are—in all seriousness—a methodological instrument of thinking. This social science thinking about the world, is genuinely imperial thinking in that it thinks about the concerns of the world of states, not through the multiple perspectives of nation state subjects, such as the citizens, but through the perspective of the concerns of state power itself vis-à-vis other states.

And because this thinking about the world, which ontologizes the citizen society, their state and their economy, can consequently only think about the world as a comparison, i.e. the relationship of individual state societies to one another, this thinking allows thinking about the world preferably as a methodological reflection on this thinking itself, such as that "cosmopolitanism" a la Beck, the "universal universalism" a la Wallerstein or the Calhoun idea of the state as a methodological instrument for reflecting about the world—which are essentially the same in their theoretical substance—and reveals in these methodological reflections on the world of states the hard core of a globalized post-colonial social science theory formation.

4.1 Imperialisms as a methodological instrument of social science theory-building

Perhaps the reason that the critics of a "scientific imperialism" of the "North", whose theories nevertheless do not criticize it as imperial thought, because the theories from the scientific "centers" indeed cultivate exactly the same world view as their word-radical opponents from those "peripheries" of the South—only without all the quirky thought tricks, to construct the adaptation of theories to the rationale of the rule of states as a liberation of science from colonial oppression and without that relativization of indigenized theories with their locally limited validity for the national societies of the former colonies. And this freedom of social science thinking about the world of states from such theoretical escapades and the local relativizations of the post-colonial theorists, which the thinkers of those old colonial states enjoy, and who have always known that "civilized societies" of the world must be citizen societies ruled by nation states, and which all the more after the end of that alternative society project, which they want to understand therefore as inevitable collapse, these connoisseurs of the science of the citizen societies and scientific experts for thinking about the world of states as a whole are then also very frank in their argumentation and confess without much if and however, on all these discourses, especially those on post-colonial thinking, whose critique of objective thinking they fully share, insofar as it concerns knowledge from the "South", whose rejection of that Marxist critique of the state and the market economy they have always advocated, and whose orientation of post-colonial thinking towards the cultivation of state identity these master minds of imperial thinking about the world of states as a whole have always supported, these master minds of post-colonial theorizing speak out without any local relativization of indigenousness, what all these state-inspired discourses and imperial theories ultimately amount to and what they as frankly support: worldwide nationalisms and wars among nation-states, or more precisely—they are after all social science theorists and not commanders—the moral justification of war, freed from moral concerns, wars, which they, like Wallerstein, academically educated, more technically call like a surgical operation, "intervention".

And this, the scientific justification of the imperialism of states, including that "intervention" of states against other states, these are the evidential goals of decolonized thinking in the scientific "centers" of the North, and this by no means by any politically right-wing outsiders of the social sciences, but by their critical exponents. Calhoun, Beck and Wallerstein, are certainly rather prototypes of critical theories, whose contributions to what characterizes imperial thinking and what it aims at enjoy worldwide recognitions in the social sciences. While Calhoun—rather politically colored formulated—propagates nationalism as the only true concept for scientific thinking about the world of states, Beck presents his "cosmopolitanism" and Wallerstein his "universal universalism" rather sociologically scientifically formulated. What they all have in common is that they construct their theories about thinking about the world as a whole as a methodically constructed imperial view of the world of states, because they want their theories to be seen without any of that local relativism of indigenous theories, rather as instructions for thinking about the world of states as a whole.

And this is why they therefore also present their instructions for thinking about the world of states with the pathos of preachers. In fact, all these gurus of theorizing about how to think about the world of states, despite all the controversies among themselves, all think fundamentally the same and in the aims of these variants of imperial thinking as well, as will be elaborated in the following part.

Needless to say, this is to be shown in these three critical thinkers of that "North", not least in order to demonstrate to the word-radical critics of a "hegemonic" science that it may be quite enlightening to really study these internationally very popular theories, to which they like to refer with their word-critical phrases of a "scientific imperialism" and similar verbiage, to find out what these masterminds of postcolonial thought actually have to say, instead of verbally scourging them to complain in this kind of criticism enviously about their unjustly high popularity, only showing that they obviously have nothing against what these theories are telling us.

If not the theoretical escapades and the renaissance of moral ideas of pre-bourgeois societies that underpin post-colonial thinking and translate them into national identity images, in order to move from the critique of the society system of state and capital of the old colonialists and the more modern imperialists to the foundation of national identity of the now own citizen societies with state and capital, if not the hair-raising argumentation may show what theoretical nonsense and what scientific regressions even behind the concept of scientificity of the social sciences must be brought about, in order to replace the criticism of the miserable living conditions of the new citizens in the new states with the search for the great ideal values of national citizen societies, then perhaps the reasons with which the scientific masterminds from the old European, i.e. from precisely those "Eurocentric" sciences, which very much welcome the learning processes of the sciences in the old colonies towards indigenized theorizing as progress of modern social sciences, may cause some irritation among the followers of de-colonialized thought.

The social science connoisseurs of societies with their nation states in the opposed scientific North not only share the criticism of post-colonial thinkers from the former colonial societies of an objective science, they are not only familiar with the theories of the meaning of state identity, these social science connoisseurs also know what national identity, also known as nationalism, is good for when it, like them, is addressed—unlike the indigenized theories do—in the view on the world as a whole.

If one then studies such statements about nationalism in the style of these connoisseurs of imperial thought about the world as a whole, one cannot help but notice at first the pastoral style of their theories, which is common to them and which deals with theorizing about the world as a whole, in which the theoretical modesty of indigenous theories theorizing about local national concerns, which is completely foreign to these thinkers, is reflected.

One of them, U. Beck, means his plea, in which he presents imperial thinking through the view of states on the world of states, which he calls "cosmopolitanism," and which he presents, knowing what he thinks citizens appreciate, as enrichment of the power of all his invented world citizens, who, as he knows very well, are nevertheless only all national citizens, because all citizens are citizens of individual states, he thinks he has to offer this philanthropic idea of a world citizenship enriching their power as nationals to his readers, who he believes, think too narrow-mindedly, he presents his ideas of "cosmopolitanism" like the enjoyment of a forbidden drug, which his readers, who are presented as if they were children, may dare to taste: "Kiss the frog"[49] is the title of this scientist's plea for his "cosmopolitanism" in the style of a fairy tale uncle; almost as if imperial thinking about the world of states were like the liberating awakening of mankind from a narrow-minded, petty-minded delusion. Why he sees it that way will become apparent in his how he advocates this kiss.

The other one, Calhoun, a little less fairy-tale-style arguing scientist, presents himself first of all as a knowing prince of science, connoisseur of his subject, with whose theories he wants to impress his readers so deeply already by the amount of time he spends digging at his knowledge, that one may hardly contradict his deep insights before one has even read them—and which nevertheless only expose the whole ridiculousness of his theory before one has read a word:

> "I have been writing on nationalism since the early 1990s and reading about it much longer."[50]

---

49 Beck, U., http://www.ulrichbeck.net-bild.net/idenx.php?page=cosmopolitan, zuletzt aufgerufen am 16.06.2018.
50 Calhoun, C. (2009), *Nations Matter, Culture, History, and the Cosmopolitan Dream*, 2007 Routledge, New York.

Impressive how irresistibly knowledgeable the man finds himself. With the term "cosmopolitanism" a la Beck this well-read writer about the world of states has his problems, because he fears that these visions of a world of world citizens beyond all nationalism of national citizens indicate to him the beginning of the dissolution of the state world order, a state world order, which for a social-scientific thinker like Calhoun deserves above all admiration, and this alone because this world order of states is for him, who argues as if he were a preacher of imperial thinking about the world of states, who has spent his life thinking through the glasses of the world of states, thus knows it uncommonly like no other, because for this connoisseur of a world of states this world of states makes possible the recognition of the world at all.

> "Nationalism is easily underestimated ... Analysts focus on eruptions of violence, waves of racial or ethnic discrimination, and mass social movements. They fail to see the everyday nationalism that ... leads historians to organize history as stories in or of nations and social scientists to approach comparative research with data sets in which the units are almost always nations."[51]

Without states there is no historical science about states, without states no data comparisons between states. In the thinking of this profound connoisseur of the world of states, the world is truly upside down. He probably read about them until he believed that without the world of states he would not have been able to read anything about them, without states there were no books and is grateful that they exist, because otherwise he would not have had anything to read since the 1990s. If you look at how this theorist explains why the world of states makes it possible to think about the world in the first place, one wonders whether this preacher of nationalism sees this nationalism as a kind of cognitive obstetrician that makes thinking possible in the first place, and whether he has developed his theories in thirty years of work under the narcotic effect of the idea of the state as a source of thinking.

It is actually true that historians, in their infatuation with the makers of the before/after of the history of rule, cannot think other than as the history of the rulers of history, because indeed, according to these thinkers, the rest of the subjects of these makers are only there to run after the makers; only, the mad idea of wanting to show, by the example of historians, that thinking about the world of

---

51   Ibid., p. 27.

states is only possible because the world consists of states, that is already a truly state-intoxicated idea, since it presents in all seriousness the reality about which thinking thinks as a precondition for thinking about it, in other words, without a world of states, not—in this tautologically sense—no thinking about it, because there were no object of thinking about states, but no thinking about the world, because without states there was no thinking about anything . No wonder, then, that all thinkers in the history of science, who have thought about the world before there was a world of states, have been able to bring about nothing—at any rate, no state supporting theories, in any case no theories which, with the fixed idea of being able to think about the state as a presupposition of thinking, give the state its deep kowtow as an enlightened scientist, whom, it must be concluded, only God can have thought up as his creation for making science possible. But that, as we shall see in a moment, is not yet enough of submissive glorification of states by this world scientist.

The third in the league of these thinkers on how to think about the world of states, Wallerstein, is in no way inferior in stylistic art to presenting his theories on thinking about the world in the same style of the preachers presenting their expertise on nationalism and cosmopolitanism with the same style of a "universal universalism" as his kind of sermon. Wallerstein presents his views on how one should think about the world as "universal universalism," that is nothing less but the worldwide worldwideness in thinking about the world, he thinks about and he introduces this pleonasm to the readers as nothing less than "the great moral task of humanity" par excellence.

> "... It is not that there may not be global values. It is rather that we are far away from yet knowing what these values are. Global universal values are not given to us; they are created by us. The human enterprise of creating such values is the great moral enterprise of humanity. This issue before us today is how we may move beyond European universalism—the last perverse justification of the existing world order—to something much more difficult to achieve: a universal universalism, ..."[52]

This scientist justifies his theory about how to theorize about the world, namely as universal universalism, that is, a globally shared single morality, so that the view of the world, founded by this scientist, is first and foremost the condemnation of every form of science, because this universal universalism consists in the replacement of

---

52 Wallerstein, I., (2006) *European Universalism, The Rhetoric of Power*, The New Press, New York, p 29.

science by morality, a world-wide empowerment of a world-wide shared morality, which he presents as nothing less than the mission of mankind, as whose little modest moral spiritus rector this scientist recommends himself with his hostility to science, and ingratiates himself to all moralists of the world as moral supreme moralist, because after all he is a knowledgeable scientists, who knows that science is the world's evil.

> "Scientism has been the most subtle mode of ideological justification of the powerful."[53]

As a result of his scientific thinking about the world, this man has come to the insight that scientific thinking about the world per se, that is, every thought that presents itself with reasons, that is, because it is reasoning it is per se an ideological justification of those in power, and therefore all reasoned thinking and the sharing of reasons must be eliminated and replaced by the sharing of moral values. And this not as sharing of moral values, shared by this one or that one, but as sharing of moral values, shared by nothing less than all of humanity.

Beyond the staging of himself as the world's scientific missionary of the moral missions of mankind, what does the man have in mind who, as a scientist, has found out that every form of theory, not because of what it has to say, but solely because it is theory, solely because it formulates thoughts about whatever, is a justification of dominating powers, and therefore advises mankind to let it be under his bulky and rather tautological academic methodological construct of a universal universalism, to turn to the question what moral values bakers, bankers, peasants, simply everyone, and this everywhere around the globe, that is, not only those who have something to do with each other somewhere, but everyone and everywhere should set out and achieve a shared moral values, shared by them all and everywhere. What for, if they have absolutely nothing to do with each other? For what, one asks oneself, does humanity need shared moral values, and this instead of science, which, according to Wallerstein, is anyway only capable of justifying anything and everything that has power, there must be a morality which, in contrast to science with its relativism, he obviously does not like for the very reason, that it does not fix anybody bindingly? Why must

---

53 Ibid., p. 77.

nothing less than the whole of mankind therefore, beyond this arbitrariness of scientific judgments, which disturb the self-proclaimed supreme moralists of the world because they are so arbitrary and justify everything and anything, and are always rubbed in the face of the weak, why and for what does mankind as a whole need values that are jointly shared and binding by it, binding also the powerful? Why this universal binding morality of everyone and everywhere, including the powerful?

Of course, when this world thinker talks about humanity on whose behalf he is thinking, he is not talking about the moral values of bakers, bankers and farmers; as for the other thinkers about thinking about the world, for Wallerstein, humanity ruled by the nation states and the states of the world are for him all the same, and after he has first accommodated himself to the criticism of the scientific thinkers from the states of the losers of the state rivalries about business and power and with his criticism of science as a subtle tool of oppression also to the plea of their thinkers for indigenous national identities, Wallerstein, this the self-appointed scientific moralizer of all mankind is confronted with the not at all indigenous question of what all these individual nation-state indigenized world views then mean for the world as a whole. Why and for what this question concerns him, why and for what it is this world of states, not the bakers or bankers or farmers, the nation states of the world as a whole that needs shared and binding moral values, shared by all individual states, this "universal universalism", so to speak, above all their indigenous national self-portraits, which he otherwise advocates, for this question the very un-indigenous thinking world moralist knows an answer that is mocking to every moral standard—and not dissimilar to his two opponents in matters of what this world view is all about.

4.2 Imperial theories—for morally clean wars

In social science thinking one does not simply think about how the world is and why it is like that, but takes the freedom that thinking actually offers and, as the number one act of thinking, creates its free interpretations of the world with the choice of a disciplinary approach, then a choice of a meta theory for thinking before any thinking, against which then as act two of thinking one measures the real world, more precisely, what this science calls empirical reality, against this chosen "meta-theory" and with these artful comparisons of two world interpretations, what one sees through the meta-theories and what one has constructed through them as the empirical reality for comparing both, this way of thinking creates all kind of legends about the world.

Beck himself knows, of course, that his idea of unpacking the old philanthropic box called world citizenship is a promotionally clever idea and that the reality of the world of states is a world of national states and of national citizens. But first of all, this is how social science thinking works, making up any catchy words and secondly, Beck's theories are Beck's scientific label and for other thinkers a kind of worldwide a very popular junk store for all those who want to give their world view a critical touch about whatever, i.e., to discover dooming "risks"—that's what he calls his worried critical view of the world, in the colloquial language one might say 'if it works out'—in everything and everyone. Even if the idea of that cosmopolitanism for such critical minds flirts with the idea of a world without nation-states, citizens, i.e. citizens of individual states, are, as he knows very well, of course all his cosmopolitans, too, and because they are and remain citizens, even if Beck would like to see them and his readers as citizens of the world, he knows of course also that the world is a world of states, i.e. his citizens are citizens, i.e. nationals, and he also knows what matters in this world of citizens of individual nation states is above all and before anything else, nationality.

Thus Beck, who has already been kissed awake by the frog, reveals to the reader his ideas on how the world of states must be viewed as a cosmopolitan and what insights this view offers about the world of states.

> "The more cosmopolitan our political structures and activities, the more successful they will be in promoting national interests, and the greater our individual power in this global age will be."[54]
> "The question then is how can states for their part win back political meta power qua states in relation to global business actors, in order to impose a cosmopolitan regime that not only encompasses political freedom, global justice, secure social order and ecological sustainability, but revitalizes national sovereignty?"[55]

---

54 Beck, U., http://www.ulrichbeck.net-build.net/index.php?page=cosmopolitan.
55 Ibid.

> This 'national sociology' is beset by a failure to recognize—let alone research—the extent to which existing transnational modes of living, trans-migrants, global elites, supranational organizations and dynamics of the world risk society determine the relations within and between nation state repositories of power."[56]

Even if this prop master of leftist vocabulary, with which he serves his readership worldwide, not least among all the decolonized thinkers from the former colonies, one should not miss the fact that he uses such twisted phrases as the interstate means of power in his talk, the "repositories of power", and not only talks about the means of power of states inwardly and outwardly, even more this concern about the means of power of states deserves attention in all the critical rhetoric, especially if this concern about the means of power of states is addressed when the world of states is mentioned. It is already clear what the world risk warner is talking about here when he is concerned about the arsenals of weapons, which he calls "repositories of power". Thus one should also not overlook behind this usually academically stilted manner of speaking that the man here is talking about nothing less than the means of violence of states in the relationship between states, that is, about military power vis-à-vis other states, and, when he speaks so sociologically abstractly about their "relations," that is, the "relations of the power potentials," the man is talking, one should not allow oneself to be fooled, in his twisted sociological way about nothing else but—war.

That for this he is striving for the old idea of cosmopolitanism, which was once conceived as a critique of the subordination of the world to the state concepts of society, that is simply Beck, who incorporates every old leftist vocabulary for his critical world view and then discreetly interprets it for his cleverer version of nationalism. Not that Beck, like his opponents Calhoun and Wallerstein, in the debates on the question of how to theorize about the world of states as a whole, makes war a natural or welcome part of all state life, as if there were nothing critical, i.e. once again "risky", to debate; however, when the critical Beck argues about his idea of a cosmopolitan view of the world does he make no great secret of the fact that the world of states debated under this philanthropic term derives its ultimate justification from this view, and only this cosmopolitan view, which he propagates, is that this is the only view that, in one way or

---

56 Ibid.

another—sometimes he talks about strengthening national sovereignty, sometimes it is the means of power of states, sometimes the "effective realization of statehood"—has in mind a strengthening of states in the world of states. And this, the strengthening of states in the world of states is what he wants to propagate, this is what only his cosmopolitanism can achieve. And this smart dialectic, that one may understand that cosmopolitanism is the cleverer and more successful nationalism, to this thinking Beck must wake up all the old-fashioned nationally thinking frogs, which must finally realize, that he, with his cosmopolitanism, is the more savvy nationalist, and that the nationalist theorists with their zombie science are in reality a barrier to the effective pursuit of states, that is, the cosmopolitan is ultimately the better nationalist.

And Beck would not be the global props man of leftist dressing-up of even imperial thinking if he did not present his more sophisticated nationalism alias cosmopolitanism as a benefit to the citizens and the state increase in power in the international wrangling of states for power and for business as an increase in "individual power" ("the greater our individual power in this global age will be.") to his critical readers. Presumably he means the individual increase in power if one wears the uniform of a state, but of course only that of a state that actually grows imperial power with its "repositories of power", otherwise one is only biting the dust.

And this a bit complicated conception, to arrive at better nationalism over the world-wide view of a world-citizen, seeing the world as a cosmopolitan, is for the scientific experts from the realistic camp how one must see the world of states, annoyance enough and their debates with their opponents a la Beck show, about which and how social-scientific discussants can argue excellently, over variants of the same view, here who knows the better nationalism in a global world of states. Even if philanthropic thinking a la cosmopolitanism then ends up with the concern for the concerns of the relations of political powers within the world of states, and with its critique of a "national view" only wants to point out that this national view is an obstacle to the successful implementation of the national concerns of states in the world of states, its theoretical concern, just like its critic Calhoun, is the success of states in the world of states and his cosmopolitanism is the more clever nationalism, alone, like Beck, even to flirt with the idea of a world-citizenship, to flirt with this idea of a world without states and all the "risks" that go along with it and that all his readers like to appreciate for their critical image, and though even the realistic thinker about what the world of states gets from its nationalism knows of this flirting with the anti-nationalism of a cosmopolitanism, admittedly. But even the mimed idea of a world of states without states and the Beck dialectic that the cosmopolitan is the better nationalist contains too much criticism of nationalism for Calhoun. Instead of this complicated cosmopolitanism, humanity needs nationalism and nothing else, and there is nothing to shake it, and certainly not morally, because for this realistic freak of nation states there is no higher morality than that of nationalism. Why and for what nationalism is the lifeblood of the world of states and nothing else, the well-read connoisseur of nationalism, Calhoun, knows.

Mankind needs nationalism for that:

> "The most basic meaning of nationalism is the use of this way of categorizing human populations, both as a way of looking at the world as a whole and as a way of establishing group identity from within ...
> The two sides come together in ideas about who properly belongs together in a society, and in arguments that members have moral obligations to the nation as a whole—perhaps even to kill on its behalf or die for it in a war."[57]

That nationalism, that is, the fatal stupidity of interpreting a nation-state as a condition of life because it does not permit any other conditions of existence than those dictated by it, even though it does not only in wartime burn up the lives of its citizens for its domination over other states and for its market economy with ultimate consequence, that this is a deadly stupidity, this concern does not even come to the pastoral advocate of nationalism when, unlike most colleagues in his sociological guild, he comes to speak of the consequence of nationalism, of war. On the contrary, with all the cynicism that sociological stupidities are capable of when they direct their sociological gaze at the world as a whole, killing the citizens of other states and dying for their state—*"to kill on its behalf or die for it in a war"*—is for the thinker of the world of states as a whole, who rejects all moral reservations, precisely the price for the state to render an existential service to its citizens, at any rate an existential service known only to sociologists.

This thinker rejects reservations of any kind about the world of states as a whole as an immoral objection to his scientific insights

---

57 Calhoun, C. (2009), Nations Matter, ... p. 39.

into nationalism, which cannot be criticized with such moral objections. There is no question for him that nationalism is the view of humans of the world, and war belongs to it. And that's it. And in order to reject all moral objections, he insists on nationalism as a scientific insight that no morality can oppose and attacks criticism of nationalism as unworldly moralism because nationalism is the highest form of morality: *"Nations matter"* and *"Nationalism is not a moral mistake"* he holds out like a religious commandment to all the scientists of his sociological guild and reminds them of what they all actually share with him in their theories of nationalism, thus rejecting their frowning at what nationalism is from the viewpoint of state authority, namely, to die for it in war, as moralism alien to life because it is alien to the state.

That nationalism is exactly what Calhoun only needs to remind every sociologist, no matter what political color, is something every sociologist shares, because it is this idea that constitutes the entire edifice of sociological thought, including all those sociologists of the "global south":

> "We need to respect the importance of belonging to nations and other groupings of human beings smaller than humanity as a whole. We need to understand that such belonging does different sorts of work for different people—inspires some, protects some, consoles some, as well as makes political opportunities for some."[58]
> "The constitution of nations—...—is one of the pivotal features of the modern era. It is part of the organization of political participation and loyalty, of culture and identity, of the way history is thought and the way wars are fought."[59]

The cynicism of interpreting one's life for the state very US—like state as a quid pro quo, as a deal, so to speak, for the state's offer to serve the search for social belonging, protection and similar needs attached to humanity by sociologists, is one of the usual beautifications of sociological state adulation. Certainly, this thinker also knows that the deepest form of serving the need to belong to a group finds its highest fulfillment when one is called up for military service—and this without any deal—and is buried under the flag around the coffin for the fulfillment of his social needs in a solemn act of state.

---

58   Ibid., p. 9.
59   Ibid., p. 49.

Not every sociologist may see it that way, but the transformation of each state's concerns about the cohesion of its society internally, with all its established exclusive interests, first and foremost the denial of the existence of the majority of its citizens by the interests of its economy, which are enthroned above everything and subjugate all other interests, for its ambitions for power against the same violent monsters around the globe, the transformation of these concerns of the political power of the citizen society about its internal cohesion, into the deeply human need for social belonging, and as a prolongation of this enforced community of conflicting interests into the interpretation of the most urgent task of the "ideal total capitalist" as a natural human need for sociality, and consequently, the interpretation of state societies, this forced community of feuding interests as an offer to the subjects to grant fulfillment to this need invented by sociologists, is of course—one is critical—never perfect, this fundamental and lethal mistake in sociological theorizing is shared by all sociologists, all the different political fractions from conservatives like Calhoun to critical sociologist like Beck share because it is the reason for sociological theorizing as an independent social science discipline in the first place.

The hardened thinker of world power reminds all the hesitating sociological comrades-in-arms of these common views shared by all sociologists and rejects their concerns about the implications of nationalism in matters of war therefore as unscientific, because pseudo-moral and theoretically inconsistent, as violating the basis of sociology. And this with success: no international congress, no scientific event at which this scientific war-monger, head of the figurehead of all sociology, of the International Institute of Sociology, to which only the noblest of all sociologists worldwide belong, does not receive his all-round applause as key note speaker. Recently: The only social science speaker at the solemn opening ceremony of the newly founded "Global Science Council", that same Calhoun, next to him, none other than the President of the Grand Nation, the state from which the leaders of all francophone states in Africa have to collect their placet if they want to govern any of these states—or are pushed away. Somewhere critical murmuring, nothing of the sort.

Not even sociologists of that "Global South" come up with the idea of putting this world thinker in his place as a war propagandist, because they deeply share everything that he otherwise knows about states and, in their post-colonial projects, with their search for national identity, they consider indigenized theories for the production and cultivation of nationalisms to be their post-colonial mission, with which they make their scientific contribution to the construction of their post-colonial state societies freed from colonialism, all sharing their concern for what they critically discuss worldwide under the notion of "social cohesion".

Incidentally, the wars of which the universally esteemed colleague Calhoun, as a morally unobjectionable department of nationalism, argues against any moral objection, are wars with which first of all the colonial societies, which have mutated from colonialism to very citizen societies and states, have been forced to adopt this colonialists' model of society and with which they are now and then brought to reason with all kinds of selected warlike violence in order to maintain this model of society and the services for the imperial states.

So, let's see also what the other world thinker, Wallerstein, with his "universal universalism" has to say about all this. Wallerstein's idea of a hyper-nationalism, a world-nationalism, his "universal universalism" is also originating from the theoretical web of sociological thought, which, since this is what he is missing in post-colonial science and its search for pure national identities, must therefore be found in the field of morality above all those individual nationalisms—the "universal" nationalism above all nationalisms.

Instead of rationalism, science, this scientist goes in search of moral values shared by the world of states, the contradictio in adjecto of an international nationalism, so to speak. It is this monster Wallerstein, who is a scientist, a sociologist, calls his political nonsense of his world view a *"universal universalism"*, a political position translated into scientific methodology. And the use of an idea, which was dished up under this messed up scientific-methodical idea, equal to the whole mankind, this definition of the mission of mankind of the creation of moral values shared by mankind, this idea as the challenge of mankind par excellence, the purpose of all this as usual twistedly social-scientifically formulated idea over the most distinguished tasks of mankind, sociologically as always generously interspersed with the world of states, the use of this task of mankind knows the global moral apostle E. Wallerstein, who converted from science to morality by its insights. Wallerstein, who, like Calhoun, is in his view on the world inspired by all the leading thinkers of the world power over all world powers, the US knows about the use of his international nationalism. So why does the world of states need a shared moral code?

> "The question—Whose right to intervene?—goes to the heart of the political and moral structure of the modern world-system. Intervention is in practice a right appropriated by the strong. But it is right difficult to legitimate and therefore always subject to political and moral challenge. ... It is not that there may not be global values. It is rather that we are far away from yet knowing what these values are. Global universal values are not given to us; they are created by us. The human enterprise of creating such values is the great moral enterprise of humanity. This issue before us today is how we may move beyond European universalism—the last perverse justification of the existing world order—to something much more difficult to achieve: a universal universalism, which refuses essentialist characterizations of social reality, historicizes both the universal and the particular, reunifies the so-called scientific and the humanistic into a single epistemology, and permits us to look with highly clinical and quite sceptical eye at all justifications for intervention! By the powerful against the weak."[60]

So why does the world of states need a globally shared moral code? Wallerstein's answer is perfectly clear: for wars, or more precisely for wars morally shared by the world. War, that is not worth the slightest question for those who know the world of states, war is a natural part of the world of states, which is why they call it "intervention", rather technically speaking.

The question that moves him is that of who has the moral right to wage war against other states, and with his universal universalism, his moral code shared by the world of states, he insists that war, i.e., the right of the strongest, must not be the sole right of the strongest, but the right of whoever has world morality on his side. To wage war, to impose the will of one state on another by the means of military force, this must in principle all be allowed, even those who do not have the means of power for it, but the morally shared right to war. As said before, this thinker has not the slightest thing to criticize about war; what moves him is that wars may be waged only by those who have the capacities to wage wars. Wars, not because they execute the right of the strongest, but because they help the moral values of mankind to assert themselves, this ennoblement of war to a morally clean mission on behalf of mankind, for this this mankind representative scientist needs his moral values shared by the world of states, his universal universalism.

---

60 Wallerstein, I., (2006) European Universalism, ... p. 79.

It is one thing that Wallerstein, with his plea for wars that not only the powerful should be allowed to wage, but all states, as long as their moral code, invented for this purpose, gives them the legitimacy to do so, does not criticize wars with this plea, but rather propagates morally cleaner wars. The other is: they already exist, after all, these moral values shared by humanity, the human rights of the UN, and there are even moral rules for morally clean warfare, and there is no war that would not be justified on all sides by the enforcement of these moral values. The one who wins wars is then right in the sense of these moral values. So what does this man want with his universal universalism, with his morally clean right to war for all states?

The fact that war is only a means for those states that have the means of war, that is, only for those that are "powerful" and not for those that do not have them, should not have escaped even the most blasé sociologist. That all former colonized states, from the point of view of these states, would have every reason to wage war against the imperialist states of the world, which they enslave with their political and economic interests, but do not do so because they cannot, because they have no power against the "powerful" and which, as one can currently study in the example of Iran, which is therefore not allowed to have an atomic bomb, also ensure that this remains so, that should not be a secret to a man like Wallerstein, who has no problems with war, if it is only morally sanctioned. That wars, then, can always be a means of their politics only for the "powerful" who have the means of war for it, is something Wallerstein knows too; so that one must conclude that what really concerns him with his moral values shared by the world is the need, present in the critical scholarly scene of all imperial states, to give the wars of the imperial states a morally clean mission, so that not only the intellectuals but all the citizens of these states can also morally endorse the wars of their states. French philosophers have recently demonstrated how this can be done using Libya as an example, and the EU with its community of values also knows how to wage wars on behalf of values and how to at least beguile its scientific community into understanding wars. So what moves this world thinker of the world power of all world powers are the pangs of conscience, above all of the intellectuals of a state world police force, and the concern for a local nationalism undivided on all sides, including the support of the world of states, which are not opponents of war in a war, but possibly cultivate their own nationalisms, how to wage wars against everything that disturbs the superintendent and judge of the world of states in his world domination, that is considered insubordinate and punished with war, how these wars of the US, about whose moral justification the politicians of this world nation do not think for a second, how these wars of the highest world power can be presented to its citizens and last but not least to its academic elite as moral missions of the world of states carried out on behalf of mankind, as wars against the violation of this moral code shared by mankind.

5. Old and New Mistakes and Their Sources: Theoretical Legacies of the Globalization and Decolonization Debates under the Preparatory Work of HistoMat

At least among professional social science thinkers, there is probably not a single one who would not criticize capitalism governing the world. Even the most hard-boiled apologists admit one or the other "it is not the best, but there is nothing else"; criticizing the capitalist social system is an everyday occurrence in the social sciences. However, those who set out to argue and advocate scientifically to get this universally criticized system off their backs will be confronted by all the critics of capitalism with the accusation of being among the eternal yesteryear and also of not having understood anything about the recent debates on globalization and de-colonization.

The message is clear: of course, you have to look at capitalism critically, but that you have to live with it and that there is nothing better, that is the assured knowledge of the thinkers enlightened by the globalized and even more so by the de-colonized view of the world, a knowledge that these debates have brought to light. It is possible and necessary to criticize capitalism, to argue for abolishing it and to think about other forms of society, or even to only find this desirable to put this into practice, testifies to a lack of knowledge about the state of knowledge of the social sciences. This savvy view of coming to terms with a society system that is continually criticized and to banish the "system question" of postwar debates to the scrap heap of history, this is the result of the globalization or de-colonization debates on the progress of social science theory formation and their insights, and these insights operate with the following—wrong—thought operations.

Even the most politically radical opponents of capitalism share with the idealists of improvements the same fundamental mistake of separating the department of the political rule of capitalism from its economic department in their talk of capitalism *and* the state, equating the economic department with the society system and adding the state to that system, just as if the capitalist economy existed without the political department, and who then endow the state, thought to be separate from the society system of capitalism, with all sorts of invented missions. In the case of the idealists of improvements the state is presented it as a lever for those who are damaged by the economy, and in the case of the radical opponents of capitalism as an instrument misused by the capitalist and, by turning this idea of a misused state reinterpreting its usage even as an instrument of overcoming capitalism.

What both conceptions have in common is the mistake of separating the distinctive elements of the political and the economic departments of the capitalist society system, a separation in which the economic department is presented as the source of its victims and therefore as the object of both kinds of criticism, and in which the political rule is presented in one case as a compensator, in the other case, the state is conceived as a violent amplifier of what its economy causes; in both cases, the criticized society system of capitalism is conceived as its economy, and political rule, the state, is conceived as a political instance added to this social system and as this added political instance beyond this society system open for all kind of policy agendas, ranging from compensations of the damages caused by the economy until overcoming the society system, sustaining this it its main mission.

And this idea of a capitalism with a state added to it, attributed for which mission ever, is already all the normal fundamental error, with which whatever kind of critique separates the political maker, the political elements of this society system, from the same system and is thought away for one kind or another of critical evaluation of its thus made-up goals as a subject independent of the society system, and thus opened up for the attribution of all possible purposes. In the manner of speaking of "capitalism *and* state", which is common even among radical opponents of capitalism, this imagined separation of the state from the society system of capitalism and its opening for the attribution of all possible missions finds its appropriate semantic expression.

To this error, which all variants of critical theory-building share even before the aforementioned postwar debates, the postwar discourses of globalization and de-colonization of social science thought have added false ideas that finally waterproof, quasi immunize, the critique of capitalism against a critique of its political department, an immunization against the critique of the political instance of capitalism, which excludes it from critique of the society system of capitalism, above all ironically thanks to the purified Marxist critics of capitalism.

And all these false judgments about capitalism are not the result of any evil intentions, but of false conclusions which the phenomenology of capitalism offers to thinking, especially to social-scientific thinking, which has committed its sort of theorizing to the "real facts," that is, to that sort of descriptive creation of thought of what the appearance of "real facts" offers to this thinking.

The construction of this fundamentally wrong thought about capitalism described above with the extraction of its state constructedness from this model of society and the subsequent attribution of all possible tasks, ranging from the ideas of making the political departments of capitalism an opponent of its economy to the—optional—subject of its abolition, this attribution of the political department of capitalism is accomplished by social-scientifically trained thinking in all its variants with the following misconceptions:

That, like all societies, capitalism, too, distinguishes its social system into an economic and a political section, already with this the theoretical neutralization of the state from the society system of capitalism by social science thinking begins by missing its actual common nature as elements of this society system: The fact that the political department actually serves neither the interests of individual capitalists nor those of the capitalist class, and yet makes the accumulation of capitalist wealth the supreme measure of all its political activities, that is, that the political department of capitalism, a model of society that makes the economic goals of its economy the primary concern of all its political activities, and which is therefore rightly accordingly coined with its economic objectives, serves the wishful imagination that these economic goals could not be the sole concern of state policy because otherwise they would coincide with the goals of the economic department, and therefore could must be explained the separate existence of a political department separate from the economy with objectives beyond this society system. But it is not: Before any capitalist can count the yield of his business, there is a political power which to the majority of the members of these citizen societies, who possess no such properties needed to produced anything they need, because everything needed for production, the nature and all means of production, are assured and secured by political power as the private property against its use by the non-owners of what any production needs, and it is therefore this political power, which, in association with the owners of all means of production, establishes with this exclusion of the majority of people from using those means for producing anything they need the blackmail that this majority of people made by the state to these non-owners, without making themselves servants of all the means of wealth production owned by a minority of people, made and secured as these exclusive owners by this political power, that these producers of this wealth will not even get the food they need for mere survival and by serving all those means multiply those properties and thus ever enlarge their exclusion from what they produce.

So, it is the political power that not only establishes the whole political basis with the establishment of property of this kind of wealth production, but also sustains this society of owners and non-owners with and despite all its self-destructive—more on this later—economic construction principles and makes this the top mission of its political agenda. The designation of the state as "ideal overall capitalist" expresses this mission of the political power of this society and its reason of state, which is committed to the achievement of economic goals, which through this power sustains its own economic foundations it questions with them.

There is something quite rational about refusing to properly imagine that the goals of political power aims at nothing but a service of its economy and then also as a service for an economy that is concerned with the (in)meaningful more of what it produces not only beyond all usefulness, but even against the needs of human lives, because it does indeed expose a very strange goal of this model of society, for which all members of society, including its political makers, struggle about what they need for a lifetime, though it produces it everything what is needed. However, to ask oneself what else the political aims of this political department must be, because it is indeed hard to believe what they are, in order to invent such aims it though must have, must make one ask oneself why the statement that the state of capitalism does indeed serve the aim of increasing capitalist wealth in everything it does, the accumulation of money, nothing else, why this unbelieving statement of what really is the aim of capitalism does not question the good faith in the aims of this political authority securing this aim as the aim of the society as a whole, as the aims of its complete society system, and instead prefers to indulge in wishful thinking that it must still be about something more reasonable. It is hard to believe, but it is not.

In order that thinking may still cling to the idea that the state in capitalist society must after all be concerned with political ends other than the service of the growth of money, the phenomenology of state politics of capitalist societies does phenomenological thinking about the "real facts" an additional favor by which it tempts this thinking to think that it is right after all with its ideas about any reasonable goals of the politics of states beyond the service of more profit.

The principle of this finding of a still somehow reasonable task of the state resembles the above logic, which, in view of the disbelief in the stated aims of state policy, may not have been true that, with all the elaborated means of power states consist of with their sophisticated political apparatus, this policy is to consist in nothing else but in harnessing the whole of society to provide for the increase of the money of a few rich people. However, this sophisticated political apparatus is needed to handle all the mess, this economy creates, that consist of the continuous de-construction of what this economy needs for its sustainability and to secure this sustainability of this self-deconstructing economy this monstrous political apparatus is needed, absorbing for this mission major parts of the wealth this economy produces to sustain this economy.

The fact that capitalist societies organize themselves in such a way that the economic subjects fight out their success in the multiplication of wealth as a competition against each other, that they need themselves for this success as buyers of their mountains of commodities and at the same time seek to eliminate them as competing producers, so that this kind of wealth production goes hand in hand with the constant destruction of the same, and that the political overseer who carefully sets up this kind of battle among all private owners and sets limits to this activity then, when—to give just one example—either basic products, such as energy or transport, such economic activity costs so much that the whole business that relies on them is no longer paying off, or when profiteering no longer offers not enough jobs to those who create all the wealth, all these are cases in which the policy of this sort of wealth production, intervenes into this economic nonsense of pulling down what it is build one, so that it can be maintained. Here too, with ones observations on how the capitalistically organized reproduction of a society functions and how the political department tames the worst excesses to ensure its free flow, one could conclude that this mode of production and its political department is not the most intelligent way of organizing a society, instead of imagining that there must be other more reasonable purposes ruling the mission of the political body of this society, because it is hard to believe that this is how this society, its politics and its economy work.

Preventing anybody from believing the unbelievable, this is what the professional thinkers in this society do, they feed the society with their legends making sense of the senseless. For the professional thinkers, it follows from these observations that the state power regulates the self-destructive dynamics of capitalist economy to ensure its functioning, that it is thus proven that the state of these citizen societies is the advocate of the interests of the citizens. It is, but it is the interests of its citizens, whom it then serves with all its coercive measures, which it calls "promoting and demanding", to spend their lives for this kind of wealth, including all its well-known impertinences. One must already have fairly accommodated one's mind to the standards of the living conditions of citizen societies and its state impositions in order to interpret the political restrictions of the quite normal everyday questioning of the existence of people by the world of profiteering, i.e., of people who spend their days working and producing, to interpret the compulsion to set oneself the task of life in spite of everything of this sort, i.e., in order to preserve their servitude, in order to interpret this preservation of their servitude fort this economy as the state's concern for its citizens, and thus to interpret the state as a political instance that protects the citizens from capitalism. They do serve their citizen, but only if one perceives this human made a citizen by the political body of capitalism, i.e., the very creature the political bodies of capitalism confront with their blackmail to spend its live as a service for the growth of capital and who they serve by forcing them to do so also in case, the very economy makes this impossible, as in the case of not even offering them a job to earn money. And this happens not only now and then, but it is the inevitable result of this economy and in the major parts of this world ruled by nations states this, making people's existence dependent on money and not even giving them any chance to earn money via working, this is daily life. So that this service of the state consists of forcing the citizen doing the impossible, serving the economy which does not want this service of citizens. This service of the state for the state objectives via the citizens, this is the source for the false conclusion, the citizen would serve the citizens objectives and it is this false conclusion that founds all the variations of false theories about the state, especially those about the therefore called welfare state.

And there is yet another institution that the state has at its disposal, one that supports this wishful thinking that the political power of capitalism is an institution that ensures that every citizen can, if not realize his life goals, at least pursue them. Indeed, the final transfiguration of the real aims of the state power of capitalism by the idea of being there for its citizens draws its evidence from the freedom granted to them to pursue their individual aims in life, just as it is enshrined in the constitutions of these societies. And also, this proof of the state as an institution acting against capitalism for the concerns of its subjects draws its persuasive power only from the political subservience that this political power has instilled in its subjects—or, which is the same thing, from the threat that it could also abolish all those freedoms.

The citizen of the citizen society is a free citizen and can live his life as he pleases. This freedom is it, which grants its political force to him and who only reads all the restrictions, which this political power imposes on itself as they are fixed in Declaration of Hum an Rights, that can overtake actually with the reading of all the paragraphs protecting people against their political power only a shower of the fear, how there the liberty is praised as a non-application of all the well sorted and well well-known means of force presented in this declaration to the citizen in the certainty of the totality of the political power of their monopoly of violence over the citizens as generous renouncement of relativating its use against them—at least not unnecessarily.[61] Certainly, for the serf who no longer has to let his wife be chosen by his feudal lord and who is now completely free to choose whether he

---

61 Article 3. Everyone has the right to life, liberty and security of person.

Article 4. No one shall be held in slavery or servitude; slavery and the slave trade shall be prohibited in all their forms.

Article 5. No one shall be subjected to torture or to cruel, inhuman or degrading treatment or punishment.

Article 14. (1) Everyone has the right to seek and to enjoy in other countries asylum from persecution. (2)

goes to work for VW or Unilever, if he lives in Frankfurt or Liverpool, the freedom of the citizen society is a gain. But to still celebrate this more than 200 years after the French Revolution as proof that the political power of capitalism is an institution dedicated to the good of the citizen, this testifies to the subservience of the thinkers that this freedom has produced on them, when they use the reference to the freedom of citizens in citizen societies as proof of the servitude of the state to its citizens. To make this generous renunciation of the use of the means of violence of the state, which it has and which only it has, while the citizens are made entirely powerless, to present this as proof of the state as servant of its citizens, thinking this is only possible only by confusing grace with liberty.

And how does this proof with the freedom that the state is the servant of the citizen and by no means vice versa, how does this proof work? This transfiguration operates with the political concession of a conceded materialism, i.e., the political recognition of all members of society as equally free subjects, even of those whose materialism in the logic of the economy of this society is actually only contrary to the societies' supreme purpose, which, with this conceded materialism of these members of this citizen society too, their equality, makes this society look as if it were about the materialism of all, even though the majority of its members with their conceded materialism, realize only the aims of this society against its own materialism, the growth of wealth, because they always only destroy their wealth in consumption and never invest it. And this counterproductive materialism of the majority of their citizen the state of this society therefore concedes, because these unproductive citizens, unproductive in the sense of what counts in this society, the growth of wealth measured in money, are inevitably needed for the production of this wealth, the workforce of those who are producing this wealth.

Because it is the political section which, despite the—in the logic of capital wealth accumulation—wealth destroyers, intervenes against the interest of growing wealth and re-stricts the use of the mere consumers of wealth for the preservation of these wealth consumers. Because the state is responsible for the preservation of its human instrument of the growth of wealth, the working part of the population, the proof of the state as servant of the citizen confuses this state's concern for the preservation of its "human capital" with the concern for the material concerns of its citizens based on the permission that their materialism is conceded to them, if they pursue this materialism as a service for this growth of capitalistic wealth.

It is true, at least if one shares the cynicism with such thinkers and forgets the masses of people around the world who are far from conquering their lives with services to the growth of this capitalistic wealth, whose existence the states of the world do not care about a second, because these citizens are never considered as servants of capitalist wealth creation, at least for the states in which the world's wealth is accumulated, it is true that in these states the state grants to those citizens who have no productive property the right to pursue their materialism—even so only in so far as the pursuit of the materialism of the non-proprietary increases the property of those who are the owners of the wealth which is the only materialism that really counts. It is this conceded materialism of the citizens which creates the appearance and which this proof misinterprets as the guarantee of the material interests of all citizens by means of its political department and its restrictions of the interests of the capitalists for the sake of the sustainability of its growth.

And still another last irrefutable final argument these scientific theories know, which know, why the state of the citizen society serves the interests of all citizens. The final transfiguration of the political body of capitalism into an institution committed to the material interests of all members of society then creates the granting of a well-calculated political power of decision making to those majorities of societies which are economically only the henchmen of the interests of the capitalists. We are talking here about elections.

Here too, before any discussion of the arguments that can be made with reference to elections in which the subjects are allowed to decide on one day every four years to whom they will cede their power of decision for four years with the consent to follow all the decisions of the people they have elected, here too one must ask oneself what is to be proven by this procedure, how much the state listens to its citizens. Doesn't it also require a certain degree of subservience to renounce the citizens' permission to intervene in the internal affairs of politics, which determines all, but also all the affairs of their lives, with the offer that they may decide on a Sunday who may make these rules for them, not only for this Sunday? Is it possibly the fact that the permission for citizens to decide about those people who have the decision power over the citizen is therefore interpreted as a proof that states are there to serve citizens, because this permission appears so generous compared to that after they elected those who decide they have nothing to decide any more at all? Or does the reference to the permission to be allowed to elect their political leaders feed on the experience that they sometimes withdraw this permission here and there with more or less force, when this political elite, together with their agents of violence, mostly the military forces, think that the citizen is not mature enough to vote because he does not choose the right ones? Is it the experience of the affinity that political elites around the world have for the ubiquitous option of refusing to vote that prompts social science theorists, is it their affinity to dictatorship, to cite the existence of elections as proof of the bondage of political powers to their citizens?

The fact that the political body, allows for the sake of the preservation of society with all those opposing subjects of all the private owners and their conflicting interests, in which the majority of the have-nots are means of the minority of the haves, to find out its political ruling personnel by the majority of the have nots, this creates all the errors that the political body of this society, despite all those always criticized capitalist impositions by the very state, must ultimately be concerned with something other than the preservation of capitalism. However, do the true sovereigns in democracies actually decide something else than the question, which political rulers in which variants of all the above conflicting goals with the always same overall goals may execute these overall goals? Perhaps the trick in democratic rule is to transfer state power to the department of the political elite that best succeeds in getting its subjects to participate in what the state's power imposes on them?

Here again, the assembled democratically elected leaders of the world of states know why political concessions to the citizenry pay off for the states. This can be read about in the preamble to the Human Rights Charter:

> "Whereas it is essential, if man is not to be compelled to have recourse, as a last resort, to rebellion against tyranny and oppression, that human rights should be protected by the rule of law."[62]

---

62 https://www.un.org/en/universal-declaration-human-rights/index.html.

Forcing people to stand up against the ruling power? Surely no democratic ruler can want that. Does this, the considerations of the world's representatives of nation states about why human rights are needed still leave anything unclear what the idea about appointing the ruling elites via elections of the majority of people is?

With these above proofs about the state of capitalist societies serving their citizens theorizing operates, departing from those false duplications of capitalism *and* state social science, false conclusions derived from the freedom thus gained, and from there create all possible idealizations of the state, which, depending on political inclination, attach across all social science disciplines imaginary missions to the citizen, their society, their state and their economy—as will be shown more detailed in volume two. These are the proofs that social science thinking has always sought to provide, and it is the legacy of the discourses on globalization and de-colonization of social science thinking that has added new theoretical views on the theorizing of the state to these state idealizations and their proofs, which now complements the old, existing social science mistakes with further developments of these false thought.

Which brings us to the discourses of the post-World War II period, while discussing the globalization and de-colonization of social science thinking: The duplication and based on this the idealization of the state as a political instrument separated from capitalism and thus opened to all kinds of political ideas is not only what drives the ideas of the political actors of the former colonies and their thinkers trained in the social sciences of the old colonial powers and what they take over from the social sciences. This idealization of the state into a means for the majority of citizens used by capitalism, freed up by this doubling of the state *and* capitalism, globalizes the foundations of the illusion of the state, arising in the old capitalist societies from the welfare state, with its discourse of decolonization also for states which do not even establish this welfare state, because the majority of their people consists of citizens, in whose preservation the idealist total capitalists of those new states have no interest, because there is no capital that wants to use these citizen societies as a whole, because only a few of them are needed for the removal of the natural resources of these countries.

But not only that: Theorizing in these societies not only adjusts thinking about them towards the idealization of the societies and their political power without the sources fueling this false judgments about nation states; the idea of this thinking in the concept of a decolonization of the social sciences also insinuates that this takeover of the social science thinking of the colonial societies and their state, their approach to sciences with its professionalization and as a matter of academics, its disciplinary nature, its cognitive form of theory-building, including its complete methodological instruments, that the adaptation of thinking in these new citizens societies to the ways of thinking in the imperialist nation states would all be a critique of this approach to social thought. And even this is not all: This discourse of de-colonization radicalizes the so far systemic affirmation of social science thinking with its theoretical operations for the refinement of the state in general, in that the masterminds of these new states, in addition to the refinement of states in general beyond any single nation state, prepare with the post-colonial interventions and here with their indigenization of theory creations the ways for the self-representation of individual states as a from now on universally accepted form of social science thinking. And finally fighting for this kind of nationally guided thinking in the social sciences against that systemic idealization of citizens societies and states as such for theorizing as the creation of self-representations of individual citizens societies and nation states as a recognized form of theory-building, these discourses wring the last remnants of objective knowledge out of social science thinking and thus radicalize it into a relative knowledge, a relativism that no longer derives its relativity from a scientific relativism via the meta-theories used for its theory-building, but from the explicitly political interests of individual nation states.

And even this is not yet the entire development that the discourse on globalization, or rather de-colonization, create for social science thinking: This release of nationalist thinking also derives its form of thinking as self-critique from theories that have so far stood for system-critical thinking. Thinking that receives its insights from explicit nationalist sources and interpreting this nationalistic scientific thought and throwing over board the critique of the society system of the imperial world via the self-critique of the system critics of capitalism, the release of nationalist thinking is presented as a further development of the critique of colonialism. This refinement of nationalist thought into a progress of social science thought interpreted as a liberation from colonialism presents by this discourse the self-critique of their anti-capitalist ideas, the revision of their critique of the society model of the colonialist and the adjustment of theorizing to the way of thinking of the imperial world as an updated version of their oppositional thinking about the society system of the imperial world.

That social science thought, which draws its theories from the inspiration of and for national self-portrayals, can be presented as a further development of an opposition against imperialism, i.e., of the Marxist critique of capitalism, cannot happen without an interpretation of this Marxist critique that has already paved the way for this self-critique of Marx with its interpretation of Marx, or phrased in a less personalized way, the presentation of a critique of capitalism as the concern of how to create nationalism in the former colonizes world, presenting the identification with the ruling power of capitalism as act of opposition against capitalism, this must be based on some preparatory interpretations of the critique of capitalism.

And indeed: In fact, it is thanks to the practical critics of capitalism and their alternative social project of the SU and their Marxist interpretation named "Historical Materialism" that the state is not an object of critique of capitalism and eliminated with the elimination of capitalism and replaced by other forms of the political organization of a non-capitalist society, it was the post-Leninist SU, which, in the face of Germany's war against itself, has made the strengthening of the state, more precisely the SU-variation of socialist state the supreme political goal of its alternative to capitalism, of its anti-capitalist project, thereby replacing criticism of the state with the political maxim that the state in its socialist variation is the central political organizer of the alternative society project of a state-driven society and economy, in which the compatibility of a production of abstract wealth under the rule of the state with the material interests of the subjects was to be proven—and has been disproved by another way of the exclusion of the people from the wealth they produced, another type of poverty of the people.

To interpret thanks to the socialist variation of a state monopolized ownership over another variant of abstract wealth and the people as a variation of a working class instead of abolishing classes, the state variation of its opposing model of society, which seeks to harmonize the maxim of abstract wealth production with the vital interests of the citizens through its political control and to conclude from there that the political power of capitalism, the nation state as a means that can be also used against capitalism, it is this prefabricated mistake which has provided the template for the masterminds of the transformation of the colonies into states for their self-criticism of an odd Marxism, who were thanks to this false critique of capitalism as practiced by the Soviet Union able to present the transformation of the colonies into just such states as a further development of the opposition to capitalism.

And it is indeed this proof that a production of wealth, measured in the growth of the wealth of money, can be reconciled with the vital interests of the citizens thanks to its maximum political control, including the takeover of all the property of this wealth by the state, it is this proof of this idea which "collapsed" there, not with its end, but with every day that it existed—not the Soviet Union. This, the collapse of this alternative society projects, is another myth, that wants to say, that capitalism corresponds to the nature of humans and any other society model does not work, originally created by the nation state politicians and then proved by social sciences.

Nationalistically inspired thinking is thus presented as the modernized form of the critique of capitalism and thus brought to worldwide recognition that the nationalism transfigured into a critique of capitalism by this courted that states are not only actually servants of the have-nots of the world, but that the national self-representation of states vis-à-vis their citizens as well as among themselves has become, with the indigenization of science, the recognized methodological principle of global critical social scientific theory-building, not only in the former colonies, but worldwide.

Nevertheless, despite of this worldwide recognition the formation of indigenous theories, the creation of theories of representation of national identity, remains the contribution to science that is reserved for the social science theory formation in the former colonized, respectively the new citizen societies as a consequence of their distancing from their systemic critical reflection on the society system of the old colonial states, as of the criticism of the exploitation and impoverishment of their national societies by the imperial states. Social sciences in the new citizen societies of the former colonies are allowed to embellish the social science canon of knowledge of the social science disciplines with the national exoticism of their indigenous theories—as long as they align their indigenous theories with the theories of the social science canon of knowledge and creating these disciplinary canon of theories for theorizing continue to be the mission of sciences of the old-established professional thinkers in the old and new imperial parts of the world.

Theories for mankind, more morally phrased for "humanity", that was and also remains the mission of social science thinkers who, like Calhoun, Beck or Wallerstein, present the desires of self-representation of citizen societies and their political powers who are ruling the world of states as the concerns of humanity and who tell the world and its states who has to do what and who has to let do what, and whose sciences tell the social scientists in the world of states what is and what is not part of the worldwide canon of knowledge as a meta-theory which count for worldwide theorizing in social science theory formation.

And in gratitude for the fact that the now civilized science of the now equally civilized societies has distanced itself from its fundamental criticism of capitalism and replaced it with the cultivation of critical, nation-state identity images, all the postcolonial thinkers with their indigenized theories may give social science thinking as a whole sufficient confirmation that the science of civilized citizen society is the natural form of thinking, which offers every scientific thought with its disciplinary science a common theoretical home shared by all, whether "North" or "South", whether nationally or imperially inspired theory, "globalized", "de-colonized" or "indigenized", or simply, like most theories, pragmatic national policy advisors and problem solvers—in other words, all variations of the same thinking about and through the concerns of a world of citizen societies.